The
Urban
Experience

Themes in
American
History

The Urban Experience

Themes in American History

edited by

Raymond A. Mohl
Florida Atlantic University

James F. Richardson
The University of Akron

Wadsworth Publishing Company, Inc
Belmont, California

To Bayrd Still

Designer: Russell Kent Leong
Editor: Sandra Craig
Cover: Nancy Benedict

ISBN 0-534-00287-0
L. C. Cat. Card No. 72-97322
Printed in the United States of America
2 3 4 5 6 7 8 9 10---77 76 75

Contents

Preface

The authors of this volume have examined some of the institutional forms and effects of urbanization in a particular national context. Modernization, industrialization, urbanization—whatever terms one wishes to use to characterize the uprooting or liberation of the bulk of the population from the land and the village—have coincided chronologically with the national history of the United States. (Both the Declaration of Independence and Adam Smith's *Wealth of Nations* were published in 1776.) Therefore, we believe that the study of urbanization and urban institutions offers useful avenues toward understanding the development of American society as a whole. Rather than organizing the study of American history around major political events, wars, or presidential administrations, we consider processes of population growth and concentration and ways in which men and women organize their lives in response to such developments. In addition to its value as a text for courses in urban history and in urban studies, this book can be a useful supplement for the second semester of the introductory survey course in American history—filling the increasing need for historical materials on urbanization.

For most of human history, urban and rural had distinct meanings; no one doubted where one ended and the other began. Cities were few, contained only a small minority of the total population, and required a constant influx of people from the countryside simply to maintain population levels. Preindustrial societies could not support a large number of city dwellers, who almost by definition are nonagricultural specialists. Inability to produce substantial food surpluses limited urban growth, as did diseases stemming from fouled water and close contact with carriers. Most people lived on the land in a style of life marked more by tradition than by change and innovation. Disruptions occurred, occasioned by famine, epidemic, and marauders, but peasant society sought to reestablish traditional patterns as soon as possible. Communal norms, which emphasized stability and continuity, took precedence over individual needs and interests. Average men and women measured time by the rhythm of the agricultural cycle and the calendar of religious festivals and penitential seasons. The best that most people could hope for was that they might escape externally imposed coercion and acquire sufficient food to sustain life.

In advanced societies in the last two centuries, these values and modes of life have virtually disappeared to the extent that it now requires a leap of the imagination or residence in an isolated rural area to recapture them. Through the exploitation of such inanimate sources of energy as coal, through the creation of more efficient tools (mechanical, organizational, and intellectual), and through the development of a value system that prizes growth, individual advancement, and innovation, modern man has transformed the texture of life. No longer are cities restricted in number and size by low agricultural productivity or by inability to cope with environmental problems caused by concentrated population.

Urbanization has been both cause and effect of this fundamental restructuring of human society. The widened pursuit of nonagricultural activities stimulated population clustering. Economic changes fostered the division of labor, the growth of specialization, and the complex web of interdependence that makes up the modern metropolis. In turn, the process of city building produced further economic development and technological innovation.

For the first century and a half of the national history of the United States, urban population remained a minority of the total. In 1860 one of five Americans lived in a city; by 1900 the proportion had reached two in five. For the whole of the nineteenth century, then, the bulk of the American people lived on farms or in village settlements, but from 1820 on, the number of urbanites grew more rapidly than total population. High rates of mobility—internal migration as well as European immigration—swelled the urban population and made it a more substantial minority each decade.

The census of 1920 indicated that for the first time more than half the American people resided in urban areas. Since that year, urbanization has reached the point where it is increasingly difficult to distinguish urban history from American domestic history as a whole. At a time when urban growth has concentrated 70 percent of our population on 2 percent of our land, only the backwaters of American society escape the impact of metropolitan influences. Writers often use the term *urban problems* as a catchall description of national social ills, and students of recent urban history wonder how to differentiate their area of interest from the entire corpus of domestic history of the last fifty years. If virtually all of American society is urban—if an Iowa farmer can be considered as an exurbanite member of an occupational subculture—our traditional categories of rural and urban may need to be scrapped in favor of terms which would describe communities more accurately. Urban history, especially that dealing with the last half century, may also require redefinition and refinement to fulfill its mission of providing historical perspective for patterns of human settlement and communal organization that are still evolving. The blurring of city and countryside, the increasing difficulty of telling where one ends and the other begins, means that "urban" no longer describes a particular kind of settlement sharply differentiated from the rest of the society.

The difficulty of finding a focal point for today's spread city that corresponds to the medieval cathedral or the nineteenth century railroad depot is matched by the urban scholar's inability to develop an adequate conceptual framework for study and understanding of contemporary urban processes. Scholars in such disciplines as economics and sociology are interested in prediction; they wish to build theories which will enable them to anticipate what is likely to happen under specified conditions. However, no one has yet constructed a satisfactory theory of urban development and processes in all their ramifications. Historians are more modest in that their concern is to determine from surviving data what happened and why. But even this more limited goal of achieving hindsight, as contrasted to the social scientist's concern with foresight, is fraught with problems. Historians must make difficult choices about the subjects they study, the questions they ask about the past, and the tools they employ to order and make sense of their materials. To date, urban historians have not agreed on the content or methodology of their specialty. A different set of authors might well have chosen quite different topics from the ones discussed in this book. We make no claim to universality, to have covered all possible subjects and approaches.

Still, these essays pose significant questions about America's past urban experience—questions that are indispensable for an understanding of the history of American cities, without which no informed view of the present or the probable future is possible. How and why have American urban areas taken the shapes they now possess? This is the question Joseph L. Arnold and Kenneth T. Jackson confront in the essays on planning and suburbanization. How have specific groups of people fared in American cities? Humbert S. Nelli, Zane L. Miller, and Neil Betten provide answers for immigrants, blacks, and workers, respectively. Bruce M. Stave and James F. Richardson examine instruments of government in cities and value conflicts over the proper organization and functioning of municipal authorities. Raymond A. Mohl focuses on attitudes toward poverty and the poor as well as the institutions created to deal with dependency. Jacob H. Dorn highlights the ambivalent experiences of churches in cities, while Selwyn K. Troen probes the relationship between the value orientation and the organizational structure of American urban schools. In the introductory and concluding pieces, the editors survey preindustrial and contemporary American cities, respectively. Taken together, the essays in this book have sought to trace the varied dimensions of the urban past and in so doing to suggest alternatives to those who will shape the urban future.

Acknowledgments

The editors acknowledge with thanks the critical reading given the manuscript by Kozmus Balkus of Florida State University, Michael Frisch of the State University of New York at Buffalo, and Mark Lapping of Virginia Polytechnic Institute and State University. Their comments have helped us shape the book for its intended audience. Our aim has been to produce a volume that is useful for courses in urban history and in American institutions, for surveys of American history, and as collateral reading for courses in urban studies programs. The extent to which participants in such courses find the book valuable will be the measure of our success. We would also like to acknowledge the assistance of Barbara Yates, a graduate assistant at Florida Atlantic University, who spent many hours at the xerox machine and in proofreading different versions of the manuscript, and Jamie Shiner, who cheerfully provided expert typing services. Finally, we would like to thank the contributors for the quality of their work and for their promptness in meeting deadlines. The editors gratefully dedicate this book to Bayrd Still. In a distinguished career as a pioneer teacher and writer of urban history, he has provided inspiration to students and colleagues and a living example of the values of academic life.

The
Urban
Experience

**Themes in
American
History**

The Preindustrial American City

Raymond A. Mohl

The discovery of the "urban crisis" in the 1960s, the dimensions of current urban dilemmas, the intensity of media coverage, and the clamor of rising public concern all suggest the immediacy of the city. Such a view, however, distorts the timelessness of urban civilization. Furthermore, it has led government officials and urban "experts" in a variety of fields to treat pressing urban difficulties as if they had relatively recent origins. In reality, of course, American society was partly urban from the beginning; the city has posed serious human, social, and political problems throughout the span of American history. The continuous demands of city life and the changing patterns of human response in and to the city form an integral and important part of the American record. The study of urban history provides much-needed perspective on the contemporary urban condition.

Unquestionably, the United States has become an intensely urban nation. From 1790, when about 5 percent of Americans lived in cities, the United States has become progressively more urbanized; by the 1970s, the proportion of urbanites was close to 80 percent. Over a period of 350 years, as both colony and nation, America grew from a society of farms and small villages to one of huge central cities and massive sprawling suburbs. From the nineteenth century on, the promise of jobs and economic opportunity, often unfulfilled, drew rural dwellers and immigrants into the cities. Stimulated by immigration, internal mobility, commercial prosperity, industrial expansion, and technological development, the process of urbanization became compelling and irresistible. Noting the "lure of the city," Horace Greeley could write in 1867, "We cannot all live in cities, yet nearly all seem determined to do so." By the middle of the twentieth century, Greeley's prophecy had become reality. The nation has indeed become "cityfied," and observers now write about "megalopolis"—great chains of urbanized areas stretching hundreds of miles in all directions and hungrily gobbling up the few remaining patches of trees and farmland. From the perspective of the urban historian, city development and its consequences for the larger society is one of the central themes of American history.

1

The history of urban America begins with the earliest establishment of colonies in the New World. Many of the first colonists had been town or city dwellers in England or Europe, and they brought to the American wilderness urban values, attitudes, and aspirations. They often sought to emulate in the New World the British or European societies they had abandoned. Thus, virtually all the first settlements took the form of organized communities. Although the populations of most such places remained small through most of the prerevolutionary period, each colonial settlement, village, or town served traditional urban functions: they became centers for the exchange of goods, services, and ideas. By the end of the seventeenth century, colonial Americans had created a dynamic and expansive urban society, and the larger seaport cities—Boston, Philadelphia, New York, Charleston, and Newport—exercised an influence on colonial society far out of proportion to their populations.

A number of forces combined to spur colonial urbanization. In the earliest stages of settlement and on every colonial frontier, new arrivals gathered together in primitive "stockade cities" for protection and mutual defense. Although most of the population lived and worked on the surrounding land, the stockade enclosed permanent leadership and institutions, provided security in times of danger, and facilitated the exchange of goods and ideas. Many such stockade communities, such as those typical of early New England, rapidly became agrarian towns. In that region a community-centered society required towns to effectively regulate social and religious life; landowners were attracted to town residence because it accorded status and prestige, and craftsmen because it supplied steady work. Town building was also promoted by English-based joint-stock companies; the sponsors of much of the early colonization, private British investors, viewed towns as necessary for effectively tapping the raw materials and resources of the New World. Thus, fishing villages, mining and lumber centers, Indian trading posts, crossroads towns, and entrepôts sprouted throughout the colonies.

Many of the colonies' largest towns grew because of their political and administrative functions. Indeed, by the end of the seventeenth century, the British government had begun to encourage urban growth, even in the colonial South, where geography and emerging agricultural patterns militated against town life. The reason for such government promotion seemed obvious—mercantilist navigation and trade regulations could be more easily implemented and enforced in towns and cities, where goods might be funneled in and out of the colonies.

Above all else, commercial activity in the colonies stimulated urbanization. Before the end of the seventeenth century, enterprising colonial merchants and entrepreneurs established a far-flung and profitable commercial network. Built primarily on the products of an extractive economy—fish and furs, tobacco and rice, wheat and indigo, lumber and livestock, naval stores and minerals—colonial trade with Britain, Europe, Africa, and the West Indies expanded and prospered. Returning ships carried slaves, sugar, manufactured goods, bills of exchange, and new immigrants. Intensive commerce of this kind promoted the growth of seaport towns and cities up and down the Atlantic coastline. These places became market cities where goods changed hands; they served as an economic "hinge," central points for the collection and distribution of exports and imports. Moreover, commercial activity encouraged a number of supportive industries in the towns. Thus, most ports also became centers for flour milling, ship building, and the processing of naval stores. Numerous trades supplementing the mercantile base emerged as well, especially shops producing rope, sails, barrels, ship fittings, and provisions. Other craftsmen—carpenters, silversmiths, blacksmiths, printers, masons, bakers, tailors—serviced expanding urban populations. As a result of these advances in craft and commerce, the economy prospered, the domestic market widened, and urbanization intensified.

Small by contemporary standards, the colonial seaport cities nevertheless grew rapidly. With a population of about 7,000 in 1700, Boston was the largest urban center in the American colonies. New York and Philadelphia each had about 4,000 residents by the end of the seventeenth century. By the mid-eighteenth century, Boston's population had stabilized at around 15,000; Philadelphia, meanwhile, had forged ahead as the American metropolis, and in 1776 its 40,000 people made it the second largest city in the entire British empire. New York ranked second at the outbreak of the American Revolution with a population of 25,000, although it soon outdistanced its neighboring rival on the Delaware River. Dominant in the South, Charleston had become a sophisticated regional center of 12,000 by the time of the Revolution. America's first "boom" town, Baltimore, also rose rapidly after 1750, primarily as a center for wheat exportation from the middle colonies. By the end of the eighteenth century, about 200,000 people lived in twenty-four urban centers of 2,500 or more. Although small, these towns and seaport cities exerted considerable economic and political influence as well as intellectual and cultural leadership.

The agglomeration of population in colonial towns and seaport cities had a significant impact on government and society. Although environment imposed a rough kind of egalitarianism on most early settlements, population growth and economic expansion eventually introduced class and economic distinctions. Compared to frontier regions and even to subsistence or commercial farming sections, colonial urban areas were highly stratified. In Boston, the class of propertyless laborers was increasing at a rate twice that of the population as a whole by the time of the Revolution. Moreover, although geographic mobility was always high, upward social and economic mobility was more limited in cities than in other segments of colonial society. The continuous influx of new immigrants tended to keep wages down and economic opportunity somewhat circumscribed.

Similar patterns prevailed even in smaller agrarian towns. In Dedham, Massachusetts, for example, the rising population imposed severe pressures on limited land resources; subdivision of farms among children over several generations reduced individual landholdings to subsistence levels and caused economic stagnation and decline. In addition, residents of larger towns and cities faced numerous problems brought by growth—housing, congestion, unemployment, threats to public health and public order, demands for wider provision of municipal services, and the need for planning for future physical expansion, among others. The collective needs of growing urban communities required the conscientious attention of civic and municipal leaders.

Municipal governments confronted serious problems of providing services, regulating economic matters, and maintaining order. Modeled upon the municipal corporations of England, colonial city governments implemented mercantilistic policies to insure orderly economic activity; thus, a small army of public officials—weighers, gaugers, measurers, clerks, inspectors, commissioners, superintendents—supervised the marketplace and administered local ordinances on wages, prices, and the quality and quantity of products. Numerous other public servants dealt with things like relief for the poor, fire protection, water supply, street sanitation, and public health— urban problems which intensified as population increased. Although local policies were more often regulatory and restrictive than positive in nature, colonial municipalities for the most part displayed paternalistic concern for town welfare.

Where the need was great but where municipal government was inadequate, voluntary and civic organizations often provided important facilities and services. In Philadelphia, for example, Benjamin Franklin, one of America's first community organizers, spurred the formation of volunteer fire companies, schools, and a hospital, as well as innovations in water supply, street cleaning, and street lighting. Colonial urbanites used associations to meet many other common problems. Thus, mutual benefit societies, often organized by trade or nationality group, eased individual concern about economic security. Men organized charities and schools, built private institutions (such as hospitals) with essentially public purposes, and in general sought to confront urban life in positive and creative ways. As historian Carl Bridenbaugh has suggested, prerevolutionary town dwellers met urban problems and demands with an increasing degree of civic responsibility and sophistication.

By the mid-eighteenth century, American urban society had matured in other ways as well. Every seaport city had become an intellectual and cultural center, supporting schools, colleges, libraries, book stores, artists, musicians, scientists, theaters, and newspapers. Upper-class social activity was fostered by numerous gentlemen's clubs; for those further down the social and economic scale, every urban tavern became a neighborhood center and a forum for local and provincial politics. City churches and their preachers influenced opinion in their congregations and in the agricultural hinterland as well. Political and administrative centers, the colonial cities provided the locale where imperial policy was transformed into colonial practice.

During the revolutionary crisis within the British Empire, colonial cities emerged as important centers of radical activity and propaganda. Colonial merchants based in the seaport cities saw urban prosperity threatened by new British economic policies and thus organized the early opposition to parliamentary legislation. The effective boycotts against British imports implemented in the port towns helped strike down the Stamp Act and the Townshend duties. The dissatisfaction and radicalism of urban workers, mechanics, and sailors, fanned by unemployment and the economic pressures of the 1760s, found violent expression in mobs and riots (the Sons of Liberty was primarily an urban group). Pivotal events such as the Boston Massacre originated in the conflict between city dwellers and British troops stationed in the cities. Such radical groups as the Boston Committee of Correspondence, along with widely read city newspapers, filled the countryside with revolutionary propaganda. And, as Arthur M. Schlesinger has suggested, the patterns of community life over the course of the colonial period accorded a "training in collective action" upon which radical leaders drew during the American Revolution.

Historians have noted that colonial society was deferential in nature—that is, it was a society in which men knew their place and accepted it. Deference shaped prerevolutionary American urbanism, and colonial towns and cities were essentially stable and orderly places. To be sure, most of the large colonial towns experienced economic depressions, poverty, disease, overcrowding, crime, violence, and social conflict. Yet colonial institutions tempered conflict and maintained more than a semblance of order and stability. Few of these problems threatened for long to upset the elite-dominated, community-centered nature of colonial urbanism. However, the egalitarian ideology and the practical results of the American Revolution destroyed deference, undermined the orderly society, and paved the way for social and economic change in the cities of the early nineteenth century.

2

More than anything else, change characterized urban America in the period between the American Revolution and the industrial takeoff of the mid-nineteenth century. Increasingly heavy immigration, commercial innovations, the beginnings of industrialism, the completion of a transportation network, and economic prosperity periodically punctured by business fluctuations and depressions all fostered the transformation of the preindustrial city. Social and economic change altered the texture of urban life. Established institutions of family and faction, church and government, social class and community became impotent and ineffective under new urban conditions. Small, usually orderly, and relatively well regulated in colonial years, the seaport cities became large, unstable, misgoverned, and socially fragmented. Meanwhile, as older cities in the East expanded at fantastic rates, newer cities sprouted in the interior, especially on the transportation arteries of the trans-Appalachian West. Increasingly, cities dominated American society east and west.

To a large degree, population growth dictated the dimensions of the changing city. People from natural increase, rural migration, and European immigration swelled cities in all sections of the nation. Indeed, urban growth rates in the early nineteenth century have never been matched since. New York, a small city of little more than 30,000 in 1790, grew by more than 50 percent each decade until 1860 except the 1810–20 period. By 1860, some 800,000 people jammed the Manhattan metropolis. Philadelphia's 42,000 people in 1790 had multiplied to more than 565,000 by the Civil War. Only a small suburb of less than 5,000 in 1790, by 1860 Brooklyn had become the nation's third largest city, with a population of 280,000. Between 1790 and 1830, New York had an overall population growth rate of 549 percent. Over the same four decades, Baltimore, Boston, and Philadelphia expanded at rates of 497 percent, 367 percent, and 266 percent, respectively. These growth rates exceeded the total rate of population expansion, the growth rate of the same cities in the forty years after 1860, and the contemporary growth rate of large British cities.

Western cities grew rapidly too, often spearheading the westward movement. River cities such as Pittsburgh, Louisville, Cincinnati, St. Louis, and New Orleans experienced similar patterns of development, emerged as regional market and manufacturing centers, and hastened settlement of the surrounding agricultural hinterland. Transportation improvements, especially steam navigation and canal building, spurred the growth of Great Lakes cities—Buffalo, Cleveland, Detroit, Chicago, and Milwaukee. Although Cincinnati ranked as the third largest manufacturing city in the nation in 1860, Chicago was rising quickly as the western metropolis. The river and lake cities of the interior became important regional processing and distributing centers and imposed an urban quality on the agrarian West.

Economic forces also fostered the growth of the preindustrial city after the American Revolution. Until about the 1830s, commerce continued to sustain prosperity and thus urban growth; world trade in American foodstuffs and cotton brought profits to urban merchants as well as to agricultural producers. In New York City, aggressive commercial activity pushed the Hudson River port firmly ahead of all competitors. In the years after the War of 1812, New York's merchants adopted an efficient auction system for imports and regularly scheduled sailing packets to Europe—innovations which increased the certainty of business transactions and made New York the center of foreign trade. In addition, New York merchants dominated the coastal carrying trade and controlled disposal of southern cotton through banking, credit, and insurance services. The completion of the Erie Canal further added to the city's commercial dominance by tapping midwestern agriculture.

The success of the Erie Canal stimulated a form of "urban imperialism," as other eastern cities rushed to complete transportation improvements of their own. Turnpikes, canals, and eventually railroads extended across the Appalachians and into the West. These internal improvements not only linked coastal cities with western farmers but fostered urbanization in the West and along the routes as well. For example, a whole string of cities sprouted between Buffalo and Albany along the Erie Canal. Equally important, the completion of the transportation network by the 1840s facilitated industrialization.

Transportation innovations created a domestic market, and urban businessmen turned their energies and capital toward production for internal consumption. By the 1830s, commerce began to give way to manufacturing in eastern cities. New York and Philadelphia led the way. Factories producing finished clothing, boots and shoes, leather items, woolen goods, cotton textiles, and iron products proliferated and became typical places of work for urban laborers. Although cities such as Cincinnati and Pittsburgh duplicated eastern factory towns, in most western cities the flour milling, meat packing, and lumber industries predominated. In New England, textiles and the boot and shoe industry fostered the development of numerous smaller factory towns. Similar developments occurred elsewhere—in Richmond, Virginia, in Lexington, Kentucky, in Paterson, New Jersey—as manufacturing supplanted commerce and as the domestic market widened. The concomitant decline of household manufacturers and locally oriented handicraft industries, along with economic specialization, division of labor, and the introduction of machines driven by inanimate sources of energy, all marked the end of the preindustrial city by the 1840s.

As cities became heavily peopled, and as the transition to an industrialized society occurred, the social complexion of urban America also changed. The stable and orderly society which prevailed in colonial years began to wear away—a social erosion hastened by rapid change. For one thing, abrupt population growth contributed to the emergence of a disorderly society. Although new transportation technology permitted the movement of the upper and middle classes to suburbs even during these early years, the cities themselves became increasingly congested. Several wards of New York City, for example, had average densities above 170 persons per acre by 1840. Most big cities experienced housing shortages; by the 1830s, European immigrants and native rural migrants crowded into boardinghouses, cellars, attics, newly converted tenements, and makeshift quarters along waterfronts and on the outskirts of business districts. These new residential patterns destroyed the homogeneity of earlier years and altered everyday relationships among city dwellers. Heavy population concentrations fostered impersonality and stimulated social tensions. Population growth also forced the physical expansion of urban centers—a haphazard process in the early nineteenth century. The rectangular gridiron pattern typically applied in Philadelphia and New York seemed efficient and businesslike, but the jumble of land uses and the absence of space for parks, squares, and neighborhood gathering places had a socially disintegrating effect.

Increasingly heavy immigration during the period contributed not only to urban population growth but also to social fragmentation. Only a small stream in the 1790s and interrupted several times in later years by war and depression, the immigrant influx hit flood tide after the 1820s. Almost 93,000 immigrants arrived in New York during the 1820s; more than 400,000 came during the 1830s. New York City annually received between one-half and two-thirds of all newcomers, although not all remained in the metropolis. By 1850, the foreign-born made up almost half of New York's total population. By the same year, Irish immigrants alone composed more than 25 percent of Boston's population. The newcomers—mostly Irish and German laborers and their families—added ethnic and religious diversity, challenged earlier majorities of English, Protestant stock, and altered the social complexion of city life in the United States. Nativists argued, more-over, that because the primarily Catholic foreigners constituted "the materi-als for mobs and rebellions," they threatened social stability and cohesive-ness. The Irish especially became the butt of nativist hostilities. Poverty-stricken, for the most part without marketable skills, seemingly averse to work, and morally offensive to old-stock Americans, they crowded growing slums in seaport cities and contributed to urban disorder.

Increasing class distinctions also fostered disorder. To be sure, upward economic mobility was always possible, but some historians have demon-strated increasing disparities in wealth and property distribution as the nineteenth century advanced, especially in urban commercial and business centers. Despite the rhetoric of egalitarianism in the "age of common man," a permanent proletariat was emerging in early nineteenth century cities, composed largely of unskilled, propertyless workers, immigrants, and blacks. Combined with the decline of deference, the reality of a larger, often discontented, lower class eroded the fixity of the old order and the values and norms which had sustained it.

Moreover, the disorder attendant on a large lower class was multiplied by geographic mobility and population turnover. According to early nine-teenth century observers, the lower stratum of society in American cities was characterized by a floating population of transients and migrants. One writer described the poor as "constantly on the wing." Many were immi-grants passing in or out of the city; others were native Americans who drifted temporarily to the city from the neighboring countryside or who sought new opportunities in the West after exhausting possibilities in the city. According to a recent study, population turnover in Boston amounted to about 30 percent per year in the 1830s and 1840s and 40 percent per year in the 1850s. Mobility undermined community as effectively as class dis-tinction and reflected the intensity of social change in the preindustrial city.

Simultaneous economic changes had a similar impact. In prerevolu-tionary times work patterns reinforced the cohesive community. Men worked in small shops with a few other apprentices and journeymen and the shop owner—a master craftsman. Such work patterns transferred skills and the incentive for shop ownership to the rising generation of craftsmen. The colonial city worker identified with his community and with the master craftsman—an employer who only temporarily stood above the worker in economic and social status. By the 1820s, however, cities such as New York, Philadelphia, and Boston were poised on the threshold of the industrial era. As the cities became important processing and manufacturing centers, the factory increasingly replaced the small shop and machines supplanted the skilled craftsman. Immigrants and farm girls took up places in the new fac-tories, further altering work patterns. At the same time, industrial beginnings produced new forms of economic complexity and interdependence. Workers, in turn, became increasingly subject to the business fluctuations, depressions, and unemployment which characterized the economic transformation of the period. Moreover, changes in the social organization of work brought specialization of tasks, lessened the importance of skill, and destroyed security, independence, and incentive for workers. In other words, the decline of handicraft industry undermined the urban worker's identification with community. These changes had a very real impact on worker behavior, as evidenced by the emergence of a strong but short-lived trade union movement complete with picketing, strikes, and labor violence in the 1820s and 1830s.

The development of factory-type work—observable as early as the 1790s—also had an impact on urban business leadership. Manufacturing in colonial years merely supplemented the commercial base of the economy, and a mercantile elite dominated political, economic, and social life of the cities through the Federalist period. But with emerging industrialism, home industries and transportation interests began to challenge entrenched merchant capitalists; new and specialized business concerns and corporations rivaled old mercantile families. By the 1820s and 1830s, "expectant capitalists" sought democratization of business life and supported President Andrew Jackson's attack on that symbol of financial power and privilege, the Second Bank of the United States. Corresponding developments occurred in American politics as state constitutional conventions made universal white male suffrage the rule by the end of the 1820s. In every seaport city, as manufacturing increasingly rivaled commerce in economic importance, and as politics became more egalitarian and subject to professional political bosses and ward heelers, the old merchant elites often suffered a relative decline in power, position, and social status.

Other developments also reflected the growing ferment and disorder of the preindustrial American city. Municipal governments failed to cope with a multiplicity of urban problems, and city services lagged far behind residential need. The essentially negative municipal controls and restrictive regulatory policies of the colonial era no longer sufficed in the larger, more diverse city of the early nineteenth century. Inadequate facilities for sewage and garbage disposal made such cities as New York "one huge pigstye," as diarist George Templeton Strong wrote in the late 1830s. Indeed, in the absence of public responsibility, roving pigs rivaled city scavengers in efficiency—a sure indication, one British traveler suggested, of "something wrong" with municipal administration. Poor water supplies and distorted medical conceptions rendered public health measures useless; epidemics of yellow fever and cholera periodically ravaged the cities. Despite constant complaints from citizens about crime and violence, no city had a professional police force before about 1840. Volunteer fire companies concentrated more on fighting one another than the frequent blazes, which could destroy whole sections of a city at a time. The city required positive government to counter disorder, but mayors and councilmen failed to provide it. As social order and the sense of community eroded, municipal government broke down as well.

Social and economic change, then, undermined the orderly, well-regulated society of the colonial town. Institutions which had fostered community, tempered conflict, kept order, and maintained social control in the small city became ineffective in the distended, disorderly seaport cities of the early nineteenth century. As a Philadelphia group noted in 1827, the ties which connected society had become "relaxed." The new conditions of an expansive but unsettled urban society imposed qualitative changes on the lives of city dwellers. Established middle-class norms and values held little meaning for the newcomers who crowded the cellars and tenements of the growing cities. The struggle for adjustment and survival absorbed most of their energies. Technology and immigration threatened the position of workers. Heterogeneity, diversity, and division marked emerging residential patterns.

By the 1820s, according to a Boston civic leader, social and economic changes had destroyed the "compact, united, and friendly community" of earlier years. Some observers thought they detected a widening gap between rich and poor—a disturbing sign of disunity and declining identification with community. For the rich, the self-interested and all-consuming concern for private wealth had corrupting influences. Yet the poor, somehow lacking this same acquisitive drive, remained equally corrupt. The role of the family seemed diminished; educators and preachers complained about the lessened influence of parents over children. Alarmed middle-class moralists noted rising rates of urban crime, violence, delinquency, and immorality. Nativists worried intensely about "internal subversion" purportedly plotted by Catholics, Freemasons, and abolitionists. Heightened ethnic, religious, class, and racial tensions resulted in a wave of urban riots and violence that reflected social unrest and fragmentation. The mob threatened the fragile foundations of American liberty. For a society which prized uniformity, stability, and order, which saw conformity as synonymous with cohesiveness and community, these social changes were especially disturbing. For those who defined the public good in terms of self-interest, disorder meant bad business, and violence posed an immediate personal danger. For those who identified with a virtuous and communal past, the signs of social anarchy seemed very real.

The forces of social and economic change shaped the preindustrial American city. In the period prior to the industrial takeoff of the 1840s, the

United States became an increasingly urban nation. Older cities expanded in the East, small villages became factory towns, and new urban centers sprouted in the developing West And, as has been suggested, the impact of urbanization was felt in a multitude of ways. Long before the Civil War, Americans were forced to confront an often harsh, demanding urban reality.

Selected Bibliography

For the publishers of the books listed in this bibliography and in those that follow, the interested student should consult *Books in Print* or the Library of Congress printed card catalog.

An important theoretical overview of the preindustrial city can be found in Gideon Sjoberg, *The Preindustrial City: Past and Present* (New York, 1960). A summary version of the book appears in Sjoberg's article, "The Preindustrial City," *American Journal of Sociology*, 60 (January 1955), 438–45. A number of other studies are also useful in providing a framework for understanding the historical dimensions of urban development: Lewis Mumford, *The City in History: Its Origins, Its Transformations, and Its Prospects* (New York, 1961); Philip M. Hauser, "Urbanization: An Overview," in Philip M. Hauser and Leo F. Schnore, editors, *The Study of Urbanization* (New York, 1965), 1–47; Oscar Handlin, "The Modern City as a Field of Historical Study" and Robert S. Lopez, "The Crossroads within the Wall," both in Oscar Handlin and John Burchard, editors, *The Historian and the City* (Cambridge, Mass., 1963), 1–26, 27–43.

Carl Bridenbaugh's massively researched volumes, *Cities in the Wilderness: The First Century of Urban Life in America, 1625–1742* (New York, 1938) and *Cities in Revolt: Urban Life in America, 1743–1776* (New York, 1955), remain indispensable for study of the colonial city. Focusing on the five largest colonial towns —Boston, Philadelphia, New York, Charleston, and Newport—both books exhaustively trace urban commerce and economic expansion, mounting social problems, patterns of municipal government, and evidences of cultural expression in the cities. Also important are: Darrett B. Rutman, *Winthrop's Boston: Portrait of a Puritan Town, 1630–1649* (Chapel Hill, N.C., 1965); G. B. Warden, *Boston, 1689–1776* (Boston, 1970); Carl and Jessica Bridenbaugh, *Rebels and Gentlemen: Philadelphia in the Age of Franklin* (Philadelphia, 1942); Frederick B. Tolles, *Meeting House and Counting House: The Quaker Merchants of Colonial Philadelphia* (Chapel Hill, N.C., 1948); Clarence P. Gould, "The Economic Causes of the Rise of Baltimore," in Leonard W. Labaree, editor, *Essays in Colonial History Presented to Charles McLean Andrews by His Students* (New Haven, 1931), 225–251; Thomas J. Wertenbaker, *The Golden Age of Colonial Culture* (New York, 1949). On smaller agrarian towns, see Kenneth A. Lockridge, *A New England Town: The First Hundred Years; Dedham, Massachusetts, 1636–1736* (New York, 1970), and Charles S. Grant, *Democracy in the Connecticut Frontier Town of Kent* (New York, 1961). Useful in explaining the lack of urbanism in the south is John C. Rainbolt, "The Absence of Towns in Colonial Virginia," *Journal of Southern History*, 35 (August 1969), 341–60. Urban economic and social developments in the colonial period are covered in James A. Henretta, "Economic Development and Social Structure in Colonial Boston," *William and Mary Quarterly*, 22 (January 1965), 75–92, and in Jackson Turner Main, *The Social Structure of Revolutionary America* (Princeton, N.J., 1965).

A number of studies suggest the important role of the city in stimulating the tensions leading to the American Revolution. Among the most important are: Hiller B. Zobel, *The Boston Massacre* (New York, 1970); Richard D. Brown, *Revolutionary Politics in Massachusetts: The Boston Committee of Correspondence and the Towns, 1772–1774* (Cambridge, Mass., 1970); Richard Walsh, *Charleston's Sons of Liberty: A Study of the Artisans, 1763–1789* (Columbia, S.C., 1959); Pauline Maier, "The Charleston Mob and the Evolution of Popular Politics in Revolutionary South Carolina, 1765–1784," *Perspectives in American History*, 4 (1970), 173–96; and Jesse Lemisch, "Jack Tar in the Streets: Merchant Seamen in the Politics of Revolutionary America," *William and Mary Quarterly*, 25 (July 1968), 371–407.

A useful introduction to the preindustrial city of the early nineteenth century can be found in David T. Gilchrist, editor, *The Growth of the Seaport Cities, 1790–1825* (Charlottesville, Va., 1967). Several more specialized works suggest the variety of the urban experience during the transition to industrialism: Richard C. Wade, *The Urban Frontier: The Rise of Western Cities, 1790–1830* (Cambridge, Mass., 1959); Richard C. Wade, *Slavery in the Cities: The South, 1820–1860* (New York, 1964); Leon Litwack, *North of Slavery: The Negro in the Free States, 1790–1860* (Chicago, 1961); George R. Taylor, *The Transportation Revolution, 1815–1860* (New York, 1951); Sam Bass Warner, Jr., *The Private City: Philadelphia in Three Periods of Its Growth* (Philadelphia, 1968); Peter R. Knights, *The Plain People of Boston, 1830–1860: A Study in City Growth* (New York, 1971); Letitia Woods Brown, *Free Negroes in the District of Columbia, 1790–1846* (New York, 1972); Robert Ernst, *Immigrant Life in New York City, 1825–1863* (New York, 1949); Charles E. Rosenberg, *The Cholera Years* (Chicago, 1962); Raymond A. Mohl, "Poverty, Pauperism, and Social Order in the Preindustrial American City, 1780–1840," *Social Science Quarterly*, 52 (March 1972), 934–48.

City Planning in America

Joseph L. Arnold

All cities are in some sense planned, whether by a single individual such as Pierre L'Enfant, who originated the plan for the nation's capital at Washington, or by hundreds of real estate developers and builders who plot streets and line them with houses and shops according to market demand. The planners of Washington wanted a noble and monumental city to house the government of the new republic. Real estate speculators, home builders, factory owners, and shippers in other East Coast cities were likewise planning for a purpose: the creation of profitable, efficient, and occasionally pleasant places of business. Consequently, few urban areas today evidence the comprehensive planning exhibited by Washington, but to call them unplanned is inaccurate. Contemporary urban form is often the cumulative result of thousands of little planning projects executed by generations of urban entrepreneurs and woven into the fabric of local ordinances created by municipal committees, city councils, and special commissions—the forerunners of modern departments of city planning.

This cumulative kind of planning has characterized the history of many American cities. The present streets of downtown Boston, for example, are laid over seventeenth century footpaths, which prudently circumvented hills now leveled and turned sharply to avoid buildings long ago demolished or pastures long since subdivided. These paths, rather well planned by those who trod them three hundred years ago, were widened and altered over the generations, but by the early years of the nineteenth century, they were frozen into the landscape as abutting properties grew too valuable to be taken for further widenings and alterations. Thus, Boston's footpaths remain, defying traffic engineers and motorists alike; yet they form an essential element in the city's unique physical charm. The street pattern is striking evidence of the hard grip of the past on the living city.

It would be misleading, however, to give the impression that Boston's incremental and somewhat random development was the norm from which L'Enfant's Washington was the rare deviant. Although truly comprehensive city planning emerged only in the twentieth century, many early American cities had carefully conceived general plans—plans which were the fruit of many centuries of European urban planning.

Colonial American planners drew heavily on Renaissance and baroque models for their cities in the wilderness. The ubiquitous gridiron street plan (or a geometric design overlaying the grid) was rediscovered by Europeans during the Renaissance; it was employed at home and abroad for much the same reason it had been used so extensively by the Greeks and Romans—it was the quickest and easiest way to impose physical order on rapidly expanding empires. St. Augustine, Florida, the oldest city in the continental United States, was laid out sometime before 1586 in accordance with the detailed plans for the establishment of new towns issued by Philip II of Spain in 1573. Philip's new town proclamation called for a rectangular gridiron focusing on a central square containing the principal public buildings —a scheme which undoubtedly drew heavily upon the recommendations of the Roman architect and engineer Vitruvius. His *Ten Books on Architecture* (circa 30 B.C.) appears also to have provided direct inspiration for the 1638 town plan of New Haven, Connecticut. In the Chesapeake colonies, Francis Nicholson, who served as governor of Maryland and later of Virginia, was responsible for the creation of new capital towns planned in the style of Sir Christopher Wren and the English baroque tradition. Annapolis, Maryland (1695), and Williamsburg, Virginia (1698), survive as living examples of this urbane governor's fine sense of proportion and geometric balance. William Penn's plan for Philadelphia (1682) is the best known of all colonial town plans, and as it was copied by countless newer towns on the nation's moving frontier, it exerted the most influence. A rectangular gridiron with two main streets (Broad and Market) intersecting at a civic plaza and with each quarter of the grid focusing on an open square, Penn's "green city" was almost an exact copy of Richard Newcourt's plan for the burnt-over district of London after the great fire of 1666. Only Savannah, Georgia (1733), the capital of James Oglethorpe's philanthropic colony for poor Englishmen, surpassed Philadelphia in its accommodation of open spaces within the gridiron; but perhaps because it was situated too far from the center of cultural influence or because it kept too much land out of the reach of urban real estate brokers, it exerted no influence on subsequent city planning in America.

In most American cities, the unrelieved gridiron became the hallmark of city planning. City surveyors marched row after row of city blocks inexorably across urban America, while their country cousins squared off farmlands in similar fashion. The unrelieved gridiron received a major boost from the New York City Commissioner's Plan of 1811, which extended twelve major avenues up the island of Manhattan and crossed them every 200 feet with a street sixty feet in width. The commission plotted 155 such cross streets, which extended a little over six miles beyond the built-up area of the city at the tip of Manhattan. The plan failed to meet the needs of late

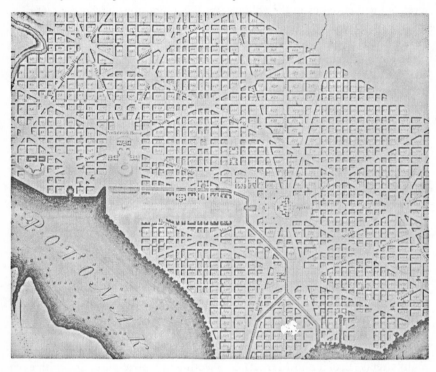

The L'Enfant Plan of Washington, 1791, Library of Congress. The greatest city plan in the United States is the brilliant creation of Pierre Charles L'Enfant, a French engineer who was given the commission to design a capital for the nation. The 1791 plan, though altered in many particulars, is still clearly recognizable in the present city. The central position is occupied by the Capitol building itself, with grand avenues leading .om it in every direction. The central design is a triangle with the Capitol, the White House, and the Washington Monument at the corners and the Mall, the White House Gardens, and Pennsylvania Avenue forming the sides. Thus, the two major federal buildings and the memorial to the nation's founder occupy the three anchors of the city design. The other major avenues were designed not only to provide grand vistas but also to facilitate rapid movement between distant points. A canal was included to encourage quick commercial expansion. Indeed, the planners of the new city were anxious that it quickly become a complete city; therefore, much land was given to private developers. A surprising 59 percent of the land area was given over to streets and avenues, which freed the capital from traffic jams until the motor vehicle finally overwhelmed it in the mid-twentieth century.

Plan of Boston, Massachusetts, in 1800. Medieval Boston's narrow, winding streets can be seen in the North End and in the area east of Tremont Street. Streets in these areas were already over a century old when this plan appeared, and they are still apparent on today's street maps of the city. But even in 1800, a new and more rational street pattern can be seen emerging on Beacon Hill

where the Mount Vernon Proprietors laid out lots designed to attract the city's
most prominent families. Streets were designed to minimize north-south traffic
because the developers did not want the poorer families then living on the north
slope of Beacon Hill tramping through the exclusive new neighborhood on the
south slope—an early case of class-oriented city planning. (I. N. Phelps Stokes
Collection, Prints Division, The New York Public Library, Astor, Lenox and Tilden
Foundations.)

nineteenth and twentieth century New Yorkers; the frequency of intersec-
tions, the narrowness of the cross streets, and the small size of the blocks
hampered movement and intensified congestion. Moreover, the New York
plan created a visually unattractive city which failed to match the capital
city then rising on the Potomac. The New York Commission's surveyor,
John Randel, Jr., explained that the chief virtue of the plan was that it facilitated the "buying, selling and improving of real estate." In his study, *The
Making of Urban America,* John Reps sadly notes that because New York
provided the model for many other cities, its street plan "was a disaster
whose consequences have barely been mitigated by more modern city planners." The gridiron typified the pell mell rush to wrest private wealth from
the city as quickly and effortlessly as possible. Buy it, cut it up, and sell out
at a profit. "Gain, Gain, Gain!" said a traveler in 1818, "is the beginning,
the middle and the end, the *alpha* and *omega* of the founders of American
towns."

Other serious planning errors stemmed from the failure to develop rational land-use patterns. During the nineteenth century, individual property
owners saw little need for land-use controls. Admittedly, comprehensive
land-use plans appeared superfluous in the small towns of the eighteenth
and nineteenth centuries. The villages of New England and their replicas on
the frontier were admirably planned for their small-scale functions of rural
crossroads of commerce and local centers of religious and social life. The
quaint clustering of church, general store, and blacksmith shop, intermin-
gled with tree-shaded homes, provided a land-use pattern that happily integrated the personal, economic, and socioreligious life of the community.
Even the largest cities of the nation maintained highly mixed patterns of

Central city traffic—nemesis of city planners. Right above, streetcars, wagons,
horses, carriages, and pedestrians jammed at Randolph and Dearborn, Chicago
1905. (Courtesy Chicago Historical Society.) Below is the "spaghetti bowl" on
the west side of Chicago's Loop, where three major superhighways intersect and
motorists exit for the central business district. This remarkable piece of highway
engineering has a sensuous sculptural quality to it (at least from the air) and is
obviously an improvement over the gridiron or the boulevard. Its construction,
however, required the leveling of several city blocks, and it creates a permanent
"dead" area in the central city that is inhospitable, untaxable, and unbreathable.
(Courtesy Portland Cement Association.)

land use in the preindustrial years. In the late eighteenth century, Philadelphia still presented the traveler with a mixture of comfortable townhouses, small laborers' cottages, taverns, and even stables crowded together on almost every block in the central city. Those few enterprises that presented a clear offense to their neighbors, such as tanneries, slaughterhouses, and brothels, had been banished by law from the built-up areas of towns since the early years of the colonial era.

But as trade and manufacturing grew, the easy-going land-use habits of property owners produced an offensive stew of factories, furnaces, and warehouses jumbled across a tangle of streets, alleys, canals, and railroads. The tannery and slaughterhouse had been joined by noisy, smoky, noxious factories, obtrusively large warehouses, and rail yards or sidings which sprang up wherever land could be bought. Lack of comprehensive planning for urban railroad networks resulted in enormous economic waste and environmental damage in the years after 1830. Tidy little commercial towns were inundated with railroads and the factories that sprang up in their wake. Whole neighborhoods were blighted and houses cut up into tiny tenement apartments for the new urban laboring class. Railroads plowed into the older established cities wherever they could obtain terminal yards and right-of-way rather than by any rational plan of transportation needs. In many cases, communities were cut in half, and adjacent open spaces became prime sites for warehouses and factories. Wherever railroads puffed in and out of the cities, they created the proverbial "other side of the tracks," often in areas that deserved a better fate.

The planning of facilities to protect public health also failed to keep up with the rush of urban growth. Colonial Boston made progress in the devel-

Golden Triangle area of Pittsburgh 1947 (left above) and 1969 (below). Rebuilding of the central business district of Pittsburgh, begun in 1947 by a coalition of local business and political leaders, provided the pattern for America's urban renewal projects of the 1950s and 1960s. As the photos of the Golden Triangle area of Pittsburgh reveal, the ugly and decayed central city of 1947 had been replaced by 1969 with an attractive and vibrant center of business and civic activity. Unfortunately, the efforts of Pittsburgh's planners to aid slum residents in the manner they aided central city businessmen was more meager and less successful. The techniques of massive demolition and large-scale reconstruction of the Golden Triangle, when applied to selected low income areas, sparked loud resistance from dispossessed residents and had no comparable impact on the other sections of the city. Indeed, Pittsburgh's housing stock was deteriorating faster than it could be renewed even with federal aid. The "Pittsburgh Renaissance" of the 1947–1969 era proved that urban renewal could cure sick central business districts, but that general urban health required more money and more imaginative planning techniques than those which saved the Golden Triangle. (Courtesy of Carnegie Library of Pittsburgh.)

opment of a sewer system to drain streets and cellars, but the system operated without municipal support and was thus available only to affluent citizens. Most urban water came from private and public wells. By 1809, New York had 249 public wells, all of them noted for their foulness. The terrible epidemics of the late eighteenth century were traced to polluted water or to inadequate amounts of water to wash the streets of accumulated filth. By the end of the eighteenth century, the need for fresh, abundant supplies of water presented cities with one of the first planning problems requiring a comprehensive solution. Philadelphia led the way in 1799 with construction of the first citywide water system in the United States, and other major cities of the East soon followed suit. But after an encouraging start, the movement failed to keep up with burgeoning population growth. The fast-growing cities of the West, racked by financial problems during the periodic panics of the nineteenth century, often lacked the basic rudiments of a piped water system. By the mid-nineteenth century, Philadelphia, New York, and other large eastern cities left whole districts without adequate water or sewage lines—almost invariably in slum areas.

In the last quarter of the nineteenth century, most major cities established citywide (and in many instances metropolitan) systems for water, sewage, parks, and transportation. Boston, New York, and Baltimore constructed long aqueducts to bring water into the cities from sources in the Appalachian mountains; smaller cities experimented with various types of filtration plants. In 1871, Chicago reversed the flow of the Chicago River and channeled its sewage into the Illinois-Mississippi system, which greatly improved the quality of Lake Michigan water but polluted the rivers. With the establishment in 1889 of the Metropolitan Sanitary District, covering 185 square miles, a regional system of sanitary canals, filtration plants, and pumping stations was constructed over the next decade. The Chicago Sanitary and Ship Canal, the backbone of the system, required more excavation than the Panama Canal.

Municipal transportation first became a citywide problem in the 1830s and 1840s, when urban areas expanded beyond easy walking distance, and intracity freight hauling grew larger in tonnage and the distance carried. Omnibuses and later horse cars drawn on rails and a few commuter railroads carried tens of thousands of workers and shoppers into and across town by the time of the Civil War. In the late 1880s and the two decades following, electric streetcar lines increased the range and efficiency of commuter travel and for the first time integrated many small transit companies into metropolitan transit systems, which operated with great efficiency despite periodic plundering by unscrupulous financiers. The movement of goods underwent no similar revolution. The electric streetcar, although it was used for a number of hauling jobs, was tied to rails and lacked flexibility. The horse-drawn company wagons that jammed city streets at the turn of the century were obviously limited in both speed and capacity, and they caused traffic jams at least as bad as, if not worse than, present ones. The only solution to this problem appeared to be wider streets and more carefully planned service entrances. Old street surveyors were gradually replaced by traffic engineers, who struggled to ease urban traffic problems with little more success than was achieved in the nineteenth century.

Planning for adequate water, sewage, and transportation made cities inhabitable, but it failed to enhance their attractiveness. The urban park movement between 1850 and 1900 was spurred by the (psychologically sound) romantic notion that city dwellers needed easy access to a rural environment and also by the desire of American municipalities to emulate the beautiful park systems of great European cities. The purchase and improvement of land for city parks began in the 1850s with New York's Central Park and Druid Hill Park in Baltimore. By 1880, almost every city in America had developed a park system. St. Louis and Chicago, each with over 2,000 acres of parkland, led the nation; New York and San Francisco each had over 1,000 acres, and many smaller cities had acquired several hundred acres each—often paying $1,000 to $4,000 per acre for unoccupied but potentially valuable land on the fringes of built-up areas. Purchasing parkland in the central city was almost prohibitively expensive; in 1872, Cleveland purchased 10.4 acres in the central city for slightly over $22,000 per acre. The first truly citywide system of parks was built in Chicago in the 1870s, but in 1893, Boston went a step further in organizing a metropolitan park commission, which soon developed a 15,000-acre park system in the central city and surrounding suburban towns. Thus, many municipalities had the foresight in the middle and late nineteenth century to buy large amounts of parkland that later became surrounded by dense construction. These acquisitions still provide most inner-city residents with the bulk of their parkland.

Out of the movement for urban parks, citywide utilities, improved transportation, and greater urban amenities came the so-called city-beautiful and city-efficient movements—the direct precursors of twentieth century city planning. This movement emerged as part of the intellectual and social reform fervor of the Progressive Era. Progressive reformers shared the perhaps naive but exhilarating assumption that the tools of the new social and physical sciences, once placed in the hands of the virtuous middle classes and enlightened businessmen, would soon produce a rational and just society crowned by beautiful, prosperous, and happy cities. Walter Lippmann, writing in *Drift and Mastery* (1914), shrewdly recognized that in a capitalistic and highly individualistic society it would be very difficult to create agencies that could master chaos without offending large numbers of the citizens upon whom those agencies depended for power. The assumption that "scientific" city planning agencies would be staffed by selfless civic statesmen directing urban affairs for the benefit of all citizens flew in the face of the realities of America's class structure and economic system. As the subsequent history of urban America reveals, city planners and municipal planning commissions have primarily served the interests of the business leaders and affluent property owners who control the urban economy. At best, city planning has until recently been of marginal value to the moderate income groups; at worst it has actively cooperated with the elite to ruthlessly exploit and destroy much of the valuable fabric of urban society.

From the beginning, it was clear that those who were interested in comprehensive city planning were motivated primarily by aesthetic and economic considerations reflecting their upper-class backgrounds. Municipal art societies (a number of which later changed their names to city planning commissions) and various civic clubs most often looked to Baron Haussman's Paris for their model of a beautiful and efficient city. The fact that the lovely boulevards, grand plazas, and architectural monuments of Paris had been built by the dictator Napoleon III to provide a suitable backdrop for his anticipated long and glittering reign is of more than passing interest.

In the United States, the great Chicago World's Fair of 1893 gave millions of citizens a fleeting glimpse of a well-planned (albeit neoclassic) urban environment. However, the parklike setting and exotic displays seemed too remote and unreal for imitation in stormy, husky, brawling cities such as Chicago. It was in the more sylvan atmosphere of turn-of-the-century Washington that the grand tradition of city planning was reborn. Beginning as a modest proposal to spruce up the Capitol area with a few new public buildings and some monuments commemorating the city's centennial, the Senate Park Commission gradually developed a plan to reconstruct the entire central city on the heroic scale envisioned by L'Enfant. The McMillan Commission's master plan for Washington became the hallmark of the early city planning movement. Daniel Burnham, the chief planner of the Chicago World's Fair, combined his talents with renowned architect Charles McKim and the nation's leading landscape architect, Frederick Law Olmsted, Jr., to draw a plan which over the next seventy years transformed the Capitol area into a shining monument of malls lined with neoclassic (or austere modern) public structures. Whether the result of this prodigious effort is attractive, noble, or pompous is a matter of taste, but in the early years of the twentieth century, it excited civic leaders; it also made Burnham and Olmsted the nation's leading city planners. These two singular individuals, along with a small group of architects and landscape designers, moved from city to city drawing sweeping plans for turning congested and frowsy looking central cities into a cross between Paris and Washington with a liberal sprinkling of Greek and Roman façades which hid railroad stations, court buildings, and museums.

Burnham's greatest effort was his spectacular Chicago plan. It revealed both the best aspects of the city-beautiful tradition and some of its most serious weaknesses. With an $85,000 grant from Chicago's prestigious Commercial Club, Burnham produced a lavishly illustrated *Plan of Chicago* (1909) calling for the development of the entire lake-front into a system of beaches and harbors and the creation of a huge civic center, from which would flow broad boulevards in every direction. Moreover, Burnham envisioned recasting the entire transportation system of the central city, even to the inclusion of a beltway around the central business district. Although it allowed for the usual emphasis on Parisian-style parks and boulevards, Burnham's plan was not simply a beaux arts cosmetic for the world's hog butcher. The "betterment of commercial facilities" and the removal of obstacles which prevented or obstructed efficient "transportation for persons and goods" provided the basic rationale for his plan. But important as many of these changes were to the economy of the city, the improvements primarily benefited the upper classes, who would find the city more efficient for business and more attractive for leisure pursuits.

Although it briefly noted the existence of a "slum problem," Burnham's plan offered no solution. Indeed, he strongly hinted that the American capitalist economy was incapable of providing decent housing for the poor! Burnham quickly passed over the whole question of Chicago's low-income residential and commercial sections; he undoubtedly knew his employers were not deeply interested in such matters. Over the next thirty years the city of Chicago spent hundreds of millions of dollars to execute much of Burnham's plan. One can only speculate on how things might have turned out if the city had given up some of its showy projects and transferred a few of those millions of dollars to Jane Addams to carry out a "city plan" for the poor. The very idea is of course absurd, for what the city was willing to spend on its physical plant (and what private citizens were willing to donate in the way of museums, opera houses, and statuary) would never have been allowed to flow into the slums. It is therefore idle to blame the early generation of city planners for catering exclusively to the elite because there was no realistic alternative.

City planning for the lower classes hardly exists in the American tradition. The poor live as they can in areas not taken up by some more important use. When city planners occasionally turned their attention to this problem in the late nineteenth and early twentieth centuries, they inevitably floundered in conceptualization or implementation. Many urban reformers of the Progressive Era remained incredibly optimistic and simplistic in their faith that the new social sciences could eliminate poverty. Charles Mulford Robinson, one of the first to offer university courses on city planning, made such contentions in his pioneer study *Modern Civic Art* (1903):

Social problems are to a large degree problems of environment. This with increasing positiveness is the conclusion of modern scientific study into the depths of sociology. Give to the boy and girl a chance; make it possible for them to work off sheer animal energy in harmless amusements; render homes pleasant, and satisfy the craving of men for brightness, entertainment, and fellowship without throwing them into temptation; let an abundance of fresh air and sunshine into living and sleeping rooms, and the slum will be ancient history and many of sociology's hardest problems will be solved. The Juvenile Court would not have business enough to keep it going; the saloon would have its vigour sapped by a substitute; the hospitals would not require constant multiplication.

Since even optimists like Robinson recognized that urban reformers could not alter the structure of American capitalism as it affected low-income families, they focused on three solutions for improving the immediate environment of the slum: housing reform, slum parks, and decentralization. Housing reformers urged the establishment of housing codes to prevent the construction of unhealthy units; they also promoted various schemes of limited-dividend "model housing," which might curb the philanthropic investor's appetite for profits while benefiting the poor. Lawrence Veiller and Robert W. DeForest's study of housing conditions in New York City resulted in the enactment of the Tenement Law of 1901, the first comprehensive building code in the United States. While it ended some of the worst abuses, the New York code was not combined with a similarly comprehensive program to stimulate construction of decent low-income housing. Almost all limited-dividend housing was too expensive for low-income and working-class people, and it failed to attract more than a handful of philanthropic investors.

A number of reformers led the movement to build small parks and playgrounds in slum areas. Painfully aware of the impact of daily street life on slum children, settlement house workers hoped the building of playgrounds would at least provide a modicum of joy and fresh air for young people living and working in airless, tuberculosis-ridden tenements. Some of the more effusive supporters of this effort, such as Jacob Riis and Charles Mulford Robinson, gave the public sentimental accounts of how slum parks transformed tough slum gangs into congeries of happy children enjoying healthy sports and tending the park greenery. Such optimism led many to the conclusion that parks and playgrounds were the panacea for the problem of juvenile delinquency.

Of all the schemes for banishing the slum, decentralization appeared at the time to offer the best hope. It was widely recognized that urban congestion resulted in high central-city land values. Since working-class people could not afford long commutes, they were doomed to pay high rents for tiny dwellings in the central city unless their jobs and homes could be removed to inexpensive land on the urban fringe. With such decentralization, furthermore, new industrial-residential complexes could be rationally preplanned without having to contend with obsolete street systems and structures or with the demoralizing effects of central-city slums. Businessmen themselves saw advantages in moving their operations out of the costly and congested central city. In the 1880s, George Pullman constructed his famous company town outside Chicago and was praised by almost all urban reform elements. However, worker discontent over Pullman's paternalism, bad publicity connected with the great Pullman strike of 1894, plus the apparent failure of the town to pay for itself convinced most large corporations that company towns were not usually good business ventures. When U.S. Steel built its huge Gary, Indiana, plant, it planned one section of the town but left most of the new city in the hands of private real estate speculators. It is unfortunate that the large corporations—the only institutions of this era that could have created a wide range of decentralized new towns—were too timid to try such experiments. The efforts to build "garden cities" in America, based on the brilliant plans of England's Ebenezer Howard, did not attract enough capital for even a single experimental town. A few small efforts were made in building moderate-income housing projects on the urban fringe, but they exerted little influence. Forest Hills Gardens, a carefully designed project in Queens, New York, built by the Russell Sage Foundation, proved that at least middle-income families could be profitably housed in an attractive environment. But as Robert DeForest, the foundation's president, admitted, the average worker's income was still too low to permit him to live in Forest Hills Gardens. Thus, most decentralization schemes failed to match the expectations of optimistic urban reformers.

The failure of city planners to serve the poor, although it upset some practitioners, resulted in no serious decline in the profession's sources of support; but the failure to serve adequately the rich and powerful carried with it the threat of premature extinction. The second generation of city planners contained a number of men who were intent on changing the character of the profession to make it even more relevant to dominant economic interests of urban areas. The tendency of the early city planning movement to draw on landscape architecture and the beaux arts tradition appeared to many business-minded and engineering-minded planners to jeopardize the entire movement. Planners such as George B. Ford, who combined an engineering degree from Massachusetts Institute of Technology with an architecture diploma from the École des Beaux Arts in Paris, worked hard during the early years of the century to turn "civic art" into an "exact science" and to transform municipal art societies into hard-headed city planning commissions that could make cities more efficient. While he was certainly not devoid of interest in aesthetic city planning or in the problems of the slum (his thesis at the École was entitled "A Tenement in a Large City"), Ford's message to city planners was that the profession would not achieve significant influence until it recast itself in the tradition of his contemporary Frederick W. Taylor, the great industrial efficiency expert. Taylor's desire was to show factory managers how they could increase production (and profits) while lightening the burden on the laborer. It was a vain hope on Ford's part that such a highly political question as the planning and control of urban development would be given over to similarly "objective" professional city planners. The modern city, unlike the modern factory, could not be "Taylorized," because no single authority held complete power. Even among wealthy property owners and businessmen there was no agreement on urban planning beyond the need for basic transportation and utility systems. Until the housing and urban renewal programs of the 1950s and 1960s, urban planners seldom did more than follow residential and commercial developers with transportation and sewer systems. The only new planning tool initiated in the Progressive Era was zoning, but its chief influence was not felt until the 1920s and 1930s.

By 1917, American city planning had established a firm foothold as a profession in service to the urban elite. Most major cities had established planning commissions, and a number employed professional city planners to draw up master plans for future development of transportation and utility systems, location of public facilities, and general land uses. Landscape architects, engineers, lawyers, and others involved in city planning began holding annual conferences in 1909. In 1917, they followed the precedent of other professions by founding a permanent society, the American City Planning Institute (ACPI) (now called the American Institute of Planners).

The dozen years between the founding of the ACPI and the onset of the Great Depression was a period of rapid urban expansion. Builders in large central cities pushed hundreds of skyscrapers high into the air, a visible sign of soaring land values. New York City had 586 buildings over twenty stories high by 1932. Home builders, industrialists, and commercial entrepreneurs, freed as never before by the internal combustion engine, flooded over the open lands of the urban fringes. City planners strained their energies to bring even a degree of efficiency to the new urban forms wrought by the automobile and truck. Not only planners but many thoughtful citizens were quick to see the disadvantages as well as the obvious advantages of the automobile. America's two million motor vehicles were already a serious traffic problem in cities on the eve of the First World War, and ten years later, there were twelve motor vehicles on the road for each one present in 1918. They clogged city thoroughfares, turning the gridiron street system into a deadly pattern of intersecting straightaways killing and maiming tens of thousands by the end of the 1920s. They forced states and municipalities into enormous expenditures for new streets and for paving and widening older ones. Automobiles began to undermine regular use of trolley lines and interurban railroads, fatally weakening many of them by the time the Great Depression struck in the 1930s. Finally, they encouraged speculators to prematurely plot thousands of acres of new subdivisions which bore no relation to previous city plans and which were of too low density to support mass transit service. Many of these auto-spawned housing developments spilled across municipal boundaries, creating regional metropolises that enormously complicated the problem of comprehensive planning.

As in the case of slum housing, city planners proved powerless to alter the fundamental "decision" to restructure the city and urban life around the motor vehicle. This choice was made by Detroit auto manufacturers and eager American consumers. What began as a luxury for the prosperous soon became a costly necessity for almost every American. Regional planning and zoning, the two major innovations in city planning during the 1920s, were to a large degree responses to the new scale of the city emerging under the impact of the automobile. The first regional planning project was begun in 1921 in New York. Charles D. Norton, a collaborator with Burnham in *The Plan of Chicago*, convinced the Russell Sage Foundation to create a master plan for the enormous twenty-two-county metropolitan region that stretched from southern Connecticut and the lower Hudson Valley across New York City to northeastern New Jersey. The Committee on the Regional Plan of New York and Its Environs issued a steady stream of reports on every major aspect of the New York region. Similar efforts were carried out by city planner Gordon Whitnall and his Los Angeles County Regional Planning Association, founded in 1922. The Chicago Regional Planning Association, established by Cook County's commissioners in 1923, expanded the scope of Burnham's original plan to include the entire tristate area surrounding the Windy City. All three organizations urged the rational preplanning of metropolitan growth, but the inevitable emphasis was on transportation, zoning, parks, and utility systems. Housing received a low priority because planners saw little hope of influencing the private housing market. Anxious to be taken seriously by the political and economic leadership, regional planners accepted basic urban trends such as the movement of the affluent into suburban areas while low-income groups stayed behind in old urban centers.

This pattern prevailed among the regional planners of New York. They made no effort to even out the dispersal of New York's population through the construction of suburban towns open to a variety of income groups. There was no challenge to the projection of the New York region's continued growth from a giant to a supergiant. The authors of the regional plan believed that their most valuable contribution would be to rationalize and facilitate the manifest trends of the region. Challenges to fundamental trends, it was thought, would simply be ignored. Thus, in terms of its limited goals, the regional plan was remarkably successful because many of its recommendations were adopted over the next several decades.

The only planning group to offer a radically different model of regional development in the 1920s, the Regional Planning Association of America, was a small organization that struggled along without funds or outside support. However, the RPAA attracted a number of people who later achieved international reputations in the planning profession—Clarence Stein, Catherine Bauer, Arthur Kohn, and Lewis Mumford. Rejecting the idea of the inevitable massing of populations in ever larger cities, these youthful, brilliant individuals suggested that cities be limited in size and that increasing population be dispersed into self-contained new towns and smaller semirural communities. The automobile and the electrical generator, they argued, freed urbanites to live in the countryside without losing the conveniences of the city. Such a major alteration of the pattern of American urbanization called for regional planning on a scale that far exceeded the scope of the New York and Los Angeles plans. The RPAA caused a brief stir within the planning profession but exerted no influence on official planning agencies or the urban elite during the 1920s. Indeed, only in the 1970s are such proposals receiving serious attention.

Zoning was the tool that first gained wide acceptance for city planners in urban America during the 1920s. The increasing velocity of urban change and the unlocking of commercial and industrial enterprises from dependence on trolley and rail lines presented a great potential threat to both urban and suburban neighborhoods. Zoning appeared to be a device for creating stability and for protecting the general public from radical, detrimental changes in land use; many early zoning supporters were people of genuinely reformist sentiment. By the end of the 1920s, though, many city planners realized that zoning also had become a tool of the rich and powerful to protect their own special interests, while it gave the average city dweller little if any security. Clarence Stein, Gordon Whitnall, and a number of other planners told the public that zoning as then practiced gave security to only a few and promoted neither efficient planning nor healthy social trends. And although openly racial zoning has been repeatedly struck down by the Supreme Court since 1917, de facto segregation of nonwhites (along with most poorer whites) through zoning has been pervasive to the present day.

The concept of zoning was not the culprit, although numerous planners found the system so corrupt and misunderstood that they recommended its abolition. Zoning ordinances in large central cities during this era were a mixture of naiveté and rapacity. Many predominately residential areas were zoned commercial or even industrial because influential realtors hoped it would increase the speculative value of their properties. Only upper-class residential neighborhoods could make their residential designation permanent. Residential suburban communities outside city limits had few problems, because most of them were middle-class areas that excluded virtually all other land uses and building densities.

Since the end of the Second World War, central cities have developed much more sophisticated zoning ordinances and have edged somewhat closer to the ideal of protecting the whole community from unhealthy mixtures of land uses. The development of historic area zoning, which prevents the destruction of priceless old sections such as New Orleans's Vieux Carré or Boston's Beacon Hill area, are positive uses of zoning. But this device insures not only that the wealthy cannot put up factories and skyscrapers in such areas but also that low-income groups will not enter because of the high cost of restoration to meet zoning requirements. Planners are forced in this case, as in almost every other, to choose between the lesser of two evils.

Even with the widespread adoption of zoning, master plans, and highway projects, only forty of the ninety-three cities with populations over 100,000 provided even minimal appropriations for their commissions during the 1920s. Most communities hired planning consultants to draw up ordinances and other project proposals but left implementation to nonprofessional planning commissions and city engineering departments. Few cities under 25,000 even sought the advice of professional consultants or bothered to establish planning commissions. When the Great Depression hit in the 1930s, planning departments were among the first to be liquidated. The profession, which was developing a comprehensive package of planning tools to help the urban elite, was still often regarded with suspicion or was entirely ignored. The depression proved that many city councils and urban business groups still thought city planners a luxury that could be liquidated to "save money." Had not Franklin Roosevelt's New Deal initiated a vast public works program during the 1930s, city planners would have suffered far leaner times.

Initially, some city planners hoped that President Roosevelt would undertake a major urban planning program. Roosevelt's uncle, Frederick Delano, was a leading figure in the city planning profession, and Roosevelt himself had often spoken of the need for more city and regional planning. However, faced with the critical unemployment problems of the 1930s and the widespread resistance to planning by Congress and local governments, Roosevelt never proposed a national program of urban planning and reconstruction. Rather, the federal government financed the construction of many urban facilities through a wide variety of independent federal agencies. Most projects were initiated at the local level by urban politicians in consultation with business groups and planners; many of them simply dusted off projects planned in the 1920s. The unemployed were put to work constructing bridges, streets, sewers, public buildings, parks, airports, and harbor facilities. In this regard, the New Deal helped the unemployed while serving the interests of traditional city planning commissions.

On the other hand, a degree of planning experimentation was evidenced by the federal public housing program, the greenbelt towns, and the work of the Urbanism Committee of the National Resources Committee. Prior to the Housing Act of 1937, the New Deal public housing program was carried out by the Public Works Administration. Not tied to any broad federal housing plan, it was conceived primarily as a useful way to create jobs for the unemployed. The passage of the Wagner Housing Act took the planning function of the housing program out of federal hands and gave it to local housing authorities, but it represented one of the first attempts to encourage cities to plan and construct something of value primarily for low-income urbanites. For the first time, city planners had at least one crude tool with which to attack slums and aid the poor.

The greenbelt town program was conceived by Rexford Tugwell, the head of the Resettlement Administration, as a demonstration of planned metropolitan growth on the general model of the British garden suburb. Three greenbelt suburban towns were constructed, one each on the fringes of Washington, Cincinnati, and Milwaukee; their residents were drawn from moderate-income groups previously living in slum housing. Each town was constructed around neighborhood units, its traffic streets were separated from footpaths, and the whole area was surrounded by a greenbelt of open land. The schools served as community centers as well as for education, and the shopping centers in each town contained consumer cooperative stores. Tugwell and the many city planners who worked on the program hoped that the success of the greenbelt towns would stimulate public pressure on Congress to broaden the program and give it permanent status, or at least to encourage private builders to imitate the large-scale economies and social innovations of the greenbelt towns. Neither hope materialized. Most Congressmen showed little interest in the program, and some expressed hostility. Private real estate interests, fearing an invasion of prime suburban land by less affluent Americans, expressed opposition. Displaying only mild interest, the public never organized to promote the greenbelt program. Public housing advocates concentrated their efforts on central-city housing, fearing that new towns were too advanced for public acceptance.

The Urbanism Committee of the National Resources Committee was a research group composed of a number of the most prestigious planners of the decade. Their major report, *Our Cities: Their Role in the National Economy*, offered a sober, low-key analysis of the nation's urban problems and suggestions of how city and regional planning could help alleviate them. Like the Regional Plan of New York, it called for building on current urban trends rather than attempting fundamental alterations. Noting how little was actually known about the urban process, the committee recommended the formation of a permanent urban research agency and the establishment of a national clearinghouse for urban information. The report appeared at the height of Roosevelt's conflicts with Congress in 1937–38, and its modest recommendations were ignored and the committee itself gradually extinguished by congressional budget cuts. Thus, New Deal ventures into city planning left a few small projects and a wealth of experience and data but no federal planning.

The planning profession itself underwent a significant change in the 1930s. The experience of the Great Depression and the intellectual currents of the decade resulted for the first time in the realization that the profession had focused too narrowly on physical planning and had ignored the social, economic, and political realities of urban life. The planning profession was castigated by sociologists such as Louis Wirth for concentrating on land use and physical structures while too often overlooking "the complex technological and social superstructure through which it has been modified." More pointedly, sociologist Edwin S. Burdell specifically complained in the *Planner's Journal* in 1936 that the city planner paid "lip service to the social and economic fundamentals underlying his engineering techniques," but he actually neither wrote nor read books in these areas. With the return of prosperity by 1941 and the renewal of the suburban exodus (before wartime restrictions halted it for another few years), Edmond Hoben of the National Association of Housing Officials asked planners how they could "moan about the loss of population from the central areas and parent cities on the one hand, and, on the other either approve of or actually propose new ways of encouraging citizens to flee the city."

The planning profession was itself divided over many of the critical issues raised during the 1930s, and its annual conferences and journal articles provided podiums for a continuing debate on questions of theory and practice. At its 1938 convention the AIP agreed to widen its official statement of goals to include metropolitan and regional planning. The emphasis, however, was still on physical planning; no agreement could be reached on the proper role of social and economic planning. Socioeconomic considerations only complicated an already difficult task, many argued; moreover, discussion of such matters opened overly wide areas of basic discord within the profession. Opponents argued that without such considerations physical planners were building on a foundation of sand.

Fundamental to the argument was a lack of a common conception of what a good city should be like—physically or socioeconomically. The grand architectural visions of Burnham that captured the imagination of the previous generation had by 1940 faded into the past as a naive utopianism, but no new vision had replaced it. The remarkably prophetic *Futurama* created by Norman Bel Geddes for the General Motors pavilion at the World's Fair of 1939 depicted the superhighways and superskyscrapers of the 1970s, but it rested for its effect on the same spectacular monumentality as Burnham's plans forty years before. It all looked clean and well ordered from a distance, but would it be the sort of city men and women would want to live in and raise their children in? Those who produced the film *The City*, shown at another building at the 1939 fair, portrayed the modern supercity as a psychotic monster and offered the greenbelt town, which was built to human scale, as the best way to achieve a healthy balance between *rus* and *urb*.

While some planners called for drastic reorientation of the entire urban process, others believed such an approach to be economically impossible and politically impractical. The majority of city planning commission members in 1940 were still businessmen and real estate dealers. Thus, more practical planners stressed the necessity of working with the urban political and economic leadership, in the process educating them about the advantages of planning in serving both private interests and public welfare. Critics of this position argued that a marriage of private profit and public good would never occur and that planners were fooling themselves by thinking that they could somehow plan away fundamental economic and social conflicts. Neither group thought seriously about wide citizen participation in the planning process. These debates between 1933 and 1945 remained largely theoretical because, with the exception of the New Deal public housing and public works projects, cities failed to initiate comprehensive planning programs. The great urban changes and the real coming of age of urban planning lay in the quarter century following World War II.

American cities have been profoundly altered by the billions of federal dollars poured into them in the past twenty-five years. In the process, the city planning profession finally overcame the barriers which kept it on the periphery of the traditional urban power structure. Federal programs soon required the hiring of professional planners who could design projects for submission to funding agencies in Washington and who could implement such programs when the money arrived. Today, approximately a thousand local planning agencies employ a small army of planners who are paid out of sizable (federally aided) planning budgets. The largest cities often have planning staffs of seventy or eighty and budgets of well over $1 million. In 1970, Los Angeles alone spent $3,184,795 on planning. The total federal contribution to planning activities across the nation in the same year came to slightly over $50,000,000. City planning, in short, has become big business.

Having thus secured a permanent place in the urban structure, planners designed large-scale projects for all major cities. Yet they found themselves attacked not only by irate citizens but by groups within the planning profession as well. Planning agencies were charged with insensitivity to human suffering, with racism, elitism, inefficiency, and political chicanery. They were called lackeys of the power structure who engaged in reverse planning —that is, the spending of millions of dollars to create an *inferior* environment. By the mid-1960s, abundant evidence had accumulated to support many of these charges. What had gone wrong with this apparent triumph of urban reform? The answer lies in a number of factors.

Planners, like many other urban experts, continued to oversimplify the difficulties of intervention in central cities. While much had been learned about the sociology and political economy of cities since the days of Burnham and Charles Mulford Robinson, research had been very spotty, and no unified theory of the urban process could (or can now) stand up under detailed application. Until recently, planning officials remained remarkably ill informed on urban research outside the area of physical planning. Few of those responsible for the programs of the 1950s and 1960s were trained in schools of city planning; even fewer made the effort to keep informed on matters such as ghetto economics, the culture of poverty, ecological degradation, and narcotics addiction. Literature on these subjects was almost nonexistent in the 1940s and 1950s, and it was certainly not easily available to busy planners. Urban planning will continue to be severely handicapped by the failure of funding agencies to promote basic research on the urban and regional environment. A great deal more has been spent investigating the moon in the past twenty years than has been spent looking into the causes of urban pathology and decay.

Planners were unable to interest suburban governments in the pressing problems of central cities; indeed, most suburbanites had moved outside the core area to escape the very problems planners sought to solve. Real estate companies, banks, and the FHA kept even middle-class blacks out of suburban areas, and local suburban governments refused to establish public housing. Thus, the stage was set for the central-city denouement of the 1950s and 1960s. Actually, neither planners nor anyone else foresaw the rapidity with which the transformation occurred under the impact of massive migrations of poor and nonwhite families into central cities and the equally rapid exodus of white middle-class families and businesses to suburbia.

It was certainly foolish and insensitive for planning officials to believe that a profession having an almost exclusively white membership could work harmoniously with segregated and exploited poor people and minority races, even with the best of programs. With the planner's one-eyed view of the city as a physical entity, of course, citizens didn't have to be poor or black to be bulldozed by inhuman and socially sterile planning projects. Where racism, elitism, and human insensitivity were combined in urban projects, the results were sometimes catastrophic. The ruins of the huge Pruitt-Igoe project in St. Louis, developed by qualified planners and designed by a world-famous architect, offer a classic case of unconscious self-destruction.

The failure of planning in central cities is also due to the crude nature of early federal programs and to the mixture of stupidity, prejudice, and avarice with which local political leaders handled federal money. The Housing Act of 1949 was the first major federal legislation aimed at the total eradication of slums and the creation of "a decent home and a suitable living environment for every American family." The act empowered local redevelopment agencies to demolish slum areas and to offer the cleared land to private developers at a subsidized bargain price, with the expectation that these entrepreneurs would build it back up on a paying basis. In order to provide for displaced residents who could not find adequate private housing, the 1949 act authorized construction of 810,000 public housing units over a six-year period. But through congressional budget cutting and local inefficiency or reluctance, it took not six but *twenty* years for the nation to get the 810,000 low-income units.

Local leaders, armed with condemnation powers and federal money, began wholesale removal of poor black and white families. Even larger displacements came under the Interstate Highway Act of 1956, but urban officials said such moves were essential to the economic health and safety of the cities. Like the railroads of a century before, superhighways plowed through areas that were only marginally substandard and that in some cases were absolutely sound; but highways required much more space than railroads and thus had a more detrimental impact. As a result, neighborhoods were blighted, potentially attractive waterfront and riverside areas were cut off, and priceless old parks and open spaces were buried under tons of steel and concrete.

Even after highways were built and renewal lands leveled and offered for sale at bargain prices, private developers were reluctant to invest in renewal areas. Private builders could not profitably construct housing at a price the poor could afford. Even commercial and industrial concerns usually chose a suburban location over cleared land in the inner city. Many urban renewal projects took from five to fifteen years to complete. Caught between urban redevelopment and the trickle of new low-income housing, evicted families were forced into other neighborhoods, where compliant landlords cut up standard housing units into instant new slums. By 1960, urban renewal and highway programs had caused more deterioration than they eliminated. A number of cities were able to build flashy civic centers, office buildings, and upper-income housing on their cleared land, but displaced residents often received nothing but moving expenses.

Small businesses also suffered from relocation. A detailed study in Providence, Rhode Island, in the 1950s found that one-third of all businesses displaced by urban renewal or highways never reopened. A seventy-five-year-old Russian immigrant whose fifty-year-old grocery business was ended by urban renewal demolition sadly commented that even though he would suffer no financial loss, his little store was very important to him and his neighbors who met and talked there. "I'm going crazy with nothing to do," he told an investigator. Similarly, a sixty-four-year-old junk dealer in the same neighborhood was forced into early "retirement" because, as he said, "one cannot get work at sixty-four years of age."

The impact on black people was staggering. In Stockton, California, urban renewal leveled an entire black community—even its thirty-two churches. A freeway in 97 percent white St. Paul, Minnesota, removed over 400 homes, of which 72 percent were occupied by black families. Dislocated blacks found it almost impossible to find new accommodations outside the ghetto, even if they qualified for public housing. Chicago, for example, openly refused to allow the construction of public housing in white neighborhoods, and the city now has a black population of 38 percent crowded onto 25 percent of its residential land area. The highest densities usually occurred among the lowest-income families, who have the fewest resources to cope with such jamming.

A number of planners foresaw these problems. G. Holmes Perkins, editor of the AIP *Journal*, hailed the passage of the Housing Act of 1949 but warned that "the broad opportunities for urban planning possible under the bill may be lost in the scramble for isolated and unrelated projects." He asked planners not to ignore the relationship between the redevelopment program and the continued flight to the suburbs; he asked how they could "avoid the head-on issue of race segregation if we are to undertake urban redevelopment on any widespread scale?" In the late 1940s, Catherine Bauer Wurster, along with a number of other planners and housing officials, predicted the dire effects of massing high-rise public housing in slum districts. At the time urban redevelopment began in 1949, economist Benjamin Higgins told planners once again that economic and social planning should be given priority and that "citizens groups should be consulted in the very first stages of forming planning programs." Lewis Mumford, whose 1938 book *The Culture of Cities* prophesied so much of the current urban malaise, focused his eloquence on the destructive effects of the highway and redevelopment programs long before they became apparent to many planning officials. It has taken almost twenty years for these messages to gain a serious hearing in the halls of power. This change has come about not simply because leaders have seen the errors of earlier plans but because aroused community groups, faced with the destruction of their neighborhoods, began fighting city hall.

The errors of commission and omission in the urban renewal programs led to a brief resurgence of antiplanning conservatism. Economist Martin Anderson's book, *The Federal Bulldozer* (1964), coupled a devastating critique of urban renewal's first decade of operation with a call for a return to the private market mechanism to solve urban problems. Anderson was joined by a number of antiestablishment critics of the left who believed that once the federal government and city hall were removed from the redevelopment field, people would somehow be liberated to do it by themselves.

Most planners and responsible public officials did not take this well-meant but naive advice, however. The problem was not too much planning but too little, and what planning there was had been too crudely and narrowly conceived. In 1954, a congressional subcommittee on urban redevelopment recommended sweeping changes in the 1949 legislation, all of which were embodied in the new Housing Act of 1954. The act substituted a combined program of demolition *and* preservation of neighborhoods through rehabilitation. Also, all urban proposals were to be accompanied by a long-range plan for the entire urban area. The tying of specific projects into a general city plan had been recommended to Congress by the American Institute of Planners in 1949, but it had been rejected.

Slowly and painfully, the federal government has continued to revise its urban program and to link it to new legislation that now comes close to giving planners a comprehensive package of planning tools for cities and metropolitan regions. With the 1954 Housing Act providing federal support for comprehensive planning, the profession began to grow by leaps and bounds from a few hundred to several thousand members. Subsequent legislation provided federal grants for planning research, and federal fellowships aided departments of city planning to expand programs to meet the new demand for trained professionals. Other revisions in the Housing Act have inaugurated new programs for urban rehabilitation, building code enforcement, neighborhood centers, a wide variety of subsidized low-rent housing, and aid to new town development. The Urban Mass Transportation Act of 1964 gave transportation planners an alternative to the inefficient and hated superhighways. Of at least equal importance was the legislation attacking socioeconomic problems. Civil rights legislation (especially as it pertained to employment and housing), education grants, and antipoverty and job training programs all focused money on areas of urban life that are essential to any program of physical renewal. The entire trend of legislation was summarized by the Task Force on Urban Problems appointed by President Lyndon Johnson, the fruit of which was the Demonstration Cities and Metropolitan Development Act of 1966 and the creation—over a half century after the first suggestion—of a cabinet-level Department of Housing and Urban Development. President Johnson appointed Robert C. Weaver, a distinguished urban administrator and long-time housing expert, as its first secretary. Weaver was assisted by an equally outstanding group of planners and urban experts, many of whom were drawn from university planning departments.

Professional planners were in the forefront of many of these changes, partly because they had won the confidence of public officials in the two decades since the passage of the 1949 Housing Act. Shaken by the rapid deterioration of the central cities, government was willing to turn to the only group that appeared to have anything approaching expert knowledge on the causes and cures of the nation's urban cancer. Fortunately, the planners of the 1960s were able to respond vigorously because the profession was dramatically broadening its activities as it became increasingly sensitive to questions of class and racial equity.

The planning generation of the 1960s executed a revolution unparalleled in the history of the profession, the effects of which are becoming increasingly apparent in the 1970s. These changes probably indicate the direction of professional planning for the balance of the twentieth century. The roots of the transformation, as with earlier ones, lie in the general evolution of American society and its urban centers in particular. They reach back to the municipal reformers of the 1920s and 1930s, who broadened city planning into a metropolitan and regional activity, and to those whose social conscience spurred them to plan for the poor as well as for the rich and powerful. The immediate stimulants, however, were the urban riots and the ecological crisis at the end of the decade. "The urban upheaval of the 1960s," wrote the editor of the AIP *Journal*, "has left an indelible mark on urban planning in the 1970s":

The last decade has seen the planning profession, like the American city, shaken to its deepest roots. Shibboleths of only a few years ago now seem distant and irrelevant. . . . It was only a few years ago that emerging analytical tools promised ever more sophisticated, ever more technically rational metropolitan utopias. . . . Today these ideas are rattling skeletons of a philosophy of man and social change which, having struggled so hard to emerge into public view, found itself smashed in the riot-torn streets of Detroit, Newark, Los Angeles, and—unbelievably—New Haven. At the beginning of 1972 the planning profession is in disarray.

During the 1960s, the American Institute of Planners carried on a spirited debate over what came to be called—even before the riots—the New Planning—social and economic planning, client-oriented planning, advocacy planning, and pluralistic planning. In 1967, the AIP broadened its official statement of goals from land-use and physical planning to include the New Planning. The AIP *Journal* reflected the trend by devoting increasing space, sometimes entire issues, to social, economic, legal, health, and environmental planning. In a special environmental planning issue, the AIP adopted an official statement endorsing firm national management of environmental resources, with "absolute protection of unique or critically endangered resources." Consistent with its new emphasis on social justice in planning, the AIP statement concludes with the caution that "environmental protection, control and restoration of quality should seek equity in the distribution of unavoidable adverse surmounted effects, in the availability of amenities, and in the provision of suitable institutional mechanisms for the representation of all citizen interests."

The hard fact is that almost every change in the urban structure involves varying degrees of disruption and sacrifice for particular areas or groups; therefore, planners will always be unpopular with someone. In a pluralistic society divided into rich and poor, black and white, suburban and urban, there are no easy compromises, but this has clearly become the goal of contemporary planners. Unlike the great urban designers of the eighteenth century or the early twentieth century, planners today do not see themselves as imposers of grand master plans. The shape of the future urban, regional, and planetary environment, many planners believe, is too critical an issue to be left solely to professionals. How much better the new urban world will be depends on the willingness of the nation's political and economic leaders to commit themselves to the goal of rational, equitable, and humane planning, and on continuing public pressure to see that the commitment is kept. Obviously, planners can never create a quality environment in cities or in suburbs unless the structure of the nation's political economy allows it. Charles M. Nes, past president of the American Institute of Architects, indicted the American system:

It is often the rules of the game, and not the men who play it, which damage the community. If the law and community custom encourage a man to line our highways with garish trash, how many men will constrain from doing it? If a man is faithless to his investors unless he builds shoddily and overdevelops a tract of land that should have been used differently or not at all, whose fault is it? It is our fault because we should not permit conditions which reward antisocial activity.

Only when America's urban institutions are forced to reorganize themselves (or are reformed from the outside) will planners be able to function as enlightened servants of the whole society rather than as the combination of technocratic elitists and bureaucratic functionaries they have too often been in the past.

Selected Bibliography

The two most comprehensive studies of urban planning in America are John W. Reps, *The Making of Urban America: A History of City Planning in the United States* (Princeton, N.J., 1965), and Mel Scott, *American City Planning Since 1890* (Berkeley, Calif., 1969). Reps surveys the development of city planning from the colonial era to 1900; Scott's volume, written to commemorate the fiftieth anniversary of the American Institute of Planners, provides a broad and detailed discussion of the whole range of city and regional planning in the twentieth century. Vincent Scully's *American Architecture and Urbanism* (New York, 1969), although it focuses primarily on architectural history, has a number of brilliant insights into the evolution of urban planning.

There are no full studies of city planning in any American city before the twentieth century, and one is forced to glean information from general histories of particular cities or from histories of public health, park, transit, and utility systems. Harold M. Mayer and Richard Wade, *Chicago: Growth of a Metropolis* (Chicago, 1969), devotes considerable attention to the physical pattern of growth in Chicago in the nineteenth and twentieth centuries. Sam Bass Warner, Jr.'s prize-winning book, *The Private City: Philadelphia in Three Periods of Its Growth* (Philadelphia, 1968), is very enlightening on the effect of the private political economy on the city's physical configuration between 1770 and 1930. William H. Wilson, *The City Beautiful Movement in Kansas City* (Columbia, Mo., 1964) is a pioneering study of this important antecedent of modern city planning. Two excellent sources of planning literature in the early twentieth century are Charles M. Robinson, *Modern Civic Art* (New York, 1903; reprinted 1970), and Roy Lubove, *The Urban Community: Housing and Planning in the Progressive Era* (Englewood Cliffs, N.J., 1967). Lubove has written two important studies of city planning, *Community Planning in the 1920s: The Contribution of the Regional Planning Association of America* (Pittsburgh, 1963) and *Twentieth Century Pittsburgh: Government, Business, and Environmental Change* (New York, 1969). The impact of the automobile on urban America is dispassionately analyzed by John B. Rae in *The Road and the Car in American Life* (Cambridge, Mass., 1971). Helen Leavitt, *Superhighway-Superhoax* (New York, 1971), is an excellent polemic on the urban freeways. S. J. Makielski, Jr., *The Politics of Zoning: The New York Experience* (New York, 1966), is the only history of zoning in a single city that has yet been published, and its major focus is on 1911 to 1938. No one has yet assessed the impact of the Great Depression and the New Deal on city planning, but Robert A. Walker's *The Planning Function of Urban Government* (Chicago, 1941) contains a wealth of information. Timothy McDonnell, *The Wagner Housing Act* (Chicago, 1957), provides insight into the origins of public housing, and Joseph L. Arnold, *The New Deal in the Suburbs: A History of the Greenbelt Town Program, 1935–1954* (Columbus, Ohio, 1971), explores one of the most ambitious New Deal planning projects and public reactions to it.

Urban planning in the postwar era has been the subject of hundreds of books. Charles Abrams, *The City is the Frontier* (New York, 1965), is an excellent introduction by one of the outstanding urban experts of the century. The problems of housing and urban renewal have been treated by a host of authors. James Q. Wilson, editor, *Urban Renewal: The Record and the Controversy* (Cambridge, Mass., 1966), and Jewel Bellush and Murray Hausknecht, editors, *Urban Renewal: People, Politics, and Planning* (New York, 1967), offer a wide spectrum of opinions. Richard O. Davies, *Housing Reform during the Truman Administration* (Columbia, Mo., 1966), throws much light on the politics behind the Housing Act of 1949. The state of the planning and architectural profession at the beginning of the postwar era is preserved in the recently reprinted 1944 symposium edited by Paul Zucker, *New Architecture and City Planning* (Freeport, N.Y., 1971). Ernest Erber, editor, *Urban Planning in Transition* (New York, 1970), and Sam Bass Warner, Jr., editor, *Planning for a Nation of Cities* (Cambridge, Mass., 1966), deal with the changing perspectives of urban planners in the 1960s. More popular studies are worth noting on this same subject. Robert Goodman's *After the Planners* (New York, 1971) is a passionate indictment of the entire postwar history of city planning. *Rites of Way: The Politics of Transportation in Boston and the U.S. City* (Boston, 1971), by Alan Lupo, Frank Colcord, and Edmund P. Fowler, is a detailed and highly partisan case study of a community uprising against the highway planners of the Bay State. A number of basic assumptions about the planning for central business districts in cities are challenged in Bruce Brugmann, *et al., The Ultimate Highrise* (San Francisco, 1971). Case studies of city planning programs that attempt objectivity are difficult to find. Alan Altshuler's study of planning decisions in Minneapolis–St. Paul, *The City Planning Process* (Ithaca, N.Y., 1965), is notable both for its sophistication and for the fact that no one else has followed his lead in producing a full study of city planning in a major postwar urban area.

Those interested in comparing European planning in the postwar era with the American experience can begin by consulting Percy Johnson-Marshall, *Rebuilding Cities* (Chicago, 1966), and Ann Louise Strong, *Planned Urban Environments: Sweden, Finland, Israel, The Netherlands, France* (Baltimore, 1971).

The Journal of the American Institute of Planners and *Planning*, the newsletter of the American Society of Planning Officials, provide the best sources for the current state of theory and practice of urban planning. The AIP *Journal* also publishes a bimonthly bibliography of books, articles, and reports on all phases of urban planning, including the history of planning. It should be noted that this bibliography contains few books published more than five or six years ago. The history of city planning is only beginning to be studied; it will be some time before we know much about city planning in the nineteenth century or about the full impact of professional planning in the twentieth century.

The Black Experience in the Modern American City

Zane L. Miller

Despite the currently fashionable speculation about the imminent death of American cities, a case can be made for the proposition that contemporary urban centers in the United States are safer, cleaner, healthier, less cluttered by slums, and politically more honest and efficient than at any time since at least the 1840s. But however successful we may have been in mitigating these evils, we have made little progress in dealing with problems of race. A myth helps explain our failure. For years, conventional wisdom has held that blacks were relative newcomers to American cities, that they appeared in significant number on the urban scene as recently as World War I and are our newest immigrants. An important corollary of this view is the belief that these black rural newcomers to our urban places, like the white immigrants before them, will after a period of acculturation adjust to the conditions of city life and disappear into the metropolitan mainstream. A lowering of voices and a policy of salutary neglect toward Negroes, this interpretation suggests, will permit the social processes of urbanization to terminate the urban racial crisis. Unfortunately, recent scholarship challenges this comforting view of the black experience in urban America.

The history of blacks in North America dates to the seventeenth century, and it begins in the city. Originally brought to these shores to work as domestic servants and laborers in coastal places, Negroes were concentrating in the Atlantic ports by the second half of the seventeenth century. As long as European immigrants remained difficult to procure, this pattern persisted, but after 1700, growing agricultural prosperity pulled many blacks into the countryside and toward the southern colonies. Indeed, by the revolutionary period the disproportionately large number of black slaves in southern urban and rural communities shaded early national politics with a North-South sectional caste. After the Revolution, the invention of the cotton gin and settlement of the Gulf states heightened the demand for slaves in the rural South, while the revival of European immigration increasingly filled the growing need for labor in cities both above and below the Mason-Dixon line. During the first third of the nineteenth century, the rural drift of the black population convinced most white observers that Negroes in America somehow "belonged" in the country.

Yet the record of urban blacks contradicted that notion. Virtually every race leader to appear between 1765 and 1820 led a distinctively urban career. Crispus Attucks earned his status as a hero of the Revolution by virtue of his participation and death in the Boston Massacre. Benjamin Banneker, who finished planning Washington, D.C., lived most of his adult life in Baltimore and Washington. Prince Hall, who left Barbados for the American colonies in 1765, organized in Boston the first black Masonic lodge, regarded by many as the initial black social institution in North America outside the black church. Richard Allen, the founder of the religious group which in 1816 became the African Methodist Episcopal church, was born a slave in Philadelphia. And not surprisingly, black newspapermen and abolitionists of the early nineteenth century clustered in cities, for only towns provided the population base, the opportunities for formal and informal education, and the personal and social interaction necessary for testing and developing leadership.

Nonetheless, the idea that Negroes thrived only in the countryside persisted among whites, and the growth of cities in the mid-nineteenth century reinforced that belief. Between 1820 and 1880, America's urban population increased at a rate never before or since matched. Equally important, cities began to occupy more space. The introduction of the horse-drawn omnibus and street railroad, the appearance of the factory on the urban scene, the expansion of commercial and central business districts, and massive infusions of foreign newcomers, largely from Ireland and the German states, provided the base for the first surge of urban sprawl in American history. In this perspective, 1820 marks a major watershed in the process of national urban development. After that date, outer wards of American cities grew more rapidly than those in the core. Simultaneously, the urban population "churned" at an unprecedented pace. During the 1840s, for example, an estimated 30 to 40 percent of city dwellers changed their place of residence annually, a figure well above the often cited contemporary mark of 20 percent. Some merely moved from one household to another within either the core or the periphery, but at the same time, a portion of those on the edges of cities pressed to the center, while others from the core shifted outward. And this internal flux coincided with a significant intercity migration.

Yet the historic social geography of the preindustrial walking city persisted well into the early industrial era. As late as the 1870s, in most cities the poor still concentrated on the periphery, the rich huddled in the core near the economic, religious, and government centers of urban life, and the middle classes occupied the space in between. Nonetheless, the mid-nineteenth century generation of urbanites ranks as the most mobile in American history, and the interplay of economic change, large-scale foreign immigration, and residential mobility produced urban disorder of unequaled magnitude. Urban blacks, like whites, found themselves caught up in an environment characterized by extraordinarily high levels of violence, poverty, congestion, crime, mortality, and political and governmental ineptitude.

These developments hit the South with a particularly dramatic impact. In 1820, urban slavery seemed a thriving institution. Blacks provided southern cities with a flexible, versatile, and disciplined labor force. They toiled on the docks, performed household tasks as domestic servants, held skilled positions in the growing construction industry, and a few served customers from behind the counters of retail establishments. In Richmond, they formed the principal source of hands for iron and tobacco factories; in Savannah, they manned the city's volunteer fire department; and in New Orleans, a black superintended the Negro labor which ran the gas works. Yet over the years, the vitality of the South's peculiar institution steadily waned in the cities, and by 1860, urban slavery in Dixie was in crisis.

At the heart of the problem lay the question of control. On the plantations blacks found it nearly impossible to elude surveillance by their white overlords, but in the cities Negroes in increasing numbers ranged beyond the master's eye. Those "hired out" by their owners to work for others often appeared before their masters only on payday, and the shortage of housing and residential congestion made the practice of "living out" away from the master's household increasingly common. This thin margin of freedom gave many slaves the opportunity to roam the streets during the day and to concentrate in small pockets among poor whites and free Negroes on the rim of the cities during the evenings. The informal associations thus afforded, the formation of concentrated black sections in southern cities, and the growth of exclusively black and often unmonitored churches fed white preoccupation with the dangers inherent in unsupervised Negro organizations and made it difficult to regulate minutely the everyday life of the black population. Moreover, the desire of politicians to appeal to the growing immigrant vote strengthened the voice of anti-Negro working-class whites, who were locked in competition with blacks for jobs and dwelling space.

The response to these conditions took two directions. On one hand, the authorities sought to control all blacks, free and slave alike, by passing increasingly stringent black laws. Much of this legislation sought to narrow the Negroes' circle of liberty, and some of it aimed at keeping the races apart. By 1860, the impulse to control and segregate by law checkered the legal codes of cities across the South with Jim Crow laws designed to supplement the growing informal etiquette governing race relations. Census returns and slave sale records traced out the other response. Between 1820 and 1860, the black proportion of total population declined in almost every southern city, and the percentage of young adult males in the black population also tended to drop. The bleaching of the southern urban population and the invention of Jim Crow testified to the accuracy of Frederick Douglass's pithy assessment of bondage under rapidly changing urban conditions. "Slavery," he wrote in 1855, "dislikes a dense population."

The Civil War eliminated slavery and intensified the urban race crisis in the South because after Appomattox blacks rushed to cities. Their motives varied. The insecurity of life in the isolated countryside, the desire to authenticate freedom by exercising the right to seek opportunity where they might, the knowledge that before the war conditions in the cities had been better than in rural regions, and the attraction of urban educational and welfare facilities provided by the Freedmen's Bureau, northern philanthropic groups, and city authorities all contributed to the blacks' push to cities. Led by liberated urban slaves and freed Negroes experienced in town life, blacks challenged the antebellum system of segregation and discrimination which had supplemented the weakening institution of slavery as a means of social control. After the war Negroes organized benevolent associations and churches, moved freely in streets and public squares, held meetings and public entertainments, sought access to public places of accommodation and street railways, and demanded the educational and civil rights so long denied them. Their numbers gave them political strength, and the appearance of white Republican allies in local, state, and national politics bolstered their morale.

For almost two decades after 1865, the attempt of blacks to construct a new pattern of race relations and to establish an improved and more secure place for themselves in cities remained the central concern of southern urban life. They faced incredible obstacles. The white response, generated by fear of the black influx and a tenacious set of race attitudes developed before the war, was overwhelmingly and everywhere hostile. A few struck a grimly Darwinian pose, arguing that the appallingly high Negro urban death and disease rates would resolve the issue "naturally." Others hoped for and sought to encourage an invasion of white newcomers, which would make blacks superfluous and would drive them ever southward into tropical climates presumably more suited to their racial aptitudes. But whatever the long-range solutions, most whites in the late 1860s seemed inclined to push blacks to the margins of town life by denying them access to public facilities and educational and welfare agencies. And in the face of what they perceived as a black threat to white civilization, Anglo-Saxons and immigrants, rich and poor, put aside old animosities which had helped disrupt southern urban politics in the 1850s. Ironically, the enfranchisement of blacks opened wide the door to political recognition for white non-WASPs. In the 1870s, a Catholic of Irish descent ruled in Richmond's city hall, and in 1880, Irish and to a lesser degree Germans manned critical posts all along the hierarchy of the Democratic machine in New Orleans.

The precise pattern of race relations which issued from this struggle to control the cities varied from place to place, but by the 1880s, a general outline had emerged. The fact or threat of military intervention from Washington softened the resolve to exclude blacks entirely from cities, and by the end of Reconstruction, an unwritten federal-urban racial compromise had been reached. According to its terms, the races would share the cities, but on a separate and scarcely equal basis. Blacks who moved in the white economy qualified only for "nigger jobs"—occupations which offered low pay and little responsibility, required few skills, and frequently involved dirty, dangerous, and extremely arduous tasks under unhealthy conditions. Middle-class Negroes found their economic, social, and intellectual opportunities restricted to the boundaries of the black community within a tightening system of segregation. And although black males could still vote, they could not exercise the suffrage freely. Economic coercion, violence, discriminatory and irregular treatment by police and courts, and a steady stream of race propaganda designed to convince blacks of their inferiority and of the validity of their subordination in the cities served not only to limit and direct the black vote but also to replace slavery as the regulator of race relations in southern cities.

Although they constituted from 25 to 50 percent of the total population in most southern cities, blacks found it impossible to resist the imposition of the new system of segregation and discrimination. Residential patterns help explain their weakness. For the most part, they lived in relatively small, scattered enclaves in peripheral slums, where they made easy targets for white intimidation. Lower-class whites who lived around them were readily mobilized into mobs, and small-scale but persistent harassment proved easier still. Moreover, black leaders found it difficult to unite the dispersed and meager resources of the Negro community for a concentrated program of economic, educational, religious, or political self-help. Divided, southern urban blacks seemed helpless, and their future appeared bleak.

By the 1880s, Negro city dwellers in the North faced a similar situation. Indeed, the black experience in northern urban centers after 1820 more closely approximated the southern model than one might suspect. The absence of slavery, of course, provided a major distinction in the antebellum period, but white northern urbanites seemed to fear and resent blacks just as intensely as southerners. In the late 1820s, a white mob in Cincinnati attacked Negroes in an abortive attempt to eliminate the growing black community from the Queen City. Philadelphia experienced five major anti-Negro outbreaks between 1832 and 1849, Cincinnati its second in 1841, and New York the most spectacular of all—the so-called Draft Riots of 1863. These cities by no means monopolized the action, and by the 1850s, white-initiated racial violence stood near the top of the long list of problems which composed the mid-nineteenth century urban crisis. To many, exclusion seemed the only solution. As one of the more sober observers expressed it, without total racial separation "rebellions, amounting to local civil wars, will carry dismay throughout our cities, and drench their streets with blood."

The mid-nineteenth century distaste for blacks among urban whites in the North also took other forms. By 1860, in cities above the Mason-Dixon line, Negroes "were often educated in segregated schools, punished in segregated prisons, nursed in segregated hospitals, and buried in segregated cemeteries." Public transport companies either excluded blacks or placed them in special sections of the cars, and the same practice predominated in theaters and other places of public entertainment. Hotels and restaurants generally refused to serve Negroes, and churches customarily relegated them to special pews or the gallery and forced them to the end of line at communion services.

Occupational opportunities for Negroes also remained restricted in northern towns during the mid-nineteenth century, although in some of the more rapidly growing cities blacks made slight economic gains for short periods of time. Between 1830 and 1860, for example, Cincinnati ranked as the nation's fastest growing major city. Though proportionately fewer blacks worked in skilled trades in the Queen City than in southern cities, the general financial standing of the Negro community improved during these years. Between 1835 and 1841, Negroes in Cincinnati accumulated an estimated $209,000 of real property, while at the same time, the percentage of black women in the work force tended to decline, which reflected marginal economic improvement within the black community and indicated a possible strengthening of the black family structure. Simultaneously, a small but significant class of black professionals and entrepreneurs developed. The most successful black bourgeoisie of this period served a white or mixed clientele as caterers, barbers, coal dealers, or photographers, but the professionals operated almost exclusively in Negro circles.

Yet after 1860, even these small signs of progress faded, and a marked tendency toward a more thorough system of residential segregation appeared. A close study of Cincinnati's black entrepreneurs in the postbellum generation shows them gradually receding from business and dwelling sites in largely white neighborhoods. Their relocation options were limited. Some doubtless retreated to the relatively stable and mildly prosperous Negro settlement in Walnut Hills near the emerging white elite hilltop suburbs. Others could only move to the less solid peripheral ghetto of "Bucktown," an occupationally diverse community on the eastern edge of the municipality which housed 20 percent of the city's black population in 1880, or join those shifting from the racially mixed river-front slums of Rat and Sausage Row into the growing neighborhood of blacks on the southwest side of town known as "Little Bucktown." Although all the evidence is not in, that which is available suggests that blacks in other northern cities in these years also had to contend with a limited, if not reduced, range of job choices in the private sector and strong pressure toward residential segregation. And above as well as below the Ohio, the continued drive of immigrants for political recognition after the war limited black accomplishments in that sphere and scarred the political process with violence and intimidation. In northern cities, where blacks seldom formed more than 5 percent of the total population, as in southern centers, where the figures ran much higher, in 1880 blacks clung to second-class citizenship. The pervasive and tightening informal and formal system of segregation and discrimination not only stalled Negroes' drive for full participation in civic life but also threatened to reduce them to an even more precarious position in the economy and residential structure of the cities.

That issue remained unresolved during the next era of American history. From the perspective of the black experience, two great developments distinguished the period between about 1890 and 1945. The first, rearrangement of the familiar social geography of the city, created the inner-city ghetto; the second, massive movement to northern cities of both rural and urban southern blacks and white response to that migration, laid the groundwork for the contemporary metropolitan race crisis.

After the 1880s, electric rapid transit completed the obliteration of the "walking" city that had been started by the horse-drawn street railway. Rapid and wide-ranging trolleys provided the means by which people and commercial and industrial establishments dispersed to locations unprecedentedly remote from the city's core. The outward push of city populations, already severe in the mid-nineteenth century, became explosive in the 1880s and 1890s, and it reversed the old urban residential pattern and created the outlines of the modern metropolis. Affluent whites resettled on the urban fringe, the less successful occupied the ground between the periphery and the center of the metropolis, while Negroes, the foreign-born, and the poor remained near downtown. Gradually too, scattered black enclaves began to merge. By 1900, blacks of all incomes and occupations found their lives increasingly circumscribed by the boundaries of the expanding inner-city ghetto. The intensity of residential segregation by race in southern areas with a history of slavery ran below that in the North, but the booming new cities of post-Reconstruction Dixie and the Southwest matched the urban centers north of the Ohio in this respect.

Migration rather than natural increase provided the population which made black districts bulge. Between 1880 and 1890, an estimated 88,000 Negroes left the South, and the figures escalated during each decade through 1940. Most of the black migrants settled in cities. In 1890, three-fifths of all nonsouthern Negroes lived in towns, and by 1910, that statistic edged up to four-fifths. But the flow did not run exclusively from South to North and from the countryside to cities. Throughout these years, the black proportion of the South's total urban population remained stable, a fact which indicates absolute urban and significant Negro population growth and suggests that some southern rural blacks probably replaced city dwellers who were seeking improved economic opportunities and racial justice in northern metropolises. In any case, the residential structure of cities in both sections fell generally into the new center-periphery mold.

Reversal of the traditional geographical arrangement of urban populations produced far-reaching changes for all elements of the metropolitan population. The outward thrust, accompanied as it was by a physical sorting out of people along lines of occupation, income, and national origin, tended to separate groups caught up in economic or cultural competition. As a result, conflicts which in the mid-nineteenth century generated riots that pitted whites against whites now more often were worked out peacefully in the partisan political arena or through negotiations between organizations of interest groups. In this sense, the modern metropolis offered the bulk of white inhabitants a safer and more secure environment than that of any urban generation since at least the mid-eighteenth century.

The emergence of the modern metropolis also produced groups of white men and women who were determined to secure a fairer deal for urban blacks. Residents of urban peripheries that were comfortably separated from dark ghettos, these white race reformers came from business or professional families of more than modest means and shared the early twentieth century enthusiasm for economic and civic boosterism. In southern centers, they sought to stem the deteriorating status of blacks and to restrain Negrophobes by securing a stable and more equitable interpretation of the separate but equal doctrine. They manned the new interracial civic committees, proposed an enlarged and improved system of public and private welfare work among Negroes, supported the establishment of secondary schools for blacks, denounced lynching, praised black economic achievements, and fought residential segregation ordinances designed to legalize and freeze the ghettos and to prevent Negroes from moving into better housing in suburban locations. In the North, similarly structured groups of whites moved beyond this agenda to praise and foster black cultural and intellectual accomplishments and to advocate full economic and civic equality for Negroes.

In both sections race reformers faced stiff odds. Middle-class and lower-class whites who lived along the cutting edge of burgeoning black ghettos refused to go along. Residential vulnerability explains their reluctance as much as any other single factor, and their numbers made them a potent political force. Affluent whites usually did not face direct competition with Negroes for urban housing. For many of the less well-to-do, their recently acquired and hard-earned residential status beyond the slums functioned as a surrogate for social and economic advances still beyond their reach. Caught between slum and suburb, the whites of the "Zone of Emergence" were ready prey for the race demagogue in politics and the twentieth century Ku Klux Klan. As blacks approached their "turf," they burned crosses, bombed houses purchased by Negroes in transitional neighborhoods, pressured realtors to uphold the color line, and either pushed for residential segregation laws or added racial covenants to home mortgages and deeds. Not infrequently, they broke loose in savage riots. Collective race violence reached almost epidemic proportions during the "red summer" of 1919, although Washington and Chicago experienced the most spectacular outbreaks. But Atlanta in 1906, Springfield, Illinois, in 1908, and East St. Louis in 1917 suffered just as intensely. For blacks, the twentieth century city was no safer than any other city, because the Negro death and casualty rate in these incidents always outstripped the white rate.

Over the same span of years, the emergence of the inner-city ghetto set the stage for the development of a new, more powerful, and more aggressive black drive for social and economic justice led by successful Negroes who had done everything society expected of them but had been denied full benefits. The growing black urban population, the enlarged physical scale of inner-city ghettos, the development of virulent Negrophobia in the Zone of Emergence, and the appearance of a handful of white allies on the urban periphery indicated to a new generation of black leaders that something had to and could be done to improve conditions under which they and their people lived. Disfranchised in the South and everywhere denied the right and opportunity to move up in the urban social structure and beyond the reach of the slums, the "talented tenth" turned back into the ghetto to organize a push to improve the quality of life and to prevent all Negroes, regardless of their educational or economic achievements, from being permanently relegated to second-class citizenship.

Strategies and goals varied, but between 1890 and 1930, black bourgeoisie in cities across the country organized an imposing array of clubs, societies, and associations. These groups stressed above all race pride, racial unity, and achievement. The urban groundwork had been laid for a series of national alliances, institutionalized by 1920 in such diverse organizations as the National Association for the Advancement of Colored People, the National Urban League, the National Negro Business League, the National Federation of Colored Women's Clubs, the Association for the Study of Negro Life and History, and Marcus Garvey's black nationalist movement, the Universal Negro Improvement Association.

The burst of organizational creativity at the national level was not the only institutional consequence of Negro concentration near the centers of the nation's great cities. The ghettos provided the base of operations for the new black middle classes. Here Negro businessmen, physicians, teachers, social workers, and lawyers found an exclusive clientele. Ironically, this situation provided the major exponent of country life for Negroes, Booker T. Washington, with a fertile urban field for cultivation of his gradualist and accommodationist racial strategy. The widespread acceptance of his approach by both blacks and whites assured black entrepreneurs and professionals that the ghetto would not disperse and gave their "buy black" campaigns a philosophical rationale. Although Washington garnered his most outspoken urban followers in the South, Negro politicians in the North such as Oscar DePriest and William Dawson of Chicago vaulted from precinct to ward and district leadership from a base in black belts of the cities, and a few even moved into city council or Congress.

Yet exploitation of the advantages inherent in the institutional ghetto bore a high cost. Black businessmen, working a generally impoverished market, could not accumulate sufficient capital to acquire real financial power in an economy increasingly dominated by corporations, and the boundaries of black districts hemmed in the aspiration of Negro politicians. The psychological burden too, although incalculable, doubtless also took its toll, because milking the system for these relatively meager economic, political, social, and prestige rewards implied an acquiesence to white-imposed segregation and the insults, humiliation, and subordination inherent in the urban caste arrangement.

The tension between the ghetto as a place of refuge and source of meager opportunities on one hand and the drive for recognition and dignity in the larger society on the other hand also helps explain the new note of militance among blacks after 1890. The new movement began with boycotts to protest southern streetcar segregation laws early in the twentieth century and peaked with threats of retaliatory violence and acts of self-defense during the race riots following World War I. Black leaders more frequently spoke of the necessity for Negroes to assert their manhood and to deny the white majority's insistence upon their inferiority. Some turned this drive into a search for self-determination. A black literary renaissance in the 1920s was one aspect of this development, a new interest in African cultural objects and African and black history provided another, and a heightened respect for black jazz music emanating from New Orleans, Memphis, St. Louis, Kansas City, and Chicago was yet another. Garvey's back-to-Africa movement in a sense represented an attempt to translate these symbolic, artistic, and intellectual assertions of roots and passion for self-expression into a nationalistic reality. The "New Negro" of the twentieth century metropolis believed that blacks were beautiful and deserved equality; that conviction bred the faith and high expectations which buoyed the sense of race pride through the anti-Negro violence, Jim Crow legislation, and race slander which stained the first third of the twentieth century.

Although optimism about the potential of the New Negro movement ran high, a retrospective assessment of its success shows that the position of blacks generally in urban society was not significantly improved. In 1930 antiblack discrimination continued in its familiar forms, and ghettos remained intact. Nonetheless, two generations of activism had raised black aspirations and had provided valuable schooling in urban leadership. Not even the Great Depression could negate these important gains.

The collapse of the economy stunned white Americans, who regarded laissez faire, free enterprise, and the upward mobility ideology as infallible doctrine. But most blacks, long accustomed to being the last hired and the first fired, viewed the debacle with more equanimity, their sense of balance strengthened by their lack of illusions about the essential beneficence of the economic system. To be sure, unemployment rates in the ghettos soared to appallingly high levels. Yet inner-city black districts continued to function as lively focuses of Negro life and as arenas of creativity and change. Politically, FDR's economic relief and welfare programs helped cut the black urban vote from traditional Republican moorings and place it among the diverse groups which made up the urban segment of the new national Democratic majority. More blacks than ever before also joined the organized labor movement, in large part because the CIO emerged as the first union in American history to successfully undertake the difficult task of attracting immigrant-stock whites, uprooted Appalachians, and blacks into one organization. And the NAACP, which had leaned heavily on legal action and public education in the years before 1929, now stressed its economic program as the most practical means of alleviating the debilitating effects of the crash on urban Negro communities.

The hardships of the depression also created opportunities for the emergence of new black leaders and of the underpinnings for distinctively black organizations. Two new religious sects, both dispensing social welfare and community organization services as well as spiritual hope, illuminated the reaction to the depression in black neighborhoods and indicated that economic disaster had not severed the strand of continuity in the black tradition. The most prominent of these two groups originated in Long Island. There Father Divine (George Baker), who grew up in the rice country near Savannah, Georgia, opened a relief and employment agency and, claiming a direct mandate of Divinity and describing himself as the Son of Righteousness, offered both material and spiritual sustenance to his followers. In 1932, near the pit of the depression, he moved to Harlem, a neighborhood played up by the national media as the mecca of blacks in America. There his spectacular exploits, including the provision of expensive free meals to destitute individuals, garnered for him a national reputation among both blacks and whites.

The other new black social gospel movement originated in Detroit and combined welfare and religion with a nationalistic stress reminiscent of Marcus Garvey. Its nominal founder, Wallace D. Fard, sold textile goods on the streets of "Paradise Valley" for three years during the early 1930s, then set up a Temple of Islam in which he taught that the black man was the original man, that the white man was a devil who imposed white religion upon blacks, and that blacks must separate themselves from white religion and turn back to Islam. Fard's successor and friend, Elijah Mohammed (Robert Poole), took up and expanded the work. After World War II, Malcolm X, clearly the Black Muslim's most famous convert, emerged as the charismatic leader who gave the movement national visibility and became a major folk hero of the postwar black civil rights movement.

World War II and the New Deal programs terminated the depression, and the emergence after the war of a "postindustrial" economy, centered on services, research and development, and light manufactures no longer geographically bound to locations near their sources of raw materials, launched a new stage in the history of American cities. From 1945 through the 1960s, the most rapid urban growth occurred around the rim of the continent in places which offered climatic, scenic, and cultural amenities as well as high-level educational facilities. In these places, as in the less rapidly growing cities of the industrial urban heartland stretching from New York to St. Louis, both jobs and population continued to push out to the periphery of the metropolitan area. At the same time, the shift from South to North of the nation's black population reached proportions which dwarfed the pre-1940 figures (see Table 1). Most Negro migrants, ironically, followed old routes to the more slowly expanding cities of the northeast and north-central states, and everywhere they tended to settle in inner-city neighborhoods, well removed from outlying areas, where the best-paying, most regular employment could be found. And few of them possessed the scientific and managerial skills required to pull down the juiciest prizes available in the new economy.

Table I. Net Migration of Negroes by Region, 1870–1970 (in thousands)

	Northeast	South	North-central	West
1870–1880	26	− 68	42	
1880–1890	61	− 88	28	
1890–1900	136	− 185	49	
1900–1910	109	− 194	63	22
1910–1920	242	− 555	281	32
1920–1930	435	− 903	426	42
1930–1940	273	− 480	152	55
1940–1950	599	−1581	626	356
1950–1960 *	541	−1458	560	347
1960–1970 *	839	−1116	514	580

Source: Reynolds Farley, "The Urbanization of Negroes in the United States," *Journal of Social History* 1 (Spring 1968):251; U.S. Bureau of the Census, *Census of Population: 1970*, PHC(2)–1, Table 7.

* Figures for 1950–70 were obtained from a different source from those for earlier decades. The figures for the earlier decades refer to Negro population, whereas those for 1950–70 refer to nonwhite population.

Yet briefly in the 1940s and early 1950s, the condition of blacks seemed to be improving. High levels of employment during World War II and the gradual broadening of opportunities in the armed forces helped. The success of the 1941 march on Washington, a black undertaking launched by A. Philip Randolph, head of the Pullman car porter's union, nudged President Roosevelt into establishing the Fair Employment Practices Commission and strengthened the case for an optimistic outlook. A trickle of desegration and antidiscrimination decisions by the courts over the same span of years wedged the door of opportunity open a bit farther. These factors, plus the general affluence of the early 1950s, produced a small but important increase in the number of blacks who achieved middle-class status, and between 1941 and the early 1950s, the relative position of Negro workers compared to white wage earners generally improved. For almost fifteen years, then, expectations of the black masses did not significantly exceed gains being made.

Toward the end of the decade, however, black frustrations and'race tensions began to intensify. The recession of 1957 and 1958 hit Negroes harder than it hit whites, and by that time the new continental and intrametropolitan patterns of urban growth guaranteed a continuing gap between Negro and white economic status. The flood of rural Negro migrants pouring into the cities stiffened white resistance to residential desegregation, and black ghettos swelled and deteriorated. Worse still, as the urban renewal program of the 1950s took hold, thousands of blacks were rooted out of the slums with virtually no provision for relocation in other neighborhoods. Instead, they moved into old and dilapidated districts recently abandoned by outwardly mobile whites, and they edged up to the borders of second- and third-generation working-class and white-collar neighborhoods.

In the postwar period blacks fell victim to a bitter paradox. As their expectations and aspirations rose, big-city ghettos expanded. Responses varied. In the urban South, Dr. Martin Luther King, Jr., established the Southern Christian Leadership Conference and launched a nonviolent crusade against the encrusted façade of public accommodation segregation in Dixie. Thereafter, black civil rights and protest groups proliferated. They ranged in character from SNCC (Student Nonviolent Coordinating Committee), which began in Raleigh, North Carolina, and specialized in organizing sit-ins, to such quasi-revolutionary and revolutionary nationalistic groups as RAM (Revolutionary Action Movement) and the Republic of New Africa, both of which opted for the foundation of a new black nation inside the United States, and the Black Panthers and other local groups of varying degrees of militancy. Many such groups emphasized community control by black people of the institutions and agencies which regulated their lives.

Despite efforts of these varied groups to find a way out of the racial crisis and the commitment of President John F. Kennedy's administration to the civil rights cause, the tensions which racked the black ghettos mounted during the early 1960s. The decade of the long hot summer had arrived. On July 18, 1964, a little over two weeks after Congress passed President Lyndon B. Johnson's civil rights legislation, Harlem erupted in its first full-scale riots in two decades. The disturbances ended on July 23, but a day later riots broke out in Rochester, New York. The action that summer climaxed in Philadelphia during the last three days of August.

By midsummer of 1965 it still seemed possible that the outbursts of 1964 were merely an incidental deviation from the main, largely peaceful path of the civil rights movement. That notion vanished during August 1965 in the smoke and death of the violence in the Watts district of Los Angeles. With thirty-four dead, over 1,000 injured, nearly 4,000 arrested, hundreds of buildings damaged, and tens of millions of dollars of property destroyed, the Watts uprising ranked as the nation's worst racial disorder since the 1917 East St. Louis massacre. Chicago and San Diego were also hit in 1965, but 1966 was worse. That summer violence struck Los Angeles, Chicago, Cleveland, and smaller cities in June, and Omaha, Dayton, and San Francisco in July and August. The following year proved equally violent: scores of cities, including Cincinnati, Buffalo, and Newark, joined the lengthening list of hot spots, and Detroit experienced the worst riots since the New York City draft fighting of 1863. After the April 1968 uproar in Washington, Baltimore, and Chicago and less serious incidents in more than a hundred other places in the wake of Martin Luther King's assassination, the violence declined.

Meanwhile, as results of government and scholarly investigations of the riots rolled in, it became clear that the race outbursts of the 1960s represented a sharp break with past upheavals. In previous cases of collective racial violence whites took the initiative, either as a reaction to black competition for jobs and housing or as a response to a black challenge to patterns of racial subordination or segregation in the cities. But in the 1960s, blacks struck out first, and they seemed less interested in attacking white individuals than in flaunting and destroying symbols of white authority and oppression. Police arrests of blacks on relatively minor charges frequently precipitated the destruction, and the burning and looting which followed focused on white-owned businesses or government agencies in ghettos, while police and fire department personnel bore the brunt of physical assaults. They retaliated with force, and blacks invariably topped the casualty lists of dead and injured.

White response to this turmoil varied. City police departments beefed up both riot training and community relations programs. The federal government under Johnson pushed hard to enact and enforce civil rights legislation and to provide jobs and educational opportunities for inner-city blacks. On the metropolitan periphery, well removed from the smoke and violence of downtown, nervous white homeowners purchased weapons, and many joined the backlash and law-and-order campaigns advocated by local and national political figures.

By 1970, few could predict with confidence what might come next, but the underlying causes of riots during the mid-1960s seemed clear. A 1967 presidential commission on civil disorders, the so-called Kerner Commission, concluded that in the final analysis, responsibility for the uprisings fell on white racism. The commission hit the mark. The federal programs of the 1960s to assist blacks in the vital areas of jobs, housing, and education fell short, partially because of continued frustration among Negroes. Like other Americans, natives and immigrants alike, since the mid-nineteenth century blacks had become an increasingly urban people. But unlike other urban Americans, they knew that even if they somehow managed to secure an education, acquire a decent job, and build a cohesive family, neither they nor their children could escape the ghettos. After six generations of experience in American cities, even the most successful blacks still found themselves restricted to the worst neighborhoods. They knew that for them the ghetto would not serve as a staging ground for mobility. In the twentieth century that growing realization produced a strong drive to enter the mainstream, some violence, and a swelling chorus of cries for revolution and black nationalism. In 1970, it was not entirely clear which direction the movement would take next.

As the last third of the twentieth century opened, the country floundered in the midst of still another urban crisis. Yet the prospects were not uniformly bleak. The problems of cities in the early 1970s were not entirely new, and in the judgment of many qualified observers, the nation lacked only the will to alleviate the most serious difficulties. Yet this account of the black experience in the modern city suggests that the persistence of the ghetto is the central domestic problem of American life. As Richard C. Wade put it in 1967, the ghetto not only stands "mockingly as a symbol of the unfulfilled promise of equality, but it also frustrates the attack on other metropolitan issues. For decisions on such questions as education, housing, and poverty are caught up in the controversy over civil rights and are often deflected or postponed." Until the metropolis is opened up and blacks are guaranteed the right to freely work out their destiny, the country will continue down the path toward two separate and unequal societies.

Selected Bibliography

Although the literature on black history continues to grow at a rapid rate, relatively few studies focus explicitly on the urban dimension. Richard C. Wade's article, "Urbanization," in C. Vann Woodward, editor, *The Comparative Approach to American History* (New York, 1968), provides a useful interpretive framework, particularly when supplemented by Sam B. Warner, Jr., *The Private City: Philadelphia in Three Periods of Its Growth* (Philadelphia, 1968). Reynolds Farley, "The Urbanization of Negroes in the United States," *Journal of Social History*, 1 (Spring 1968), 241–58, lays out in a few pages the essential facts on black rural-to-urban and South-to-North migration patterns, and David Ward, *Cities and Immigrants: A Geography of Change in Nineteenth Century America* (New York, 1971), briefly and lucidly describes and analyzes the patterns and processes of interregional and intrametropolitan migration from a broader perspective. Peter R. Knights, *The Plain People of Boston, 1830–1860: A Study in City Growth* (New York, 1971), details the astonishing volatility of mid-nineteenth century city dwellers.

The key works on race relations and the black experience in the cities during the antebellum period are Richard C. Wade, *Slavery in the Cities: The South, 1820–1860* (New York, 1964), and Leon F. Litwack, *North of Slavery: The Negro in the Free States, 1790–1860* (Chicago, 1961). On the emergence of the ghetto and the development of problems, including riots, related to that subject see Gilbert Osofsky, *Harlem: The Making of a Ghetto* (New York, 1966); Seth M. Scheiner, *Negro Mecca: A History of the Negro in New York City, 1865–1920* (New York, 1965); Allan H. Spear, *Black Chicago: The Making of a Negro Ghetto, 1890–*

1920 (Chicago, 1967); Elliott M. Rudwick, *Race Riot at East St. Louis, July 2, 1917* (Carbondale, Ill., 1964); William M. Tuttle, Jr., *Race Riot: Chicago in the Red Summer of 1919* (New York, 1970); John M. Bracey, Jr., August Meier, and Elliot M. Rudwick, editors, *The Rise of the Ghetto* (Belmont, Calif., 1971); and Robert M. Fogelson, *Violence as Protest: A Study of Riots and Ghettos* (Garden City, N.Y., 1971). Dwight W. Hoover, *A Teacher's Guide to American Urban History* (Chicago, 1971), contains discussions and bibliographies on the urban blacks in both the antebellum and the postbellum periods. My views on the black experience in the modern American city stem principally from my reading of these secondary accounts, from my own research and that of my students on blacks in Cincinnati from 1820 to the present, and from my research on the black communities in five southern cities (Richmond, Savannah, New Orleans, Birmingham, and Louisville) from 1865 to 1920.

European Immigrants and Urban America

Humbert S. Nelli

During the century that followed the Napoleonic wars and ended with World War I, approximately 35 million European immigrants entered the United States. Some left their homeland because of religious persecution, some to evade military service or prison sentences, and others to escape the death penalty imposed for political or criminal activities. For most newcomers, however, economic factors ranked first in importance. Numbers of immigrants felt the pull of America's rapidly expanding opportunities; others found themselves unable to cope with Old World conditions, where rural economies defeated the individual's efforts to better himself, and governmental attempts at reform proved beneficial only to the wealthy. The rise of large-scale scientific agriculture—which dispossessed laborers and small farmers to the advantage of the well-to-do—initially affected northern and western Europe. During the latter part of the nineteenth century, the new agriculture had its impact on the southern and eastern portions of the Continent as well. These scientific developments separated large masses of people from the soil. Millions remained in Europe, drifting from the countryside to nearby or distant cities, but many decided that personal betterment and financial gain lay in the new world.

Whatever their place of origin, newcomers tended to settle in American cities, where they formed a highly visible segment of the population. Even those who intended to farm often remained temporarily in eastern or midwestern cities, living in tenements and working as unskilled laborers until they were able to replenish depleted economic resources. Newcomers from northern and western Europe—the so-called old immigrants—arrived in the decades between 1815 and the 1880s. Their pattern of settlement was followed later by "new" immigrants from southern and eastern Europe, who arrived during the thirty-five years prior to World War I. On the eve of the Civil War, foreign-born residents formed approximately half (and in some

61

cases more) of the populations of Chicago, Detroit, Milwaukee, St. Louis, Cincinnati, and New York City. For example, along with its other nationalities, New York City was more than one-fourth Irish and one-eighth German. In 1910, when the federal census showed that fewer than half the country's native Americans lived in cities, 68.3 percent of the "old" and 78.3 percent of the "new" immigration resided in urban areas. Eastern European Jews and the Irish, of whom five-sixths lived in cities, formed the most heavily urbanized groups; more than three-fourths of the Italians and Hungarians, seven-tenths of the English, Scots, Austrians, and Greeks, two-thirds of the Germans, and three-fifths of the Swedes chose to settle in urban America.

Like their predecessors during colonial times, immigrants in the early nineteenth century resided at the city's outer limits. Early American cities were "walking" settlements, most of them measuring no more than two miles outward from the core. The heavy use of centrally located land drove up its value to premium levels. The high cost of property combined with the absence of inexpensive public transportation made property ownership in the most desirable location—the city's center—prohibitively expensive and thus unaffordable to all but financially secure residents. Immigrants, along with other low-income urban dwellers, generally lived in shanties located at the outskirts.

Outlying shanty areas contained some of the most disreputable living conditions in the New World, a situation generally blamed on the aliens residing there. In 1819, a report of the Society for the Prevention of Pauperism in the City of New York complained that immigrants arriving in the United States were poverty-stricken, ignorant, incapable of self-support, and criminally inclined, placing an intolerable burden on the community and forcing better elements to despair of coping successfully with the whole immigrant problem.

The introduction of the horse car, which facilitated the movement of the middle and upper classes away from the central city, affected the other end of the economic ladder by making formerly inaccessible upper-income core neighborhoods available to low-income groups—in particular, the masses of foreigners swarming into the cities. The first groups came from northern and western European countries, particularly Germany and Ireland; after the 1880s, Italians, Poles, and other southern and eastern Europeans swept in. For these new urban dwellers, housing had to meet two essential conditions: it must be cheap, and it must be within walking distance of work. Central-city neighborhoods provided ideal locations, and the large, single-family structures of the departed middle- and upper-income groups (as well as warehouses and stables) were quickly converted into multifamily, low-rent dwellings. These buildings returned handsome profits to owners because of their heavy population densities; little, if any, money went into improving structures or facilities. New construction took the form of tenement housing, designed to concentrate many people into the least space possible.

New York contained the largest and most congested immigrant areas. Walk-up tenements rose to five and six stories and occupied all the property except for a narrow strip at the rear of the lot. In most other cities, tenements generally had two or three stories, but an additional hazard in the form of the rear tenement threatened the welfare of the inhabitants. In order to provide cramped living space for even more tenants, property owners tacked one or more flimsy structures onto the back of larger tenement buildings. The congested rear tenements of Chicago, St. Louis, and Philadelphia were as disastrous to the health and lives of the residents as were New York's multistory firetraps.

The former upper- and middle-income core area neighborhoods quickly turned into unsightly, overcrowded slums. They exhibited social disorganization and personal degradation, poverty and pauperism, crime and corruption. Contemporaries expressed deep concern about the future of their cities and, indeed, about the nation itself. A report prepared in 1857 commented on tenement area conditions in New York City:

> These immigrants . . . are destitute, sick, ignorant, abject. They demand immediate food, garb, shelter, and not only immediate but permanent means of obtaining these necessities. . . . The men of families or feeble widows with three or four children, are forced to remain in the neighborhood of the landing-place, because absolutely unable to move away from it. . . . They swarm in filthy localities, engendering disease, and enduring every species of suffering. . . . They are often habitual sots, diseased and reckless, living precariously, considering themselves outcasts, and careless of any change in their condition.

This report referred to "old" immigrants, principally Irish and German; later reports used similar (sometimes identical) wording to describe conditions among "new" immigrant groups before World War I. In 1922, John Palmer Gavit, a reformer who had been a resident of the Chicago Commons Settlement House, described the repeating pattern: "Each phase of immigration has been 'the new immigration' at its time; each has been viewed with alarm; each has been described as certain to deteriorate the physical quality of our people and destroy the standards of living and of citizenship."

"Old" or "new," most immigrants came of peasant stock. They had had little contact with urban life before leaving Europe (with the exception of the Jews, who had formed an urbanized group before they crossed the Atlantic). Often the family circle formed their entire world. In the United States, the neighborhood of the immigrant generation served as a receiving and staging area where new arrivals remained until they absorbed the ideas and habits that made possible their adjustment to the American environment. The immigrant community therefore fulfilled a vitally important (and generally unrecognized) function both to its inhabitants and to the receiving society. It bridged the gap that lay between rural, Old World traditions and the new urban world, and it acquainted a succession of immigrant groups with American ideas and values.

Many Americans mistakenly assumed that ethnic districts and institutions reproduced homeland surroundings and perpetuated isolated group life. In actuality, the immigrant community and its institutions represented an important step *away* from Old World patterns. Family-centered in Europe, the newcomers remained so in the United States, but they soon discovered that the family unit was unable to deal effectively with most of the problems encountered in urban America. They had to cooperate with other newcomers and other family groups in order to survive. The community awareness and group consciousness that developed through this cooperation did not arrive with the immigrants but developed in the new world in response to the American environment. "In America," sociologist Robert E. Park reported, "the peasant discards his [Old World] habits and acquires 'ideas.' In America, above all, the immigrant organizes. These organizations are the embodiment of his needs and his new ideas."

Because the city prevented isolation, the community and its institutions were neither fully European nor fully American in character. Constantine M. Panunzio, himself an immigrant, noted this fact when he described an Italian colony in Boston as being "in no way a typical American community, [but] neither did it resemble Italy." Immigrants attempted to cling to what was familiar from the European village, but in the American urban environment they found it impossible to recreate village life; yet they, and most Americans, believed that they had done so. Edith Abbott and Sophonisba P. Breckinridge, both reformers and college professors, voiced their apprehensions in 1912. They feared that through "churches and schools, and in social, fraternal and national organizations," immigrants could maintain "the speech, the ideals, and to some extent the manner of life of the mother country."

Despite American anxieties, community institutions of the various immigrant groups in the United States more closely resembled each other and native American counterparts than they did homeland organizations (these were essentially middle class in origin and character and seldom touched the lives of the groups from which immigrants came). Mutual benefit and fraternal societies existed among Poles, Lithuanians, Germans, Irish, Jews, and others and provided them with companionship as well as sickness and death benefits. Immigrants—and native Americans—who joined mutual benefit organizations contributed small monthly sums, usually between twenty-five and sixty cents, to guarantee that the group would look after them when they were sick and provide a decent burial when they died. Societies required all members to attend funeral services or pay a penalty fine, thereby assuring each member of a well-attended burial. Over the years the funeral service grew into an opportunity for old acquaintances to gather and reminisce about old days. Since young and vigorous members predominated during the early years of the organization, most deaths resulted not from old age but from accidents or disease growing out of employment and housing conditions. Societies also generally handled other related activities, including the payment of sickness and accident expenses.

Foreign-language newspapers in immigrant communities addressed themselves to people who had seldom (if ever) read newspapers in the mother country. Language was simple, direct, phonetic. Americanized and slang versions of the mother tongue appeared frequently. The papers that survived longest generally lost their European appearance and style in order to imitate the style and format of successful American dailies, with illustrations, headlines, and bizarre or dramatic stories. The ethnic press served as a causeway between life in the European village and that in the American city, providing identifiable leadership for the immigrant community and voicing group demands and complaints. Newspaper editors consciously fostered group awareness and pride, sometimes to a point that more sophisticated readers of following generations found to be laughable or irritating. As the immigrant generation moved into the American community or died out, the need for ethnic language papers declined, and the journals disappeared, combined, or changed into monthly publications.

Many newcomers depended (often with misplaced trust) on the immigrant banker, a neighborhood resident able to read and write English as well as the mother tongue. He safeguarded immigrant savings, wrote letters, remitted money abroad, bought steamship tickets, and handled business affairs too complicated for his compatriots to manage on their own. Most immigrant bankers operated a business or two—a store, barbershop, saloon, or other concern—in addition to their banking activities. These last were unlicensed, unregulated, and often directed toward cheating the clients. Like the ethnic press, the immigrant banker dealt with the immigrant generation, and American-born children of the immigrants turned away from his services.

Religion played a central role in the lives of most European peasants, whether Catholic, Protestant, or Jewish. However, the ocean crossing profoundly affected religion. The separation of church and state in the United

States necessitated radical changes, especially among Protestants but also among Catholics and Jews. In contrast to Europe, where the state church often played a formal, open role in politics, churches functioned as purely voluntary organizations in America. This difference tended to bring about a shift in emphasis from dogma to evangelism, and it focused the parishioner's attention upon his personal religious experience. There was also a movement toward democratization of church government, a tendency toward lay influence over church operations that would have been out of the question in Europe.

Sectarianism, another major tendency in American religious life, formed a particularly serious problem for Protestants. Catholics also experienced bitter factional disputes between the Irish, who controlled the church in the United States, and their fellow communicants of German, Italian, French-Canadian, Lithuanian, and Polish backgrounds. National consciousness, which developed among these groups after they arrived in the United States, strongly influenced ethnic attitudes toward religion. While for most groups—Irish and Poles, for example—religion was a central and fervent aspect of national loyalty, nationalism and Catholicism for Italians and Czechs exerted opposing forces that reflected church-state relations in the homeland. American Judaism experienced division into Reform, Orthodox, and Conservative groups. Reform resulted from an effort, especially on the part of German Jews, to conform to middle-class Protestant forms of religion. It clashed with Orthodox Judaism, the strict, formal, all-encompassing way of life brought into the United States in the years after 1890. Conservatism represented a halfway house, largely for second-generation eastern Europeans, for whom Orthodoxy was too restrictive and tradition-bound but Reform too cold and unemotional.

Identification with the colony and use of its facilities and institutions indicated not only a growth away from homeland outlooks but also a vital step in the assimilation process of many newcomers. We now recignize that immigrant institutions speeded the process of adjustment by enabling newcomers to function within the American environment, but contemporary opinion held that the opposite was true. Since immigrant institutions appeared to prevent Americanization or at least to retard assimilation, Americans and the children of immigrants regarded them with derision and contempt. It is important to note, however, that not all members of any group reacted in the same way to the colony, its available institutions, or the larger urban environment. Some ignored all community institutions and never expanded their loyalties or interests from the European village or district of birth. Others made full use of some or all available community institutions and widened their village interests by developing national self-awareness and group identity—concepts, as one social historian noted, that were "the product of American conditions, not the importations from abroad." A third group preferred to make limited use of press, societies, and churches as intermediaries through which to learn American customs and ideas. Often these first-generation arrivals came as children or young adults and absorbed or consciously adopted American habits and speech from politics, schools, settlement houses, and the streets.

The tremendous amount of immigrant mobility was a major reason for the waning of community institutions. "A given race, closely settled and extensively organized," wrote an Illinois Health Insurance Commission investigator in 1919, "sooner or later scatters and perhaps surrenders its locality to another." Mutual aid groups, immigrant banks, and ethnic newspapers rapidly disintegrated as immigrants moved to better neighborhoods. Of all community institutions, only the churches grew in strength and membership with succeeding generations. Acceptance and respectability in American society, especially in the 1940s and 1950s, demanded church affiliation of some kind.

Contrary to the viewpoint held by most Americans, no set, unchanging, or rigid colonies existed, because immigrant areas of settlement expanded and shifted location over the years. Movement occurred not only inside colonies and from one district to another but also, in the decades following 1850, from the early, centrally located neighborhoods toward outlying areas of the city and even to the suburbs. A few settlements did exist in outer areas of cities and in suburbs from the first years of immigration, generally formed around an industrial complex providing jobs. With rare exceptions, contemporaries did not recognize the extensive amount of residential mobility among the Irish, Germans, Swedes, and other "old" elements or later among the various "new" groups. Some groups dispersed from ethnic colonies more rapidly than did others, but even Italians and Poles, regarded by contemporaries as the most immobile of all immigrants, exhibited a high degree of residential mobility. The 1915 City Department of Public Welfare survey of an Italian and Polish district in Chicago's Seventeenth Ward noted that nearly half the community's residents changed their dwelling places each year.

Newcomers in each immigrant wave shifted from central-city areas toward peripheral residential neighborhoods with their economic and social advancement. The process was neither orderly nor absolute. Many residents resisted any change in location even after succeeding ethnic waves had inundated the neighborhood. Only the large-scale invasion of a totally unacceptable group or the conversion of a district to industrial or commercial use could eliminate the hard core of earlier inhabitants. Closely related to this mixed character of immigrant communities was the fact that—except for New York—most cities had no areas occupied exclusively by one ethnic group (with the exception of Negro districts). Native Americans resided with recent arrivals and remnants of earlier ethnic waves in neighborhoods that contemporaries labeled Irish, Italian, German, or Greek.

When they arrived in the United States, immigrants generally understood little about the English language. They also lacked contacts with potential American employers and knew nothing about American labor practices. To compensate for these deficiences, they looked for an intermediary in the same way they sought out the immigrant banker for financial assistance. This intermediary was the private labor agent or labor boss, who spoke both languages, understood Old World customs and New World business operations, and could communicate with American employers in need of unskilled workers.

From at least the 1880's, some form of boss system seemed to be typical of non-English-speaking immigrant elements newly arrived in urban-industrial America. Bossism existed among Germans, Norwegians, Swedes, Italians, Greeks, Austrians, Turks, Poles, Bulgarians, Macedonians, and others. The boss operated unofficially, in private, and often dishonestly. He took an "order" from an American employer for a specified number of men, gathered the men from the ethnic community (after receiving a cash commission in advance from each one), and supervised them at the job, often doling out their pay after extracting an additional "commission" for himself. When out-of-town construction kept the men away for days or weeks, the boss received boarding fees for whatever housing he chose to provide, and he usually operated the only available food commissary, where prices were high and the quality inferior. Increased familiarity with the English language and American labor practices and the resultant rise in economic status brought to an end the immigrant's need for the boss. At the same time, pressures applied by social workers and other Americans anxious to improve immigrant living conditions tended to reduce or prevent padrone abuses.

Popular opinion held that newcomers, both "old" and "new," displaced native American workingmen and depreciated wage rates. This argument appeared as early as the 1850s against new arrivals from Ireland, England, and Germany. Its foremost proponent, Francis A. Walker, superintendent of the census in 1870 and later president of Massachusetts Institute of Technology, maintained that immigration held down the native-born population because immigrants accepted lower wages and worse living conditions than did Americans. With its pronounced bias against "new" immigrants, the United States Immigration Commission (the Dillingham Commission, 1907–11) echoed Walker's prejudices. Dillingham researchers "showed" that new groups were in the process of forcing out older elements from industrial jobs, especially in the eastern portions of the nation. The commission concluded that such displacement adversely affected both workers and the country. However, this conclusion had only a tenuous connection with the commission's evidence. Facts collected by researchers indicated that immigrants neither underbid nor competed with their predecessors; furthermore, the increased economic activity permitted by a large labor force enabled earlier groups to improve their economic levels. Displacement indeed occurred, but the movement was generally upward or outward, as earlier groups and native Americans became foremen, executives, partners, owners, and the like or moved to higher-paying jobs in other states. Examining the coal industry, the commission found that native-born and "old" immigrant workers moved to the Midwest or Southwest and brought about a tremendous expansion in mining operations. "Those that remained in the bituminous mines," noted the commission, "have in most cases attained to the skilled and responsible executive positions created by the development of the industry, such as those of engineers and foremen." Not every worker improved his position; immobile ones provided the discontented voices that blamed the unfair competition of foreigners.

During the decades before the Civil War, some groups arrived in the United States in order to engage in particular lines of work. As a result, during this period the particular skills or training possessed by members of these groups often determined job distribution. After the 1860s, job concentrations in the United States owed little to earlier employment in Europe. Generally, "old" as well as "new" immigrants arrived without skills valued by American business and industry and started as laborers at the bottom of the pay scale. The significant point is that over the passage of time, *all* immigrant groups moved up that scale, although at differing rates of speed. Some, like eastern European Jews, improved their economic status much more rapidly than did other groups that arrived at about the same time.

Popular opinion attributed ethnic job concentrations to specific physical characteristics: Slavs had great size and strength and so went into heavy industry; Italian physiques necessitated lighter labor; Jews worked well with textiles. Physical attributes did, of course, play some part for each worker, but the situation was far more complex. Among the factors that helped to explain ethnic job concentrations were the cultural and economic background of each immigrant group, which made certain lines of work more appealing than others; the time of arrival of each group and the extent to which this coincided with the expansion needs of American industries; the structure of the industries themselves, which might accept female and child labor or require workers to be on the job outside the city for long periods of time; and worker mobility, which bore a direct relationship to the number of unmarried males in the group. At any rate, by the turn of the century, immigrants or the children of immigrants provided 75 percent of the labor force in twenty-one leading American industries.

Immigrants played a vital role in the formation and growth of labor unions in the United States. Following the Civil War and continuing into the years after World War II, foreigners provided the major driving force behind organized labor, both as rank-and-file members and as leaders. With few exceptions, immigrant leaders of American unions in the post–Civil War decades came from the British Isles, usually England or Ireland, because during this period, England led the industrial nations of the world, and British labor was well organized. This leadership greatly influenced the character and direction of American labor development, giving the movement a moderate, nonrevolutionary, essentially middle-class nature that has traditionally shown little sympathy for socialism. It should be noted that the radical movement as well owed much to the efforts of migrants, especially from Germany and (after 1900) of Jews from eastern Europe. The Finnish immigration, although relatively small, also featured prominently in the radical movement in the United States.

In the late 1870s and 1880s, the Knights of Labor attempted to bring together in one national organization all skilled and unskilled workers, foreigners and natives, whites and blacks, women and men. In the wake of a series of unsuccessful strikes in the mid-1880s, the Knights declined, and the American Federation of Labor emerged as the dominant labor group in the country. Samuel Gompers, the long-time president of the union, decided that unionism in America could succeed only if it concentrated its organizational efforts on skilled workmen and emphasized bread-and-butter issues such as higher wages, shorter hours, and improved working conditions. The AFL thus concerned itself primarily with protecting the position of skilled labor, which in the 1890s and after the turn of the century consisted largely of "old" immigrant groups. "New" immigrants, especially Italians and Slavs, gained a reputation for strikebreaking and for an inability to organize. Under Gompers, the AFL made little effort to organize the "new" immigrants, most of whom were unskilled. These unskilled "new" groups did not have an effective labor union to represent them and to look out for their interests until the 1930s, when the Congress of Industrial Organizations was organized. Where unionizers made diligent efforts to attract "new" immigrants and in industries where unions could give some assurance that effective leadership would obtain union objectives, immigrants joined labor organizations. By World War I, the International Ladies Garment Workers' Union and the Amalgamated Clothing Workers of America ranked as powerful organizations; the largest part of the membership of both consisted of immigrants from southern and eastern Europe.

Valuable economic benefits accrued to immigrants, and especially to their children, from politics and criminal activities; in core areas of American cities, the two often intertwined. Early in their settlement process, immigrant groups recognized that economic advantages came after naturalization and participation in politics and as a result of both. In order to win and hold immigrant support, political machines made available to a succession of ethnic groups patronage positions and jobs with private companies doing business with the municipality. Work included street cleaning, garbage collecting, and custodial jobs in public buildings; building and maintaining roads, public transportation networks, and sewage systems; and constructing tenements, bathhouses, and parks. This employment generally offered unskilled workers relatively steady incomes and job security; to immigrant groups it gave immediate proof of the benefits to be gained from local politics. Professional police and fire-fighting forces, which emerged in urban America during the middle decades of the nineteenth century, quickly fell under the control of local politicians and provided additional sources of patronage for the machine. By the 1870s, this connection had evolved into a working relationship among criminals, politicians, and the police that has plagued American cities ever since.

Although by the 1830s immigrants, especially the Irish, exercised the franchise in sufficient numbers to cause concern among middle- and upper-class Americans in New York City, not until the decades following the Civil War and the growth to maturity of the second generation did ethnic groups begin to exert a dominant influence in municipal politics. The boss system, a familiar part of the urban scene by the 1880s and 1890s, grew out of conditions in core area neighborhoods. In 1894, the United States commissioner of labor published the results of a survey of slum areas in four major American cities (Baltimore, Chicago, New York, Philadelphia). In each city, investigators found serious overcrowding in tenements, high rents for inferior housing, barely adequate sanitary conditions, and extremely poor social relations. In these neighborhoods, the great press of people compounded all existing problems, but in politics, the mass of humanity was a benefit rather than a disadvantage. When organized and directed, tenement residents proved to be a powerful voice in city affairs. The momentum and organizing power came from ambitious, upwardly mobile members of the second generation who had reached maturity only to find economic advancement in the professions and business world made difficult (but not impossible) by inadequate education, lack of money, and ineffectual family connections. In the words of George Washington Plunkitt, the sage of Tammany Hall, young men like these "seen" their opportunities and they "took 'em." Along with crime and sports, politics offered fame and fortune to slum youngsters despite their financial and educational shortcomings. By winning elective office, an individual could gain esteem and power within his home district as well as American recognition of his position and that of the ethnic group.

An effective, enduring political machine provided a variety of services and favors for constituents. In addition to jobs, the successful political boss obtained exemptions from city ordinances for core area businessmen; arranged bail and obtained pardons; sponsored dances, parades, picnics, social, and athletic affairs, bazaars, and community church functions; distributed turkeys at Christmas; gave food and fuel to needy residents; sent flowers to the ill, and attended funerals. The harsh and painful life in tenement areas made residents extremely sensitive about the manner in which one started his journey to the hereafter. A politician who saved deceased constituents from "that awful horror" of a pauper's burial gained admiration and respect from the living. Those who received patronage positions or favors felt obligated to vote for the machine, and although they seldom formed a majority of a ward's eligible voters, they provided a loyal, disciplined, and effective nucleus. The high degree of residential mobility displayed by immigrants discouraged many from taking an active interest in precinct or ward politics. Bosses attempted to encourage this general apathy in order that the votes of the faithful could determine election outcomes. Members of the underworld figured prominently among the most loyal supporters of the political machine.

In exchange for a free hand in operating gambling halls, saloons, and houses of prostitution, criminal elements not only helped get out the votes on election day but also kept many opposition voters from reaching polling stations. In addition, through hoodlum muscle and cash, bosses used intimidation, bribery, violence, and trickery to prevent the rise of effective competition, particularly rivals from more recent ethnic groups.

Second-generation Irish achieved great successes in ward and city politics. Reformer John Paul Bocock published an article in *The Forum* (1894) entitled "The Irish Conquest of Our Cities." It clearly reflected middle-class fears that the Irish had captured control of urban politics and crime in the United States. Although Americans pictured Irish political bosses as officers leading phalanxes of dutiful immigrant voters to the polls, the politicians themselves never found political realities to be so simple or pleasant. Ethnic rivalries and antagonisms characterized urban politics as they did the Catholic church in America, and no boss could afford to relax his vigilance, efforts, or cash outlays.

Shrewd political realists such as Graham Taylor, the head of Chicago Commons Settlement House in the city's seventeenth ward, made extremely effective use of ethnic antagonisms against the Irish, who although numerically in the minority, still retained control of politics at the time that Taylor moved into the ward. Uniting other ethnic groups against the Irish, Taylor and his forces overthrew the local machine and elected effective, intelligent candidates to the city council, where they aided the forces of reform to push through needed legislation in housing, health, and labor. Taylor attained greater successes than most settlement workers who engaged in politics; nevertheless, reformers in New York, Boston, and many other cities did reach and influence immigrant voters. Their successes came when they concentrated their efforts on concrete, understandable objectives affecting the lives of slum dwellers. Reformers who emphasized abstractions like justice or democracy found little support among immigrants.

Social workers achieved only limited results in practical politics. However, settlement houses offered a wide variety of activities and services that many immigrants and their children utilized. Settlements generally maintained social, civic, political, domestic, musical, athletic, and dramatic clubs for adults and provided lessons in English and citizenship for the foreign-born. They also offered music lessons, gymnastic facilities, arts and crafts classes, concerts, lectures, and forums. Lighter entertainments included festivals, pageants, and dances. Many settlements kept libraries and study rooms available. Some, including all the larger establishments, maintained playgrounds, camps, and vacation houses and took members on summer outings. These activities usually won steady, if not overwhelming, immigrant support and participation.

With few exceptions (among them Jane Addams of Hull House), social workers rallied behind President Woodrow Wilson and ardently supported the American war effort after the declaration of hostilities against the Kaiser's Germany in April 1917. Settlement houses then served their immigrant neighborhoods as clearinghouses of information about wartime legislation; they saw to the needs of families with relatives in the services and operated as Red Cross stations, draft boards, and Liberty Bond drive sponsors.

World War I profoundly affected immigration and immigrant colonies in American cities. Manpower needs in the belligerent countries of Europe and the extreme difficulties of passage during wartime cut sharply into the numbers of newcomers arriving from overseas. European immigration declined precipitously from 1,058,391 in 1914 to 197,919 in 1915 (the first full year of war) to 31,063 in 1918. The virtual cessation of immigration ended the constant replenishment of labor reserves in the United States. Combined with military manpower demands in the period after April 1917, labor needs offered immigrants already in the country and their children wider job opportunities than ever before and at higher wages.

Immigrants generally showed great interest in the war fortunes of the mother country. Some returned home to fight, and many more served as volunteers or draftees in the armed forces of their adopted homeland. Sacrifices on the battlefields increased ethnic pride and prestige, and—spurred by President Wilson's often reiterated promises of self-determination for the peoples of Europe—raised high hopes among immigrants in the United

States. With the end of hostilities, the various ethnic groups competed with each other in attempting to influence the president's foreign policies, either to create new and independent states or to increase the territories of existing nations. With the exception of the Poles and Czechs, these hopes died quickly. Immigrant hostility to Wilson's actions at the Paris Peace Conference played a significant role in the 1920 presidential election. The president's unfulfilled promises and actual or supposed slurs against Germans, Irish, Italians, and other groups received extensive and continuing coverage in the foreign-language newspapers in the United States and proved too heavy a burden for Democratic candidate, James M. Cox, to bear. Poles and Czechs generally supported Cox, but other ethnic groups vented their frustrations and rage by staying away from the polls or by casting their ballots for the Republican, Warren G. Harding.

America reversed its traditional policy of free immigration during the postwar years. Social workers and other liberal elements among the American population joined urban ethnics, under the guidance of Jewish organizations, in the fight against immigration restriction; but the outcome was never in doubt when business groups aligned themselves with organized labor in support of restriction. Organized labor traditionally supported federal legislation to restrict immigration in the belief that the constant stream of unskilled labor undermined unionizing efforts. During the war years, with traditional overseas sources of unskilled labor cut off, American industry discovered the availability of alternate sources of labor. Migrations of Mexicans and of Negroes from the American South removed the need for European immigrants. This development, along with emotional factors like antiradicalism, religious bias, and racism, brought about the closing of America's gates and the adoption of clearly discriminatory quota laws.

As a result of World War I and the immigration laws of 1921 and 1924, core area communities declined in importance and population as immigrants and their families continued to move to the peripheries or suburbs of American cities. The general prosperity that began during the war and continued until late 1929 (except for the recession of 1920–21) facilitated the socioeconomic mobility of "new" immigrant elements. Movement away from central-city slums proceeded rapidly.

Despite the bitter cries of protest in the decades since the passage of the National Origins Act of 1924, immigrants and their descendants accepted the end of the era of free immigration. Protest after the 1920s centered on the implication that some groups were more acceptable than others and thus should receive larger quotas, whether or not these quotas were filled. These complaints dwindled, but did not entirely disappear, with the enactment of the 1965 immigration law, which sets an overall yearly quota but permits the entry on a first-come, first-served basis of immigrants possessing skills needed in this country.

Significantly, recent demands by white ethnic group leaders (often self-appointed) do not include a return to the policy of free immigration. They concentrate rather on recognition by the American population of the importance and uniqueness of their particular group, insist that real or imagined slurs against the group be discontinued, and demand that areas of economic, political, or cultural activity hitherto closed to that group (or in which it seems to be underrepresented) be opened forthwith. The resurgence of white ethnic group consciousness, an outgrowth of increasing Negro awareness, is also a result of the belief that through pressure blacks have gained benefits that other ethnic groups ought to share. As one group member maintained in the ethnic press in November 1971: "The revolution of the '60s has seen the blacks achieve some measure of acceptance in their struggle for equal treatment. . . . Is it too much for Italo-Americans to ask for their fair share of human dignity from that same community?"

Movement out of ethnic districts slowed during the 1930s because of the depression and during the 1940s because of housing shortages. By the 1950s, the process again accelerated, and the formerly heavy concentrations of "new" immigrant groups has thinned drastically. Some communities broke up under the physical reconstruction of urban renewal, others because of settlement within them of blacks, Puerto Ricans, and southern whites. "New" immigrant groups prefer not to associate with these newer arrivals; they regard the latest in the succession of newcomers with the same attitudes that Anglo-Saxons and "old" immigrants had previously exhibited toward them. Some European ethnic neighborhoods remain in American cities, but as pale reflections of the pre–World War I districts that overflowed with people and teemed with vitality. Except for a handful of American cities, the torrent of immigrant newcomers has slowed to a trickle.

Selected Bibliography

A vast literature covers immigration to the United States. In order to stay within manageable limits, this bibliography is limited to books and published reports written in English. For the same reason, titles will be mentioned only once, although many of the volumes examine a variety of topics within the immigrant experience.

Among the general studies dealing with American immigration are: Maldwyn Allen Jones, *American Immigration* (Chicago, 1960); Carl F. Wittke, *We Who Built America: The Saga of the Immigrant* (Cleveland, 1939); George M. Stephenson,

A History of American Immigration, 1820–1924 (Boston, 1926); Marcus Lee Hansen, *The Atlantic Migration, 1607–1860* (Cambridge, Mass., 1940) and *The Immigrant in American History* (Cambridge, Mass., 1940); Oscar Handlin, *The Uprooted* (Boston, 1951), *The American People in the Twentieth Century* (Cambridge, Mass., 1954), and the essays on immigration in his *Race and Nationality in American Life* (Boston, 1957); David F. Bowers, editor, *Foreign Influences in American Life* (Princeton, N.J., 1944); Philip Taylor, *The Distant Magnet: European Emigration to the U.S.A.* (New York, 1971). During the 1920s, Edith Abbott of the University of Chicago School of Social Work edited two invaluable collections of documents: *Immigration: Select Documents and Case Records* (Chicago, 1924) and *Historical Aspects of the Immigration Problem* (Chicago, 1926).

On the experiences of particular immigrant groups see: Rowland T. Berthoff, *British Immigrants in Industrial America, 1790–1950* (Cambridge, Mass., 1953); John A. Hawgood, *The Tragedy of German-America* (New York, 1939); Carl F. Wittke, *The Irish in America* (New York, 1956); Florence E. Janson, *The Background of Swedish Immigration, 1840–1930* (Chicago, 1931); Theodore C. Blegen, *Norwegian Migration to America, 1825–1860* (Northfield, Minn., 1931); Emily G. Balch, *Our Slavic Fellow Citizens* (New York, 1910); Samuel Joseph, *Jewish Immigration to the United States from 1881 to 1910* (New York, 1914); Robert F. Foerster, *The Italian Emigration of Our Times* (Cambridge, Mass., 1919); Marcus Lee Hansen, *The Mingling of the Canadian and American Peoples* (New Haven, 1940); Theodore Saloutos, *The Greeks in the United States* (Cambridge, Mass., 1963); and the classic sociological study by William I. Thomas and Florian Znaniecki, *The Polish Peasant in Europe and America* (5 vols., Chicago, 1918–20).

Studies by contemporaries of living conditions in slum areas of American cities include: U.S. Commissioner of Labor, *Seventh Special Report: The Slums of Baltimore, Chicago, New York and Philadelphia* (1894); Charles Loring Brace, *The Dangerous Classes of New York, and Twenty Years' Work Among Them* (New York, 1872); Robert A. Woods, *et al., The Poor in Great Cities* (New York, 1895); Robert W. De Forest and Lawrence Veiller, editors, *The Tenement House Problem* (2 vols., New York, 1913); Edith Abbott, *The Tenements of Chicago, 1908–1935* (Chicago, 1936); Jane Addams, *Twenty Years at Hull House* (New York, 1910); Robert A. Woods, editor, *The City Wilderness* (Boston, 1898) and *Americans in Process* (Boston, 1902).

Over the decades, sociologists have produced extensive amounts of literature dealing with the immigrant experience in urban America. Among the most noteworthy are: Thomas J. Jones, *The Sociology of a New York City Block* (New York, 1904); Robert E. Park and Herbert A. Miller, *Old World Traits Transplanted* (New York, 1921); Louis Wirth, *The Ghetto* (Chicago, 1928); William F. Whyte, *Streetcorner Society* (Chicago, 1943); Herbert Gans, *The Urban Villagers* (New York, 1962); Gerald D. Suttles, *The Social Order of the Slum: Ethnicity and Territory in the Inner City* (Chicago, 1968); and Nathan Glazer and Daniel

P. Moynihan, *Beyond the Melting Pot: The Negroes, Puerto Ricans, Jews, Italians, and Irish of New York City* (Cambridge, Mass., 1963; rev. ed., 1970). Following the lead of Oscar Handlin's landmark work in urban immigration history, *Boston's Immigrants: A Study in Acculturation* (Cambridge, Mass., 1941; rev. ed., 1959), historians have begun to examine the urban dimension of the immigrant experience. Among these are: Robert Ernst, *Immigrant Life in New York City, 1825–1863* (New York, 1949); Moses Rischin, *The Promised City: New York City's Jews, 1870–1914* (Cambridge, Mass., 1962); Humbert S. Nelli, *The Italians in Chicago, 1880–1930: A Study in Ethnic Mobility* (New York, 1970); Stephan Thernstrom, *Poverty and Progress: Social Mobility in a Nineteenth Century City* (Cambridge, Mass., 1964); Gerd Korman, *Industrialization, Immigrants, and Americanizers: The View from Milwaukee, 1866–1921* (Madison, Wisc., 1967); Donald B. Cole, *Immigrant City: Lawrence, Massachusetts, 1845–1921* (Chapel Hill, N.C., 1963); Earl F. Niehaus, *The Irish in New Orleans, 1800–1860* (Baton Rouge, La., 1965); Peter R. Knights, *The Plain People of Boston, 1830–1860: A Study in City Growth* (New York, 1971); Arthur A. Goren, *New York Jews and the Quest for Community: The Kehillah Experiment, 1908–1922* (New York, 1970). Important studies by geographers are: Walter I. Firey, *Land Use in Central Boston* (Cambridge, Mass., 1947), and David Ward, *Cities and Immigrants: A Geography of Change in Nineteenth Century America* (New York, 1971).

For a focus on urban politics see, among others: Harold Zink, *City Bosses in the United States* (Durham, N.C., 1930); Samuel Lubell, *The Future of American Politics* (New York, 1952; 3d ed. rev., 1965); J. Joseph Huthmacher, *Massachusetts People and Politics, 1919–1933* (Cambridge, Mass., 1959); Arthur Mann, *La Guardia: A Fighter against His Times, 1882–1933* (Philadelphia, 1959) and *La Guardia Comes to Power* (Philadelphia, 1965); William L. Riordon, *Plunkitt of Tammany Hall* (New York, 1963)—this edition contains a discerning introduction by Arthur Mann; Lawrence H. Fuchs, *The Political Behavior of American Jews* (Glencoe, Ill., 1956); Lloyd Wendt and Herman Kogan, *Lords of the Levee: The Story of Bathhouse John and Hinky Dink* (Indianapolis, 1943); Frederick G. Luebke, *Immigrants and Politics: The Germans of Nebraska, 1880–1900* (Lincoln, Neb., 1969).

On the immigrant economic experience consult: U.S. Senate, *Reports of the Immigration Commission* (41 vols., 1911); Jeremiah W. Jenks and W. Jett Lauck, *The Immigration Problem* (New York, 1912); Isaac A. Hourwich, *Immigration and Labor: The Economic Aspects of European Immigration to the United States* (New York, 1912); Charlotte Erickson, *American Industry and the European Immigrant, 1860–1885* (Cambridge, Mass., 1957); Peter Roberts, *Anthracite Coal Communities* (New York, 1904); Clifton K. Yearley, Jr., *Britons in American Labor* (Baltimore, 1957); Victor R. Greene, *The Slavic Community on Strike: Immigrant Labor in Pennsylvania Anthracite* (Notre Dame, Ind., 1968); William M. Leiserson, *Adjusting Immigrant and Industry* (New York, 1924).

Studies of immigrant community institutions include: Robert E. Park, *The Immigrant Press and Its Control* (New York, 1922); Carl Wittke, *The German-Lan-*

guage Press in America (Lexington, Ky., 1957); Edmund G. Olszyk, *The Polish Press in America* (Milwaukee, 1940); Mordecai Soltes, *The Yiddish Press: An Americanizing Agency* (New York, 1925); Thomas Capek, *The Czechs in America: A Study of Their National, Cultural, Political, Social, Economic, and Religious Life* (Boston, 1920); Grace Abbott, *The Problem of Immigration in Massachusetts* (Boston, 1914); Gerald Shaughnessy, *Has the Immigrant Kept the Faith?* (New York, 1925); Robert D. Cross, *The Emergence of Liberal Catholicism in America* (Cambridge, Mass., 1958); Colman J. Barry, *The Catholic Church and German Americans* (Washington, D.C., 1953); George M. Stephenson, *The Religious Aspects of Swedish Immigration* (Minneapolis, 1932); H. Richard Niebuhr, *The Social Sources of Denominationalism* (New York, 1929); Oscar Handlin, *Adventure in Freedom: Three Hundred Years of Jewish Life in America* (New York, 1954); Nathan Glazer, *American Judaism* (Chicago, 1957).

For examinations of nativism and efforts to restrict immigration see: Edward A. Ross, *The Old World in the New* (New York, 1914); John R. Commons, *Races and Immigrants in America* (New York, 1907); Madison Grant, *The Passing of the Great Race* (New York, 1916); John Higham, *Strangers in the Land: Patterns of American Nativism, 1860–1925* (New Brunswick, N.J., 1955); Ray Allen Billington, *The Protestant Crusade, 1800–1860: A Study of the Origins of American Nativism* (New York, 1938); Barbara M. Solomon, *Ancestors and Immigrants: A Changing New England Tradition* (Cambridge, Mass., 1956); Henry J. Desmond, *The A.P.A. Movement* (Washington, D.C., 1912); Donald L. Kinzer, *An Episode in Anti-Catholicism: The American Protective Association* (Seattle, 1964); Roy L. Garis, *Immigration Restriction: A Study of the Opposition to and Regulation of Immigration to the United States* (New York, 1927); Robert A. Divine, *American Immigration Policy, 1924–1952* (New Haven, Conn., 1957); William S. Bernard, editor, *American Immigration Policy* (New York, 1950).

Urban Workers and Labor Organization

Neil Betten

Workers and unions are formidable forces in the contemporary American city. The recent surge of unionization among municipal employees, for example, has resulted in a spate of crippling strikes by teachers, firemen, policemen, social workers, sanitation men, hospital workers, even bridge tenders. Labor's political endorsement and financial support is often crucial to victory at the polls, especially in state and local elections. Labor's political education committees provide propaganda, field workers, and funds for the labor movement's allies. Important city commissions and boards are often staffed with labor representatives. Even citywide charity drives benefit from organized labor's assistance. In sum, in major cities the labor movement has become part of the establishment. Organized labor's considerable influence and high status is a relatively recent phenomenon, however, a product of the last forty years. The worker's role in society evolved slowly, and his early organizations were often considered little more than subversive challenges to the system.

In colonial towns, the working class consisted of diverse elements. Indentured servants and apprentices had similar standards of living, worked long hours (usually from sunup to sundown), and had little social status, although apprentices had greater esteem because they would eventually be craftsmen. Skilled workers, or journeymen, and their employers—the master craftsmen—worked and lived together. Until the latter part of the eighteenth century, they also belonged to the same economic and social organizations, which sometimes had the character of benevolent societies, employment agencies, or price-lobbying agencies. Although an incipient capitalist, the master craftsman labored with his hands six days a week. To society, the man behind the workman's leather apron was neither aristocratic nor bourgeois. Yet with increased income, the master craftsman could gain social standing, because class lines were more fluid in colonial America than in Europe. Thus, some colonial craftsmen became part of the upper-middle-class elite, whereas others remained on lower rungs of the socioeconomic ladder.

A scarcity of free laborers and skilled workers, particularly in the seventeenth century, kept wages in America high relative to those in Europe. Nevertheless, inequities existed, and alternatives to such inequities were not easily pursued. Those whose freedom was severely limited—indentured servants and apprentices—might protest poor food, inadequate living accommodations, and physical abuse through the courts; they might ultimately become runaways, a course, although hazardous, that provided the only realistic alternative to urban slaves who sought improved conditions. Free unskilled workers likewise faced hardship: periods of unemployment, harsh winters in which fuel costs soared, and the economic inability to flee when yellow fever and typhoid periodically decimated the cities. Seamen were in a class by themselves, with low incomes, crowded living conditions, and little freedom of action.

Although organization among the lower rungs of the cities' working class remained rare, skilled journeymen and master craftsmen attempted to improve and protect their economic status by organizing well before 1800. Whole trades pooled resources to provide welfare benefits for members such as income for the sick, disabled, widowed, and unemployed, and these benevolent associations also served as embryonic credit unions, loaning funds to members in need.

Journeymen and masters had closely allied economic interests as well. Throughout most of the colonial period, town officials regulated wages, prices, and fees for necessary services. Thus in some crafts, increases in the journeyman's and the master craftsman's income depended on government concessions. In other trades, a lack of trained masters in the developing society resulted in monopolies or near-monopolies. In such cases, employers passed high wages on to the consumer, providing many colonial workers with an income substantially above that of his European counterpart. Likewise, the scarcity of skilled workers bolstered bargaining power, not only keeping wages high but also keeping working hours low—at least according to the European standards of the day. In fact, in 1670 Massachusetts legislation declared ten hours the minimum work day, curtailing the bargaining leverage of free labor. The colony's elite would not have found it necessary to pass such a law unless a significant portion of the working class labored less than a ten-hour day.

The interests of journeymen and masters gradually parted, however. Improved roads and river connections in the eighteenth century, coupled with a thriving coastal trade, permitted town entrepreneurs to sell products beyond earlier, limited geographical limits. Instead of producing "bespoke" products—custom-made for each individual local buyer—masters from different towns and cities found themselves competing in the production of ready-made goods for distant markets. This competitive market pressed working conditions and wages downward. As merchants with commercial expertise and credit resources replaced the master craftsman as the central agent in the distribution and control of the products, the journeyman's role gradually deteriorated further.

Journeymen thus emerged as economic adversaries of the master craftsmen who employed them and formed their own organizations, at first similar to the older benevolent societies. The new associations provided minor benefits such as sick pay, widows' pensions, and corresponding social activities, but they did not deal with workers' basic grievances. Thus, early in colonial history, the strike, or "turn-out," conducted by ad hoc associations resulted. When monopolistic conditions still prevailed, master and journeymen often jointly turned out against what they considered unfair government price rates, and less skilled workers whose incomes the city controlled followed the same pattern. In 1684, New York City's scavengers refused to remove dirt from the streets unless they received a wage increase. In this case, the strike was broken because the garbage entrepreneurs were "suspended and discharged . . . for not obeying the Command and doing their Duties as becomes them in the Places." Savannah carpenters struck in 1746, and in 1770 New York City coopers (barrel makers) refused "to sell casks except in accordance with the rates [we] established." In 1763, black chimney sweepers of Charleston, the local *Gazette* reported, "had the insolence by a combination amongst themselves, to raise the usual prices."

By the mid-eighteenth century, urban workers had carried out several conventional strikes against employers. As early as 1734, female domestic workers in New York organized and struck because "we think it reasonable we should not be beat by our Mistresses' Husband[s], they being too strong, and perhaps may do tender women Mischief." The Journeymen Caulkers of Boston struck in 1741 because their employers paid them in company scrip rather than currency, and the Philadelphia printers walked out in 1788. The court records of one Philadelphia shoemakers' strike reveal the similarity of the eighteenth century turn-out to modern industrial conflict. The shoemakers struck for a closed shop, socially ostracized the "rats" (as strikebreakers were called), and organized "tramping" committees (like picketers) to inspect shops and inform workers of the strike.

Strikes occurred infrequently and usually erupted as spontaneous reactions to local grievances within one trade, occupation, or service; rarely were they organized by permanent labor unions. Government, courts, and employers all opposed turn-outs by workers. Although they were occasionally successful, ad hoc strike groups did not yet have a profound effect on urban life. The immediate issues involved in strikes, whether carried out by skilled or unskilled workers, did not stimulate permanent organization. Urban workers might temporarily turn to riots or radical politics to settle major grievances, but more often they formed associations to deal with common problems. The benevolent society continued to provide welfare and social functions for its members.

By the late eighteenth century, American wage earners still earned more than European workers, but high prices in the New World eroded much of the differential. America's respect for craftsmen and more fluid class lines generally allowed American workers to achieve higher social status than their Western European counterparts. During the first half of the nineteenth century, skilled workers fought to prevent erosion of their social standing; simultaneously, they also sought to protect established avenues of upward mobility. They demanded free public education for all children, not just those of the upper and middle classes; they attacked monopolies and banks because such institutions blocked the rise of small entrepreneurs; they demanded a shorter work day, local governmental and political reforms, and the abolition of imprisonment for debt. Nevertheless, skilled workers—like unskilled workers—were affected by the machine; their status fell, and their income diminished in newly mechanized trades.

Although commerce dominated the early nineteenth century American city, after 1830 manufacturing emerged as a major urban economic activity, particularly in the Northeast. In addition to the commercial cities which took on manufacturing functions, distinct factory towns also emerged. Cities such as Lowell and Chicopee in Massachusetts attracted workers to new textile factories. At first, entire families found work in the factory towns, but between 1810 and 1815, some mills began using young, unmarried women from nearby farms as operatives. Factory employment became "women's work," at least for a time. In the 1820s and 1830s, the female factory operatives labored approximately twelve hours a day. The women lived in company boarding houses, and employers regulated the factory girls' lives by such means as establishing curfews, directing the women's social activities, making attendance at the company church obligatory, providing propagandistic reading material, and punishing outspoken malcontents. Working conditions further deteriorated as employers cut costs in response to increased competition in the industry. However, not until an alternative cheap labor supply emerged—Irish immigrants fleeing the potato famine of the 1840s—did poor wages and intolerable conditions drive American farm girls from the mills.

For nineteenth century American workers, unionism provided one means of dealing with labor problems. After several false starts stemming from unfavorable court decisions and a highly cyclical economy, throughout most of the century labor organizing generally followed a definite pattern closely related to the business cycle (although some exceptions occurred). Unions were organized and took strong stands during periods of prosperity and little unemployment, during which businesses were reluctant to sacrifice profits and disrupt long-standing, profitable commercial relations by engaging unions in long strikes. In addition, workers could find alternative employment during labor stoppages. Thus, management more easily succumbed to strike activities. But in times of economic stress, employers could easily recruit strikebreakers from among the large pool of unemployed, whereas strikers without work for long periods faced starvation. During economic reversals traditional union activities proved ineffective.

Between 1821 and 1828, a multiplicity of labor organizations emerged in American cities and towns. Semiskilled and unskilled women and girls organized in textile mill towns, and skilled workers formed local craft organizations for members of their trade. During this same period, local unions representing many trades combined to form citywide trades unions. The first central labor federation appeared in Philadelphia in 1827, an outgrowth of attempts by the city's workers to establish a maximum ten-hour day. The workers made other demands as well: they petitioned for reforms such as free public education, elimination of compulsory military service which discriminated against workers (who could neither purchase substitutes nor afford to miss regular working days), a mechanics lien law to protect workers' wages against loss resulting from a firm's bankruptcy, and an end to government sanction of monopolies.

Between 1828 and 1831, the embryonic city unions stagnated, and many disillusioned workers turned to urban workingmen's political parties, which were often led by reformist and radical intellectuals. However, such parties were split by competing factions and infiltrated by political hacks and middle-class opportunists, and they soon disintegrated as the economy revived by mid-1831. In an economic climate of full employment, numerous urban workers again turned to labor organizations. Between 1831 and 1837, at least 200 local trade unions were established, with a membership of over 100,000. Once again, skilled workers joined citywide federations. New York City's Trades Union emerged as the most important, but significant city centrals also blossomed in such urban centers as Philadelphia, Boston, Baltimore, Washington, D.C., Cincinnati, Pittsburgh, and Louisville. The federations of New York City and Philadelphia each included over fifty member unions.

These trades unions developed generally uniform activities and procedures. Each local union in the federation contributed a portion of membership dues to the central organization to be used for legal suits, propaganda, and aid for striking workers. Sometimes city centrals aided unions in other cities, organized boycotts of "unfair employers," raised additional funds in support of striking unions, and publicized such actions in newspapers owned and operated by the local labor federation. Some city federa tions established political parties, but most centrals rejected this thrust. In many New England towns, workers and farmers joined together in associations similar to city centrals. Providence, Rhode Island, for example, spawned a group called the New England Association of Farmers, Mechanics, and Other Working Men. Even a few nationwide or national unions appeared in the 1830s. These associations of unions, which presaged the present city labor federations (whose activities are similar) were killed in the panic of 1837 and the subsequent depression.

Most economic indicators portray the middle and late 1840s as an economically expanding era with little unemployment, but labor's advancement can be described only as marginal. The influx of Irish immigrants crowded the cities and the job market; one historian has estimated that New York City's density quadrupled in the 1840s. Although incomes went down in the factories of small cities such as Lowell, skilled workers held their own economically in industries that were still unmechanized. In the forties, however, increased population added significantly to the supply of potential strikebreakers and prevented union growth corresponding to generally improved economic conditions. Many urban workers thus turned to political action to achieve the ten-hour work day, and some advocated utopian socialist alternatives to escape intolerable conditions.

A complex chain of advances in communication, transportation, and technology nourished the industrial city, and by the 1850s, all major American cities had entered the industrial phase. New York and Philadelphia soon emerged as the largest manufacturing centers in the nation, and Cincinnati, Hartford, Syracuse, Newark, and Richmond stood among the many cities expanding on a manufacturing base. However, unionism continued to ebb and flow in relation to the business cycle, with organizational advances between 1847 and the early 1850s, from 1862 to 1865, and between 1870 and 1873 but major losses between 1837 and 1842, between 1857 and 1862, and from 1866 to 1868.

The emergence of national unions constituted the major structural change in the decade preceding the Civil War. As markets expanded, and as businessmen either competed more with distant entrepreneurs or expanded to other geographical areas, independent local labor unions were forced to expand their operations to a national level to successfully confront large entrepreneurs and deal with local business elements which had to compete with distant nonunionized competitors. Not all occupations followed this general pattern, and antiunion firms crushed numerous collective bargaining attempts irrespective of the product market. At the same time, some unions, particularly in printing and the building trades, organized nationals while their industries remained local. These national unions resulted from the ability of workers to move from place to place, and they controlled work standards, established uniform admission policies for dispersed locals, and imposed penalties on workers expelled or suspended from their original locals.

Thus by the 1850s, unions moved toward national organization, and with evolution in structure came some changes in approach. The new national craft unions focused on "bread-and-butter" issues—wages, hours, and working conditions—rather than on cooperative ventures, political involvement, or currently fashionable panaceas, a formula that led to moderate organizational success. By 1873, total union membership exceeded 300,000, every major city had a labor federation, and over thirty national unions existed; one national federation had already failed, but another had recently emerged. Then, from mid-1873 to late 1878, the United States suffered the first extensive economic collapse of the industrial period.

The depression following the panic of 1873 illustrated the extremity of nineteenth century problems. One student of the period estimated unemployment at 4 million in 1877, with an additional 100,000 on strike—the largest ratio of unemployment to total population to that time. The New York Association for Improving the Condition of the Poor reported that between one-fourth and one-third of the city's workers were unemployed during the first two winters of the depression. At least 20 percent of the work force remained permanently unemployed during the depression years; others worked only part of the year. But even those who found work faced severe economic pressures. Recent studies indicate that wages fell at least 25 percent, although contemporary estimates placed the wage drop at 50 to 60 percent; retail prices decreased only 20 percent at most from 1873 to 1877. During the same time period, incomes of elite railroad workers and furniture carpenters plummeted 30 to 40 percent; between 1873 and 1880, the textile industry reduced wages 45 percent. Newspapers of the day printed many stories documenting the seriousness of the problem. The *New York Sun* suggested that masons and stonecutters go to Scotland for work. "How the unemployed . . . have got through this," the *New York Tribune* queried early in 1878, "God only knows." The *New York World* printed a survey of conditions showing that thousands "lived [on] from 70 cents to $14.00 a week; that hundreds subsisted on the refuse from the city."

Sometimes the urban unemployed gave up searching for work and became vagrants who begged food from door to door and in some cities secured temporary or overnight shelter in city jails and police stations. Others lived in camps near railroads, where they found temporary housing in box cars. Freight trains also served transportation needs as the unemployed and unhoused migrated to warmer climates in winter. These tramps and hoboes, as the middle class called them, numbered about one million.

Workers had few alternatives in facing the cyclical poverty of the industrial age. Labor unions collapsed, often after losing hard-fought strikes. Only seven weak, floundering national unions survived the depression of 1873 to 1878, and local unions disappeared even in the strongest union towns. In New York, only five locals remained of the twenty-five in existence before the panic; Cleveland did somewhat better with ten surviving units, whereas Cincinnati had only one. Most cities no longer had any local unions by 1876. While some workers turned to radical politics—even to terrorist organizations such as the Molly Maguires—others sought release first in demonstration and then in spontaneous riots. The riots of 1877, which began as an unorganized strike of nonunionized railroad workers, devastated large areas of numerous cities, including Chicago, Indianapolis, Buffalo, Reading, Pittsburgh, and St. Louis.

The risks taken by the urban workers who committed acts of violence or simply gambled with the blacklist when on strike indicated the desperation of many. Nevertheless, for others, especially from 1879 to the mid-1890s, the work environment provided a means of adjusting to American and urban society and of accumulating some capital and moving upward economically. To be sure, the Horatio Alger myth rarely functioned in reality—most industrial leaders of the day came from the middle or upper middle class—but periods of sustained prosperity affected the working class as well. Recent studies of social mobility, usually in small, nineteenth century cities, do not permit many generalizations; however, it is clear that a significant portion of working-class people bettered their position over time. Two studies of mobility in Southern cities agree that whites could rise significantly on the economic ladder, but at the expense of immobile black workers, who were kept at the bottom of an expanding economy by job and promotional discrimination. Historian John A. Garraty sees the late nineteenth century as a period of mobility. He estimates that real wages rose 25 percent in the 1880s, but skilled workers earned 50 percent more than unskilled workers, and white-collar workers made almost twice as much as manual laborers. Although further studies on different segments of the working class are needed, it seems reasonable that even the unskilled advanced economically. Several studies of the late nineteenth century residential mobility suggest that the poor frequently moved to sustain employment; indeed, the poor had a considerably higher rate of geographical mobility than those who were better off. For example, numerous migrants arrived in American cities with no income; for them there was nowhere to go but up or out.

Although a short, serious recession occurred in the early 1880s, urban migrants arriving between 1879 and 1893 could adjust to city life during a period of general prosperity and full employment. Responding to the favorable turn of the business cycle, a multiplicity of labor organizations competed for workers' loyalty. The national labor unions of the 1880s, with their efficient organizations of skilled workers, high initiation fees, elaborate strike funds, and short-run economic goals, differed little from their predecessors of the 1850s. However, in reaction to an organizational rival—the Knights of Labor—craft unions banded together, first in 1881 as the Federation of Organized Trades and Labor Unions and then in 1886 as the American Federation of Labor (AFL). The AFL and the autonomous national unions which constituted it had little effect on the lives of most urban workers in the nineteenth and early twentieth centuries. It engaged in strikes, a weapon it fully accepted, and even stimulated the 1886 general strike, which in some cities exploded in violence and death; but it acquiesced to the craft-oriented elitist philosophy of its nationals, succumbed to their racist exclusionary policies, and generally ignored the interests of ordinary workers. In a sense, the AFL hoped to turn history backward. Larger firms began dominating American enterprise, and industry combined in trusts and other forms of consolidation as the economy evolved from a competitive to an oligopolistic stage, but structurally, the AFL had divided the working class by crafts, each confronting its industrial opponents virtually alone in autonomous unions.

AFL national unions, with few exceptions, completely omitted the bulk of each industry's work force—the unskilled and semiskilled workers. National union leaders assumed that such workers could not be organized, mainly because they could be easily replaced, but some union leaders simply discriminated against southern and eastern European immigrant workers. Likewise, black workers were excluded from many AFL unions and were segregated in Jim Crow locals in others. In some cities, union contracts forced blacks out of crafts in which they seemed firmly entrenched, such as the building trades of New York. To the urban worker, the AFL might have appeared a hope—but a distant and perhaps false hope.

However, there were organizational alternatives. The Knights of Labor organized originally as a secret society in 1869 and came into national prominence in the mid-1880s. It attempted to confront bigness in industry with bigness of labor; it combined the power of skilled with unskilled, native-born with immigrant, black with white, men with women, and bread-and-butter unionist with radical visionary. It accepted national unions composed of skilled workers, but it also included the unskilled. It was particularly attuned to the urban dimension, where local assemblies often consisted of individual workers who, irrespective of skill or occupation, lived in the same neighborhoods. To the urban worker, the Knights provided a fraternal organization's social activities, a union's meetings and occasional strikes, and a hope for a better society achieved through consumer and producer cooperatives.

After winning two dramatic strikes in 1885, the Knights of Labor was suddenly inundated by workers seeking admission and membership. Laborers who viewed the Knights as a panacea swelled its ranks to 700,000 by mid-1886, only to be disillusioned when the organization soon disintegrated. Damaging publicity associated with the Haymarket affair, failure and controversies surrounding the Knights of Labor producer cooperatives, and loss of key strikes, combined with the uncertain and high-handed leadership of Terrence V. Powderly, led to the organization's virtual disappearance from the urban scene by 1894. However, the AFL continued to grow, although slowly, because of its limitations on membership. By surviving the depression of the late 1890s (1893–97), the AFL became the first American labor federation to successfully cope with a sustained economic collapse, and thus ended the movement's close tie to the business cycle.

Despite the AFL's clear commitment to the strike, which indicated greater tactical militancy than the Knights of Labor, the Federation completely accepted the capitalistic system. In this sense, the AFL was the more conservative of the two groups. While both organizations had significant socialist factions, the Left had greater influence in the Knights. Thus, the Federation more easily rejected such radical proposals as cooperative industry and compulsory arbitration. It viewed political involvement with extreme caution and stressed immediate economic issues. Since the AFL defended the economic system, one might have expected establishment support for the Federation. Indeed, after the turn of the century government occasionally intervened in behalf of AFL unions, and the AFL hierarchy joined industrial leaders in the reformist National Civic Federation. Nevertheless, on the whole, firms both large and small bitterly and violently opposed collective bargaining even by the AFL.

During the first decade of the twentieth century, American business, particularly on the local or urban level, made a concerted effort to destroy the Federation. Local business organizations like the Chamber of Commerce, with considerable press support, pictured the AFL as subversive of American institutions. The industrial counterattack on AFL gains was spearheaded by quasi-legal law enforcement units, private police, and outright vigilante groups. Violence against labor organizers and discrimination and blacklisting of union members slowed AFL advances. The government and the courts also did their best to retard union growth.

Yet American employers had visions of greater enemies. Industrial unions that combined skilled and unskilled workers, such as the American Railroad Union, or those with avowed radical goals, such as the early Western Federation of Miners (WFM) and the Industrial Workers of the World (IWW), provided a more ominous specter. The WFM and the IWW assumed important roles on the urban frontier. Radical miners had considerable influence in cities such as Denver and politically controlled many small mining and lumber centers. Although less active in the East, the IWW carried out dramatic strikes of unskilled workers in textile centers such as Lawrence, Massachusetts, and at the silk mills in Paterson, New Jersey. But the freewheeling radicalism of the IWW had little lasting influence in urban life. The IWW committed itself to basic change in the economic system. It viewed strikes as educational devices to mold class solidarity and rejected collective bargaining contracts as an accommodation to the system. Although committed to all workers and especially to the unskilled, the IWW was most effective in occupations that depended on migratory labor, such as lumbering or agriculture. But on the urban scene before World War I, industrial workers consisted of immigrants and others who desired a degree of security as well as traditional economic goals. Ignored by the AFL, they sometimes turned to the IWW, but when other unions presented a viable alternative, the IWW lost much of its appeal to urban immigrants.

By World War I, several industrial unions had emerged in large industrial cities, including the Amalgamated Clothing Workers in Chicago and New York City, the International Ladies Garment Workers Union, and other nationals in the needle trades, mainly centered in eastern cities. Originally led by socialist reformers, such unions faced less opposition than the IWW, partly because they posed less of a threat to business. The traditionally antilabor Hearst and Pulitzer newspaper chains called for the AFL to organize industries threatened by the IWW. The anti-AFL movement was also somewhat blunted in the East by the psychological effect of the tragic fire at the Triangle Corporation sweatshop in New York City, where 145 young immigrant working girls needlessly perished because fire regulations had not been enforced. Also, anti-industry Progressives publicized poor working conditions in order to control expanding capitalism. Thus, traditional unions, including some industrial ones, continued their growth after 1910. The economy appeared strong, with little unemployment and slightly improved real wages.

By the end of World War I, the AFL had become a respectable institution. Given de facto recognition and some aid from the Wilson administration and represented on the planning boards that structured the wartime economy, the AFL had an increased impact. It came out of the war with a higher membership than ever and with its coffers filled with strike funds. Simultaneously, during the "great Red scare" of the postwar years the federal government, state agencies, and local vigilantes attacked and severely damaged radical institutional alternatives to the AFL. The Justice Department destroyed the efficiency of the IWW leadership through imprisonment, and deportation and jail sentences forced newer communist rivals underground.

Once the effects of antiradical hysteria ended, the future looked favorable for the AFL. Its labor movement competition was weak and confused, and the economy had recovered from a brief recession: the 1920s seemed ideal for labor expansion. But the AFL did not expand; indeed, it declined measurably. Total union membership dropped from over 5 million to 3,443,000 at the height of the 1929 prosperity. Undoubtedly, upward economic trends and lack of AFL commitments hampered organization. While the AFL remained primarily concerned with organizing skilled workers, semiskilled industrial workers increasingly constituted the bulk of the work force. As immigration slowed, southern blacks and rural whites entered industrial plants in greater numbers. Such workers, the AFL contended, were difficult to organize because of their hostility to unions and the traditional individualism of rural Americans. Industry also went on the offensive, attacking unions through traditionally repressive tactics coupled with some benefits provided by welfare programs and company unionism. The courts gave employers strong support in their antiunion activities; sweeping injunctions made organizing difficult.

Yet such factors alone could not thwart organization. The IWW and the unions in the needle trades demonstrated that rural workers and immigrants made militant unionists and that diverse groups could be unionized despite hostile employers. But the AFL leadership seemed to lack commitment to change, for no major organizing campaign began during the 1920s. Even where the will existed, as in the 1919 steel strike, energetic strike administrators and courageous organizers could not overcome the AFL's self-imposed handicaps. The Federation leadership, for instance, demanded that newly organized steel workers be parceled out to craft unions, which proceeded to squabble about jurisdictional prerogatives rather than devoting efforts and finances to organizing. The massive economic and human investment needed to confront the considerable power of the United States Steel Corporation was simply lacking. Thus, in the 1920s the AFL moved from its earlier tactical militance and instead sought to convince management that labor organization would profit both workers and business—an unrealistic approach given the climate of opinion in the 1920s.

It was difficult to convince management to temper its antiunion stand on economic grounds, especially since American business seemed to be achieving new successes. A federal agency announced in 1927 that "the highest standard of living ever attained in the history of the world was reached last year by the American people." Technological change accelerated; young industries like chemicals, synthetics, automobiles, electric light and power, and chain stores surged ahead. From 1923 to 1929, while prices remained steady, corporate profits rose 62 percent, and dividends went up 65 percent. Between 1921 and 1929, national income rose from 50.7 to 88.1 billion dollars.

Some of the prosperity trickled down to the workers—average real income rose 11 percent from 1923 to 1927—but the worker fell below the average. Economist Paul Douglas discovered that real hourly earnings in all industries rose 7.2 percent between 1923 and 1928, but real weekly income advanced only 2.5 percent. The National Industrial Conference Board found that real wages in manufacturing rose 2.1 percent from 1928 to 1929, but only .7 percent weekly. Differences between hourly and weekly incomes reflected fewer hours worked per day, although fifty hours per week remained common. Nevertheless, employed workers enjoyed a slightly larger income than in previous years, and most immigrants achieved a significant improvement over living standards in their less developed homelands. Other factors, such as improved public health measures, increased number of recreation facilities, even installment buying, affected living standards. The 27.4 percent rise of employed women workers between 1920 and 1935 meant that many families had increased incomes. Studies of low-income federal workers in five cities found that from 15 to 33 percent of family breadwinners held two or more jobs. Prosperity drifted down, but only with hard work and sacrifice.

In 1929 the spiral of American economic growth came down in a crash. Within a year, it proved to be not another mild recession or even a short-lived financial panic but a major catastrophe. By the election of 1932, all but the Republican establishment admitted that the country faced the "Great Depression."

The depression's massive poverty resulted primarily from a lack of jobs. In 1933, 13 million were unemployed; between 1934 and 1936 the total fluctuated between 10 and 11 million. At the end of the decade, nearly 10 million still lacked work. *Fortune* magazine, a voice of the American business elite, estimated that 11 million unemployed workers meant that one out of every four employables had no jobs. Counting wives and children, more than 25.5 million people saw their regular sources of livelihood cut off by the depression. The rate of unemployment rose from 3 percent in 1929 to 25 percent in 1933; it never fell below 14 percent during the decade.

In some areas of the country, virtually all members of a community were without jobs. In Coello, Illinois, with a population of 1,350, two people had jobs in 1932. In the same year Donora, Pennsylvania, had 277 employed out of a population of 13,900. Larger cities fared better but still faced an enormous problem of unemployment. Representative George Huddleston reported in 1932 that in his congressional district, which included the steel center of Birmingham, 25,000 of 108,000 workers remained jobless and 60,000 to 75,000 others worked only part time. The *National Municipal Review* pointed out the same year that between 600,000 and 700,000 Chicago workers (about 40 percent of the city's employable) remained without jobs. The journal added that unemployment reached 298,000 in Philadelphia and 178,000 in Pittsburgh; New York City reported that one million of the city's 3.2 million labor force were without work.

Unemployment was a traumatic experience. Social workers called the panic that engulfed men as they looked for nonexistent jobs "unemployment shock." Workers perhaps dreaded the lay-off more than any other aspect of the economic crisis, yet those who were working also faced problems. Although wage rates differed in each industry and also reflected the cost of living in different parts of the country, on the whole, income dropped considerably below prices. At the same time, the number of hours in the work day increased for those working full time. Some industries reintroduced the twelve-hour day; in others the ten-hour day and the six-day week became commonplace. Fear of unemployment forced workers to accept an increased work pace.

In response to the catastrophe, the AFL remained faithful to its nineteenth century heritage. It called and lost strikes, decreased in membership, and viewed government intervention in the economy with suspicion. Section Seven A of the National Industrial Recovery Act helped organized labor somewhat, particularly in chaotic industries such as garments and mining, but on the whole, Seven A aided company-controlled unions more than worker-controlled organizations. After Senator Robert Wagner of New York maneuvered his National Labor Relations Act through Congress and past a cautious and at first hostile president, possibilities improved for massive organization of urban workers. Among other advances, the Wagner Act protected the right of workers to join unions and eliminated company unions as collective bargaining agents. Although the depression continued, industrial workers appeared increasingly anxious to join the ranks of organized labor. AFL inaction and procrastination culminated in the 1935 split in the labor movement. With John L. Lewis of the United Mine Workers in the lead, the Committee, later the Congress, of Industrial Organizations (CIO) was established.

The CIO accepted support from various elements in the labor movement. Because he needed to quickly establish a base of organizers, John L. Lewis depended in great part on communist-trained activists who had gained experience with the Trade Union Unity League, an embryonic but active communist labor federation established during the 1920s. Their success in organizing part of the CIO helped lead to the establishment of industrial unionism, altering the history of American labor. To confront complex and economically ponderous corporate giants, all workers of an industry, irrespective of craft or skill, combined. An ideological commitment reinforced this structural pragmatism. Unlike the AFL leadership, CIO leaders pledged themselves to organize the unorganized. Competition between the two labor federations not only stimulated the old guard of the AFL but added to the zeal of CIO activists. In addition, the Wagner Act, in protecting the worker's right to join a union, provided security to industrial workers who already had accepted the desirability of organization. Thus, the CIO organized such basic industries as steel, auto, textiles, oil, and shipping. By 1937, the young organization claimed a membership of more than 3.7 million. This achievement is especially dramatic when the figure is juxtaposed with the less than 3 million members of all trade unions just four years before. By the end of the decade, American unions counted 13 million members, mostly urban workers.

Organized labor, which had preferred the Democratic party to the Republican party since the Wilson administration, viewed Franklin D. Roosevelt's defeat of Herbert Hoover as a victory for the labor movement. And although New Deal politics eventually led to unofficial but close ties between the Democratic party and organized labor, the alliances on the urban level grew more slowly. Entrenched urban political bosses had traditional links with the more conservative AFL and viewed the CIO as a dangerous upstart. Democratic Mayor Frank Hague of Jersey City, for example, carried out a vendetta against the CIO. His declaration that no good Catholic should join this communist conspiracy had ramifications throughout the Catholic church in the United States, as well-known clerics such as John A. Ryan and Charles Owen Rice came to the defense of the CIO organizing effort in New Jersey. Boss Edward Hall Crump of Memphis welcomed the CIO to the city in 1942 after it achieved respectability, but he had opposed the young organization during the thirties, especially after 1937. In Pittsburgh the Central Labor Council demanded the removal of Mayor William McNair because he "aided and abetted strikebreakers hired to break the ranks of organized workers." In Chicago, it took the 1937 Memorial Day massacre, in which police killed or wounded over a hundred peaceful picketers, to subdue Mayor Edward Kelly's hostility to the CIO. Powerful Thomas J. Pendergast of Kansas City and Mayor James M. Curley of Boston also opposed the CIO.

Northern urban political leaders—whether bosses, strong mayors, or local oligarchs—eventually accepted the CIO's role in the city. The influence of organized labor, first separately and then somewhat unified in the AFL-CIO, became greater in time. Labor's support in industrial and manufacturing cities usually became a necessity for election victory. With power came considerable influence; organized labor has emerged as an unofficial partner in city government. Its representatives sit on city councils, welfare commissions, education boards, correction and parole agencies, special investigatory panels, and the other abundant committees that are necessary in governing a city. Although organized labor may not always be able to deliver the votes of its members, it fills city council chambers with lobbyists, supplies workers to staff candidates' organizations, and provides some of the funds necessary to win elections. From one segment of the New Deal coalition, the CIO evolved into an important part of the urban establishment. But not all urban workers belong to the AFL-CIO or other unions, nor are they always satisfied with AFL-CIO direction.

Although the labor movement made major advances in the 1930s, numerous urban workers—particularly those in southern cities and manufacturing towns—remained unorganized. In northern cities, the old elitist craft unions, even after the merger between the AFL and the CIO, still controlled entry into numerous skills. Discriminatory apprenticeship programs and other racist union practices effectively excluded blacks and other minorities from many trades. But racial conflict was not limited to traditional skills. As the black urban population grew, demands for equality increased throughout the middle years of the twentieth century. Hopes for improved schools and neighborhoods were coupled with the assumption that blacks could wrest job improvements and their share of union leadership from the American industrial system of the 1960s and 1970s. Racial conflict in plants not only led to black worker caucuses and even separate unions but, combined with other social trends, contributed to the growing racial discord affecting urban America. The alienation and conservatism of a large portion of the working class could be seen in the support George Wallace received in the 1964 and 1972 primaries and in his American Party bid of 1968; it is even clearer in the contemporary political polls. The support of the labor establishment for the American war in Viet Nam further weakened the New Deal alliance between workers and middle-class liberals.

Yet the liberals had cherished the old CIO as a defender of the downtrodden and champion of all workers, irrespective of race or politics. Had its ideals and energy been so dissipated by its merger with the AFL that it had become ideologically bankrupt? Actually, the CIO had never been a unified organization with clear and generally accepted goals. The successes of the 1930s had sublimated divisions between the socialists, communists, and more conservative trade unionists. With the emergence of the cold war, the noncommunist factions joined together in attacking communist and pro-communist labor units. By the time of the AFL-CIO merger, communist-influenced unions had been expelled from the official labor movement; individual communists and their allies were purged from the ranks of noncommunist unions. The socialists had become liberals, and the conservative CIO leaders differed only marginally from their ideological brothers in the AFL. With one of the strong voices of the Left silenced, much of the labor movement marched to complacency on numerous vital issues.

Organized labor became part of the urban establishment, but recent developments in the cities reveal a new labor militancy. Unionized workers employed by cities must compete with other urban elements for a share of city revenue. The assumption that government employees should receive lower wages than workers in private industry in return for job security and low productivity has been challenged by such unions as the American Federation of State, County, and Municipal Employees. Although AFSCME has concentrated on municipal clerical employees, it also serves as an umbrella for municipally employed groups ranging from social workers to garbage collectors. Strikes by such unions, it is sometimes argued, threaten the general health and safety of a city. Garbage piles up when sanitation workers go on strike, menacing public health. When the Transport Workers Union struck the New York City subways, business in the city ground to a crawl. In frequent strikes, which often sent participants to jail, locals of the American Federation of Teachers shut down school systems of large and small cities. In addition, numerous associations of municipal workers act more like unions each year. Policemen's benevolent associations have achieved collective bargaining status in some cities, often following epidemics of the "blue flu." Firemen have struck in numerous northern cities, as have independent associations of social workers, and affiliates of the National Education Association increasingly emulate the more effective American Federation of Teachers.

Aggressive city unions and independent employee associations sometimes conflict with the older union establishment. In Gary, Indiana, for example, a militant independent union of social workers struck in 1968 against the county (which administered welfare for the city). Although the agency's paraprofessionals, the local welfare rights organization, and the city administration supported the union, the strike failed. The local of the United Steel Workers, through its influence on the welfare board (a USW representative served as chairman), directed the crushing of the union, the firing of the strikers, and the blacklisting of both the leadership and rank and file throughout northwest Indiana. Although they were once little more than outlaw organizations, unions use the tools workers traditionally condemned in order to preserve their position in the urban establishment.

Many complacent unions retarded change, but some established locals have organized workers in industries that previously had proved difficult to penetrate, such as health care. Other unions have conducted organizing campaigns in parts of the country that were traditionally hostile to unionization, notably the South. Such unions often worked with black community organizations and stressed long-range social goals as well as immediate economic advance. Thus, the labor movement continues to embrace many different and often divergent forces in American urban life.

Selected Bibliography

Both historians and economists have examined the history of the worker in the United States. The works of Carl Bridenbaugh, *Cities in the Wilderness: The First Century of Urban Life in America, 1625–1742* (New York, 1938) and *Cities in Revolt: Urban Life in America, 1743–1776* (New York, 1955), provide considerable insight into the worker's social surroundings; his *The Colonial Craftsman* (New York, 1950) contains an invaluable description of early workers. Bridenbaugh should be supplemented by studies which depict the social inequality of the period: James A. Henretta, "Economic Development and Social Structure in Colonial Boston," *William and Mary Quarterly*, 22 (January 1965), 75–92; Jackson T. Main, *The Social Structure of Revolutionary America* (Princeton, N.J., 1965); and Jesse Lemisch, "Jack Tar in the Streets: Merchant Seamen in the Politics of Revolutionary America," *William and Mary Quarterly*, 25 (July 1968), 371–407. David Montgomery, "The Working Classes of the Pre-Industrial American City, 1780–1830," *Labor History*, 9 (Winter 1968), 3–22, presents a thorough synthesis of labor's early role.

Traditional American labor history grew out of institutional labor economics. Richard T. Ely and John R. Commons trained many of the first labor historians at the University of Wisconsin. The economists of the "Wisconsin School" subsequently dominated the study of labor history. Primarily, they traced the history of unions, and to a lesser extent, they examined radical groups traditionally involved in the labor movement. The first major work directed and edited by Commons was the four-volume *History of Labor in the United States* (New York, 1918–35), which was supplemented by Selig Perlman and Philip Taft, *A History of Trade Unionism in the United States, 1896–1932* (New York, 1935). Commons and his students also produced the monumental ten-volume *A Documentary History of American Industrial Society* (New York, 1910–11). The Commons analysis and the questions it promulgated dominated much of the pre-New Deal labor history. The intricacies of the emergence of national unions has been further examined in Lloyd Ulman's *Rise of the National Union: The Development and Significance of Its Structure, Governing Institutions, and Economic Policies* (Cambridge, Mass., 1955). Philip Taft, one of the most successful of Commons' students, in a two-volume history of the AFL, *The AF of L in the Time of Gompers* (New York, 1957) and *The AF of L from the Death of Gompers to the Merger* (New York, 1959), paints a totally positive picture of the AFL as practical, hard-boiled, and successful. Gerald N. Grob's *Workers and Utopia: A Study of Ideological Conflict in the American Labor Movement, 1865–1900* (Evanston, Ill., 1961) illustrates the complexity of the Knights' activities and personalities and tends to support the Commons school, which viewed the Knights as ideologically unrealistic, structurally unwieldy, and tactically inefficient.

The Commons school analysis of nineteenth century unionism did not go unchallenged. Sociologist Norman Ware, in *The Labor Movement in the United States, 1860–95* (Gloucester, Mass., 1959), argued that the Knights' structure could and did accommodate national trade unions. Philip S. Foner, in the second volume of his four-volume Marxist *History of the Labor Movement in the United States* (New York, 1947–67), points out the chauvinism of the AFL national union leadership and thus balances the apologetics of the Commons school.

Conflict over the Commons analysis has provided the major benchmarks for nineteenth century labor history, but other issues have arisen. The role of the worker in Jacksonian politics concerned both labor and political historians. Recently, nineteenth century social and urban historians have begun examining working-class mobility. The emergence of quantitative techniques and the availability of data, especially nineteenth century manuscript censuses, have opened up this long-awaited phase of labor history. Among the new quantitative studies, Stephen Thernstrom's *Poverty and Progress: Social Mobility in a Nineteenth Century City* (Cambridge, Mass., 1964) illustrates the lack of economic and social mobility in a small manufacturing city. Other quantitative historians have used similar approaches: Paul B. Worthman, "Working Class Mobility in Birmingham, Alabama, 1880–1914," in Tamara K. Haveren, editor, *Anonymous Americans: Exploration in Nineteenth-Century Social History* (New York, 1971); Richard J. Hopkins, "Occupational and Geographic Mobility in Atlanta, 1870–1896," *Journal of Southern History*, 24 (May 1968), 200–213; and Peter R. Knights, *The Plain People of Boston, 1830–1860: A Study in City Growth* (New York, 1971).

To supplement recent quantitative studies of the nineteenth century see Norman Ware, *The Industrial Worker, 1840–1860* (Boston, 1924); William A. Sullivan, *The Industrial Worker in Pennsylvania, 1800–1840* (Harrisburg, Pa., 1955); Hanna Josephson, *The Golden Thread: New England's Mill Girls and Magnates* (New York, 1959); Vera Shlakman, *Economic History of a Factory Town: A Study of Chicopee, Mass.* (Smith College Studies in History, 20, October 1934–July 1935); Robert W. Smuts, *Women and Work in America* (New York, 1959).

Analysis of twentieth century workers, in contrast to analysis of unions, has not seen the breakthrough that Thernstrom's work stimulated for the late nineteenth century. However, there have been successful nonquantitative approaches. Economist Ely Ginsburg and historian Hyman Berman used oral histories and government investigations to produce a collection of valuable documents, *The American Worker in the Twentieth Century: A History through Autobiographies* (New York, 1963). More recently, Staughton Lynd directed a writers' workshop which concentrated on workers in the industrial area of northwest Indiana. Oral history constituted a significant part of the source material used for his *People's History of the Calumet Region*, which will appear shortly.

Traditional union histories provide the bulk of twentieth century labor history, however. Several general studies of the Industrial Workers of the World have appeared since Paul F. Brissenden, *The I.W.W.: A Study of American Syndicalism* (New York, 1919), and John S. Gambs, *The Decline of the I.W.W.* (New York, 1932). Two books by Joseph Robert Conlin, *Bread and Roses: Studies of the Wobblies* (Westport, Conn., 1969) and *Big Bill Haywood and the Radical Union*

Movement (Syracuse, N.Y., 1969), add some interpretive insight. Patrick Renshaw's *The Wobblies: The Story of Syndicalism in the United States* (New York, 1967) is a readable narrative. Melvyn Dubofsky's *We Shall Be All: A History of the Industrial Workers of the World* (Chicago, 1969) is the most valuable analytical synthesis now available.

There have been a multitude of union and industry studies by both historians and economists. Among the most valuable are Jack Barbash, *Unions and Telephones* (New York, 1952); David Brody, *Steelworkers in America: The Non-Union Era* (Cambridge, Mass., 1960); Brailsford Brazeal, *The Brotherhood of Sleeping Car Porters* (New York, 1946); Elmo P. Hohman, *History of American Merchant Seamen* (Hamden, Conn., 1956); Leo Huberman, *The National Maritime Union* (New York, 1943); Mark Perlman, *The Machinists: A New Study in American Trade Unionism* (Cambridge, Mass., 1961); and Reed C. Richardson, *The Locomotive Engineer, 1863-1963* (Ann Arbor, Mich., 1963).

The New Deal years and the emergence of the Congress of Industrial Organizations stimulated numerous works in labor history. Walter Galenson, *The CIO Challenge to the AFL: A History of the American Labor Movement, 1935-1941* (Cambridge, Mass., 1960), is a thorough study by an institutional economist. Also see Milton Derber and Edwin Young, editors, *Labor and the New Deal* (Madison, Wis., 1957), and Herbert Harris, *Labor's Civil War* (New York, 1940). Two volumes by Irving Bernstein, *The Lean Years: A History of the American Worker, 1920-1933* (Boston, 1960) and *The Turbulent Years: A History of the American Worker, 1933-1941* (Boston, 1970), best synthesize two complex decades and the emergence of the CIO. *Labor Radical: From the Wobblies to CIO, A Personal History*, by Len De Caux (Boston, 1970), analyzes the CIO and the expulsion of the communists from the point of view of a leftist CIO official.

On the CIO conflict with the urban Democratic Party politicians see Barbara W. Newell, *Chicago and the Labor Movement: Metropolitan Unionism in the 1930s* (Urbana, Ill., 1961); Bruce M. Stave, *The New Deal and the Last Hurrah: Pittsburgh Machine Politics* (Pittsburgh, 1970); Harold B. Hinton, "Crump of Tennessee: Portrait of a Boss," in Ray Ginger, editor, *Modern American Cities* (New York, 1969).

Of recent issues of concern to labor historians, race and ethnicity have superseded questions of corruption, automation, or communist influence in labor unions. Julius Jacobson, editor, *The Negro and the American Labor Movement* (New York, 1968), contains a number of incisive articles by labor and black history specialists. Likewise, the journal *Labor History*, 10 (Summer 1969), devoted an entire issue to blacks and the labor movement. W. I. Thomas and Florian Znaniecki, *The Polish Peasant in Europe and America* (rev. ed., New York, 1958), provides five volumes packed with useful insights. Victor R. Greene, *The Slavic Community on Strike* (Notre Dame, Ind., 1968), disagrees with Thomas and Znaniecki and argues that the Polish immigrant became a militant labor unionist. A special issue of *Dissent* (Winter 1972) examines "The World of the Blue Collar Worker," providing important perspectives on the laboring man in contemporary society.

Poverty in the Cities: A History of Urban Social Welfare

Raymond A. Mohl

Few domestic problems plague American society as deeply as poverty, dependency, and social welfare. The "welfare mess" is a troublesome and persistent ingredient of the larger urban crisis, but it is one most Americans have become pervasively aware of only in the last decade. Following the lead of Michael Harrington's shocking book, *The Other America*, President John F. Kennedy declared a "war on poverty" in the early 1960s, spurring a social consciousness largely dormant since the Great Depression and the New Deal. Lyndon Johnson's Great Society and Richard Nixon's more recent efforts at welfare "reform" have kept the issue of poverty in an affluent society in the public spotlight, as have ghetto riots, racial turmoil, and demands for minority group power. Widely reported investigations, such as that of the National Advisory Commission on Civil Disorders, have identified inadequacies of the welfare system as contributing to a climate of powerlessness, oppression, and violence in urban ghettos. Proposals for a guaranteed income, a negative income tax, a family allowance system, public employment programs, and liberalized welfare benefits have been debated extensively in the mass media, in the political arena, and by average Americans. Poverty and the present state of the welfare system, in short, have become matters of urgent contemporary concern.

As public awareness has grown, so have the welfare rolls. In a recent book entitled *Regulating the Poor*, Frances Fox Piven and Richard A. Cloward have demonstrated a virtual welfare "explosion" in the 1960s, with the relief rolls doubling and tripling in the largest American cities. The Social Security Administration, which collects statistics on poverty and income levels, categorizes as poor a family of four whose annual income falls below $3,972 (a figure said to be three times a minimum food budget for that same family of four). Government studies revealed that more than 25 million people were living below the poverty level in 1970. Just over half of these—

some 13 million—are on the welfare rolls; the rest, although most are eligible for benefits, are not enrolled. More than half of the nation's 25 million poor live in metropolitan areas—central cities and surrounding suburbs. It is estimated that an additional 25 million Americans live just above the poverty level. Many of these are made "nonpoor" by virtue of government payments in the form of social security, unemployment compensation, and veteran's benefits. Relief costs have skyrocketed, reflecting expanded welfare rolls; public assistance absorbs the largest chunk of most big-city budgets. Welfare has become a way of life for millions in urban slums and in rural regions like Appalachia, yet benefits remain well below the minimum necessary for a moderate or decent standard of living—a minimum set by the Social Security Administration at above $9,000 for an urban family of four.

Government officials and policy makers are confronted, then, with the paradox of widespread poverty in the world's most affluent society. Simultaneously, they must wrestle with the complementary issue of the function and extent of public assistance in a competitive, work-oriented economy—an issue which generated great controversy in the 1960s.

The idealism of the war on poverty and the community-action orientation of the Great Society exposed the welfare system to minute examination, subjecting it to increasingly vigorous attacks from the Left. Reform-minded social workers (as contrasted to welfare workers with an investigative and bureaucratic focus) have long known of the deficiencies of the welfare system and have complained bitterly of the impersonality and inhumanity of the welfare bureaucracy. Even government investigations have criticized a system that is "designed to save money instead of people, and tragically ends up doing neither." Some, like Piven and Cloward, have argued that public welfare serves capitalistic purposes by manipulating the poor and forcing them into low-income, menial work. Welfare rights organizations, allied with and sometimes formed by activist social workers and community organizers, have attempted to redress these grievances; simultaneously, they have tried to break the system of its own weight by enrolling all eligible persons for welfare benefits. Many concerned big-city mayors who are close to the problem and liberal in their politics have called for more state and federal money to aid poor people and to improve the quality of life in urban slums.

But a more popular, contradictory response has also emerged, one which derives from a mythic view of the American past and conforms to established American values and ideals. The still vigorous conception of the United States as a land of opportunity holds that any hard-working, industrious man or woman can labor, earn, save, and get ahead. Adherents of the American work ethic refuse to accept as worthy those who cannot, or will not, earn a wage. The poor should be made to contribute to their own support, this argument runs; life on welfare should be made less attractive, should pay fewer returns, than the most menial kind of work. Deterrents of various kinds—mainly work, but also humiliating and degrading treatment by the welfare bureaucracy—have been developed to discourage welfare applicants and to reduce the financial drain relief payments now imposed on productive members of society. Articulating middle-class fears and prejudices, conservative and middle-of-the-road politicians at every level of government have translated these attitudes into policy and programs. They have called for lower taxes, welfare cutbacks, stricter residency and work requirements, punishment of welfare chiselers, termination of such controversial programs as the OEO Legal Assistance Project (which has sued government agencies on behalf of the poor), and quick action to move the poor from relief rolls to payrolls.

The controversy about welfare, then, has revealed underlying tensions at work within American society. Essentially, the current debate reflects sharp disagreement about the causes of poverty, proper methods of relief, and the nature of a responsible society. Some want to make the welfare system more humane, to permit the poor to live in dignity through higher payments and better services. Others, who seem most concerned about welfare cheaters, want to force the unemployed and unemployable into jobs—any job—to build character and reduce relief costs.

1

It comes as a surprise to most Americans to learn that most of these problems are not new, that poverty is rooted deep within the American past, and that people have long differed about its causes and prevention. The idea of the United States as the land of opportunity has rarely corresponded with reality. From the colonial period onward, most immigrants came poor and stayed poor. Significant social and economic mobility might be achieved within a family over several generations, but for most Americans survival meant excessively long working hours, rigorous underconsumption, poor housing, putting wives and children to work, perhaps taking in boarders. Those who failed to meet such tests became society's dependents, living on public relief and private charity. Thus, from a very early date, pauperism and dependency plagued American cities, fostering numerous social problems, draining municipal treasuries, and stimulating public discussions which bear a strikingly modern appearance. The "welfare mess," in variety of forms to be sure, has long been an inseparable part of the American urban experience.

In a sense, poverty accompanied the earliest colonists to American shores. Most British settlers had been small farmers, agricultural workers, or urban laborers; few were even moderately wealthy. During the hard, early years of colonization, new settlers remained dependent on the British connection for even the bare necessities, and not all survived. It has been estimated that over the whole colonial period almost half of all colonists came as indentured servants—surely a measure of the extent of economic deprivation among new arrivals. As the colonial economy matured, and as small colonial towns grew into large seaport centers, the proportion of unskilled laborers and helpless dependents requiring permanent assistance increased accordingly. Urbanization made every colonial town a marketplace for goods and services, yet the larger the marketplace grew, the more interdependent it became, leaving those on the lowest rungs of the economic ladder with few protections against hard times. Ironically, as commercial profit stimulated prosperity, the uncertainties of a more complex economy also brought business fluctuations, low wages, and periodic unemployment for those without skills. Thus, while some in the colonial city—mainly merchants and large landholders—grew richer, and a few spectacularly so, most colonial urbanites were not so fortunate.

Several recent studies have demonstrated these patterns. Historian James Henretta's investigation of economic development and social structure in eighteenth century Boston illustrated the trend toward greater economic class distinctions. Using original tax lists from 1687 and 1771 (which contained information on property ownership), Henretta documented the simultaneous emergence of a small but wealthy merchant elite and a large proletarian, non-property-owning, wage-earning class. Over the entire period, the group of propertyless laborers increased at a rate twice that of the city's population as a whole. By 1771, this group totaled 29 percent of Boston's population. Even in smaller agricultural-oriented towns, the same process was repeated because of the pressure of rising population on limited land resources. Another historian, Jackson Turner Main, reached a similar conclusion in *The Social Structure of Revolutionary America*. On the basis of research in tax lists and probate records, Main estimated that by the end of the revolutionary period as much as one-third of the population in the northern colonies could be categorized as poor.

Most of the poor, of course, lived independently at subsistence levels, but increasingly larger numbers went "on the town" as the colonial period progressed. Intensified pauperism confronted the municipal governments of most colonial cities by the beginning of the eighteenth century. As early as 1700, the New York City common council complained that "the Crys of the poor & Impotent for want of Reliefe are Extreamly Grevious." Again, in the winter of 1713, they reported the poor to be "in great Want & a Miserable Condition & must inevitably perish unless some speedy Method be taken for their support." By the 1760s, a combination of colonial wars, postwar depression, restrictive British legislation, and American boycotts on British trade had aggravated social welfare needs in every colonial city. The seriousness of the problem was reflected in rising relief rolls and increasing poor taxes. In 1769, for instance, the Boston poorhouse sheltered 270 dependents. New York City's almshouse contained 425 paupers in March 1772. Other major seaports also had overcrowded poorhouses, and all supported hundreds of additional dependents by noninstitutional means.

Colonial Americans responded to poverty and dependency in predictable fashion, drawing upon British poor laws and humanitarian traditions. In England, as feudalism gave way to a wage-oriented economy, and as ecclesiastical relief broke down during the Protestant Reformation, government assumed responsibility for social welfare. Elizabethan poor laws saddled the parish—the unit of local government—with care of the poor, required local taxes for this purpose, and recommended apprenticeship for pauper children and institutional facilities (poorhouse, workhouse, house of correction) for various categories of dependents. By the middle of the seventeenth century, residency requirements for relief had been added as well, stipulating that only those who had obtained a "settlement" (acquired by birth, apprenticeship, land ownership, tax paying, or office holding) were eligible for local assistance. Private philanthropy in England provided a second set of benevolent institutions by the mid-eighteenth century; some voluntary associations established schools, hospitals, infirmaries, and asylums for the poor, while other humanitarian organizations aided debtors, seamen, orphans, widows, and other dependents.

The American colonies duplicated both British assistance patterns. Every colony in British North America enacted poor laws modeled on those of the mother country. The principles of public responsibility for the poor, local taxation, settlement, apprenticeship, and institutional facilities where necessary prevailed throughout the colonial period with very little change or modification. Outdoor relief—that is, noninstitutional assistance to the poor in their own homes—remained the most common form of public aid, but the largest colonial towns all had well-filled poorhouses by the 1730s. Other relief practices were also utilized: for children, apprenticeship and indentured servitude became common; under the "contract system," local officials boarded helpless dependents in private homes at a fixed rate; under the "auction system," cities and towns sold pauper labor to the highest bidder. By the mid-eighteenth century, public relief had become one of the largest annual expenditures in cities like New York and Boston, leading municipal officials to place great emphasis on the removal or "warning out" of "unsettled" dependents. Long before the American Revolution, then,

British poor law experience shaped the public response to dependency in the colonies.

Similarly, the associative pattern of private benevolence found widespread expression in British North America. Colonial urbanites organized by trade, nationality, and religion for mutual relief. Specialized charities aided blacks, Indians, debtors, and orphans; others supplied work, education, medical care, and evangelical religion to the poor. Numerous ad hoc groups sprouted during periods of crisis or temporary distress. Thus, for example, Boston had a Scot's Charitable Society as early as 1657, and a Charitable Irish Society was organized in 1737. Charleston had a Society for the Relief of Widows and Orphans of the Clergy of the Established Church, and Philadelphia a Society for the Relief of Poor and Distressed Masters of Ships, their Widows and Children. Typically, New Yorkers sponsored the New York Hospital Society and, in the early years of the revolutionary crisis, a Society for Employing the Industrious Poor, and Promoting Manufactory. British humanitarian tradition became the American practice as well.

2

Between the American Revolution and the Civil War, several broad themes in social welfare history emerged. First, colonial patterns of public relief and private humanitarianism continued but became ineffective in dealing with intensified need in large urban centers. Increasing pressures on inadequate welfare institutions stimulated a search for alternative methods for assisting the poor while simultaneously reducing municipal costs. By the 1820s, many urbanites in rapidly expanding cities associated the increased visibility of paupers and dependents with the rise of serious urban problems, especially the noticeable decline in social order. The benevolent attitudes toward the poor which prevailed in colonial times gave way to a harsh moralism which blamed poverty on the poor. Statewide investigations of public assistance in Massachusetts and New York and local inquiries in Philadelphia and Baltimore urged abolition of outdoor relief, institutionalization of all paupers, and a work requirement for relief recipients, primarily as a deterrent. Most private humanitarian organizations, also affected by the new moralism, limited or abandoned the relief function and sought instead to purge the poor of their presumed vices, to bring moral uplift to growing urban slums, and to end poverty with virtue and religion.

A century and a half of colonial experience determined the direction of welfare practice in postrevolutionary years. The essential ingredients of the old British poor laws remained intact well into the nineteenth century. State-mandated poor laws imposed the burden of public assistance upon local government, while residency provisions theoretically protected communities against dependent outsiders. Yet city fathers in the seaport cities— which were swarming with poor immigrants after 1790 and were increasing in population at startling rates—found little consolation in ineffective, unworkable settlement laws originally designed to stifle mobility in a modernizing society. Points of debarkation for European newcomers, the nation's largest cities were forced to provide relief to resident and non-resident dependents alike, simply because there was no place for immigrants to go. The laws of some states—New York, for instance—which required ship captains who brought pauper immigrants to return them to Europe were obviously unenforceable, since enterprising captains simply landed new arrivals unobtrusively outside city limits. Not surprisingly, immigrants comprised a substantial portion of every large city's dependent population.

However, immigrants were not alone in stimulating an increased incidence of urban pauperism. In most northern cities, seasonal variations in labor patterns had the same effect; winter weather often suspended commerce and forced many urban workers into temporary unemployment and their families onto the relief rolls. Workers most affected in this way included day laborers, cartmen, dock workers, seamen, fishermen, building tradesmen, and numerous craftsmen who worked outdoors or whose livelihood depended on a busy harbor. In addition, the intensified interdependence of a competitive, wage-oriented economy made most urban workers —skilled as well as unskilled—subject to business fluctuations and depressions. During the embargo crisis of 1807–9, a New Yorker reported "thousands of mariners, mechanics, and laborers . . . ranging the streets in search of employment, destitute of cloathing, food, and a lodging." In the midst of the panic of 1819, journalist Hezekiah Niles estimated a total of 50,000 unemployed in Boston, Philadelphia, and New York. Unemployment and general hardship of similar proportions occurred in the depressions following 1837 and 1857. Even in good times the possibilities of upward economic mobility remained limited for most urban workers. Class stratification increased in the first half of the nineteenth century, a pattern often masked by the strident egalitarian rhetoric of the period. Ironically, at a time of rapid urban growth and economic advancement, the larger lower class became less independent and less self-sufficient. Consequently, the welfare problems of the nation's largest cities became catastrophically modern in intensity.

Rising welfare rolls reflected social dislocations and economic changes in the early nineteenth century. New York City serves as a case in point. In February 1784, a local newspaper reported more than 900 families on the relief lists, a result of the social and economic turbulence produced by the American Revolution. During a severe yellow fever epidemic in 1798, the city supported more than 2,400 destitute citizens. In January 1805 Mayor DeWitt Clinton sought legislative appropriations for 10,000 impoverished New Yorkers who were forced on the public bounty by severe winter weather. City records show that between April 1814 and April 1815 more than 16,000 individuals received public outdoor relief, while the new municipal poorhouse supported almost 3,000 others. In that single year, more than one-fifth of the city's inhabitants sought public relief, and private charitable societies aided thousands more. Investigators in 1817 estimated that 15,000 people depended on public and private charity. By that time, poor relief annually topped all other items in the city budget. In the depression year of 1848, outdoor relief alone aided more than 45,000 persons (almost one-tenth of New York's population) at a cost of $95,000. Massive welfare problems and heavy expenditures similarly confronted municipal governments in Boston, Philadelphia, and Baltimore in the years after 1820.

The early welfare explosion accompanied other disturbing changes in nineteenth century urban society. Heavy immigration, increasing ethnic and religious diversity among city populations, rapid urbanization, the beginnings of industrialization, and tremendously high rates of internal mobility combined to undermine the generally stable, orderly, well-regulated cities of colonial years. Old institutions no longer served society effectively; established middle-class values and norms had little impact on pauperized immigrants. Preservation of social order became a matter of serious concern for merchant elites and the urban middle class, who linked the societal disorder of the transitional city to the rising numbers of urban poor.

These disturbing changes, and the ways in which early nineteenth century urbanites perceived them, fostered hardened public attitudes toward poverty. Like the contemporary British political economists from whom they borrowed intellectually, Americans began to accept the idea of permanent economic inequality among men. But they postulated an essential distinction between poverty and pauperism. Poverty seemed natural and ineradicable, the normal condition of the laboring classes. Few expected unskilled working men and immigrants to live much above a subsistence level. Furthermore, the self-reliant, laboring poor outwardly conformed to the Protestant work ethic and presented little threat to established order.

Pauperism, however, meant dependency—an unacceptable kind of inequality which contradicted the basic assumptions and requirements of a stable society. It undermined virtue and order and violated the work ethic; it represented a constant economic drain on productive members of society. It denied the optimistic and often-repeated assertions of American progress.

Paupers were idle, ignorant, immoral, impious, and vicious, urban spokes-men said. They begged, stole, disturbed the peace, drank to excess, and, in the parlance of the times, committed "shameful enormities." They sought charity but avoided work. They refused to conform. Because a good portion of them were the same foreigners blamed for other disturbing changes, they were labeled un-American too. Pauperism, in short, seemed a destructive evil which threatened social values and norms and thus became intolerable.

New social perceptions also generated a conservative reaction against the humanitarian attitudes and charitable patterns of colonial years. Previously, poverty had been viewed as providentially determined. Thus, most had recognized charity as a Christian duty; municipal relief represented a societal obligation to those in distress. However, the rising incidence of urban dependency and pauperism—and the social fears and higher taxes it caused—undercut earlier benevolent arguments and fostered a close-fisted moralism. If the poor pauperized themselves through drunkenness, impiety, idleness, extravagance, and immorality, public relief and private charity would only reinforce such "vicious and immoral habits." The conviction that the poor brought poverty upon themselves implied that moral improve-ment would cure dependency. The fear of suffering, some urban reformers argued, was "a whole-some moral discipline" which forced the poor to work and save, but the certainty of relief in time of need tended to destroy char-acter and self-reliance. Charity simply deepened dependency; poorhouses made paupers. Stemming from individual moral defects, pauperism could be ended only by forcing the poor to work and by character-building moral reforms.

Social welfare developments in the early nineteenth century city reflected these new beliefs. Troubled by mounting evidence of entrenched pauperism in urban centers, state and municipal officials took actions tem-pering the humanitarianism which primarily underlay poor relief in colonial years. The hardened moralism of the period demanded welfare cutbacks, limiting aid only to the "worthy" poor—presumably a relatively small group of people who became dependent through no fault of their own. To insure that public aid was the last resort of the poor, life on relief had to be made less appealing—"less eligible," in the terminology of the time—than the worst kind of independent existence. Convinced that numerous "unde-serving" applicants lived comfortably on welfare, public officials sought to purge the rolls as much as possible, forcing those remaining into a de-grading institutionalized existence. Welfare "reform" in the 1820s in New York State, for example, although abolishing archaic settlement clauses, eliminated outdoor relief and required poorhouses in every county. A si-multaneous investigation of Massachusetts poor laws, conducted by Boston mayor Josiah Quincy, similarly condemned outdoor relief and recommended poorhouses "having the character of Work Houses, or Houses of Industry" as an economically and morally superior relief technique. An 1827 inquiry in Philadelphia concluded that outdoor relief destroyed ambition and fostered idleness and dependency. The tradition of local responsibility for the needy continued, but by the 1820s city governments hoped to deter relief-seekers and save money by providing only for those who were willing to submit to the regimen and discipline of the poorhouse.

During these years, city officials turned the relief system into a work-enforcing device. In a competitive, wage-oriented economy work became a prime requisite for the maintenance of public order. Legislation in most states permitted local officials to impose a work requirement for relief. Every urban almshouse became a workhouse; forced labor became routine. The work test applied indiscriminately to all paupers—children, aged, blind, and disabled as well as able-bodied. When Boston's city government established a "house of industry" in the 1820s, a local organization enthusiastically supported the idea: "It is believed there are but few of our poor who, notwithstanding the imbecility induced by previous habits, cannot do something, and very many of them a great deal towards their own support." In 1830 the New York City common council not only tried to maximize pauper labor by turning "to some advantage the labour of the more feeble" but argued as well that work positively improved health and character. In 1834 the Philadelphia Guardians of the Poor refused to replace the almshouse "treadmill" with a steam engine, preferring human power because of the "constant employment" it necessitated. In every city plagued by pauperism in the first half of the nineteenth century, outdoor relief was limited or terminated, and work became the indispensable condition for institutional aid.

Moreover, the work test seemed to have other positive advantages. Municipal leaders clearly saw it as a deterrent to relief, one which would encourage relief applicants to seek, as city fathers in New York said in 1830, "a course of voluntary industry of their own choice to a systematic Service under the Overseers in the Poorhouse." The very mention of the workhouse, a Boston philanthropic group contended, "impressed with a salutary terror the minds of several, who might justly be considered candidates for admission to it." Thus, relief costs would go down, while the "idle and vicious poor" would be forced into jobs in order to survive. Resulting conformity to the work ethic would wean the poor from former bad habits, would build character and self-reliance, and would help stabilize the deteriorating social order.

Similar impulses affected private charitable endeavor during the period. A fantastic array of new voluntary associations institutionalized antipauperism energies in every city. Groups organized for every imaginable purpose: to aid widows and orphans, immigrants and blacks, debtors and prisoners, aged females and young prostitutes; to supply the poor with food, fuel, medicine, employment, Bibles, and religion; to promote morality, temperance, piety, thrift, and industrious habits; to educate poor children in charity schools, free schools, almshouse schools, and Sunday schools; to reform drinkers, gamblers, criminals, juvenile delinquents, ungodly sailors, and Sabbath-breakers. Concerned about social order and drawing upon new social perceptions about the causes of poverty, these societies consciously combined charity with moral and religious exhortation. Convinced that relief undermined character and multiplied the poor, many abandoned charity altogether for moral reform. Evangelical preacher Lyman Beecher saw in these voluntary societies "a sort of disciplined moral militia" which would "uphold peace and good order in society" and would "save the nation from civil war and commotion." They became, as one historian has suggested, "special kinds of defense organizations."

Fairly typical of urban benevolence in the early nineteenth century was the Boston Society for the Moral and Religious Instruction of the Poor (later the Boston City Missionary Society), which was begun in 1816 with the conviction that moral reforms would solve the temporal problems of the city's poor while improving their chances in eternity. Headed by prominent merchants, professionals, and clergymen of Boston, the society embarked upon a wide-ranging program of humanitarian activism. Since, as the society argued, "nine tenths of the pauperism in our country is occasioned by vice," true benevolence demanded moral and religious instruction rather than charity and relief for the poor. Thus, the organization sponsored Sunday schools, distributed Bibles and religious tracts, hired missionaries to visit and exhort the urban poor, established a chapel and "temperance" boarding houses for seamen, and promoted antiliquor and antiprostitution campaigns. Reflecting the protective functions of philanthropy, the society envisioned positive returns from such programs: elimination of "numberless outrages" in the city, the "protection and security of property," and reduction of "the greater part of the public expenses for the support of the poor."

Along the same lines, societies for the prevention of pauperism in New York, Boston, and Baltimore made comparable efforts to end dependency, save money, and reform the poor. Philadelphians sponsored a Society for the Promotion of Public Economy, which focused on the problem of pauperism, and a Society for Bettering the Condition of the Poor. Most groups eschewed relief-giving and depended primarily on district visiting to achieve their goals, dividing their city into small sections and assigning voluntary "visitors" to advise, counsel, encourage, and exhort the poor in each. Religion-oriented groups—Bible and tract societies and urban missionary organizations—were especially zealous in visiting families in poor neighborhoods. But whatever their techniques, spokesmen for private charities throughout most of the early nineteenth century, like municipal officials everywhere, agreed on the necessity for individual reform. Only at the end of the preindustrial period did the newly organized New York Association for Improving the Condition of the Poor (AICP) grudgingly admit possible environmental causes of dependency—unemployment, low wages, disease, unsanitary housing. Yet even the New York AICP and similarly named groups in other cities continued to emphasize idleness, extravagance, and alcoholism as responsible for most lower-class dependency. Also using district "visitors," the urban AICPs applied most of their energies to uplifting the morals of the poor.

Thus, "benevolent" citizens as well as city functionaries viewed the poor with a new set of assumptions in the early nineteenth century, assumptions which dictated urban antipoverty programs centering on forced labor and moral reform. These social welfare patterns deeply affected governmental and institutional responses to poverty throughout the rest of the century. Indeed, it is hard to avoid evidence of the old moralistic attitudes and accompanying work-enforcing programs even in the welfare controversy of mid-twentieth century.

3

Urban social welfare practice between the Civil War and the Great Depression of the 1930s retained much of its earlier form. Although change affected both public benevolence and private philanthropy, and although new institutions emerged, these seemed merely superimposed upon the framework established in earlier years. Despite markedly different social and economic conditions, old assumptions continued to prevail and affect decision making. Urbanization became a national rather than an East Coast phenomenon, and by 1920 more than half of all Americans lived in cities and towns. Industrialization transformed the United States, aggravating urban social problems in the process. At the same time, cyclical business depressions affected ever greater numbers of workers—low-paid as well as skilled and semiskilled. Poverty, pauperism, and periodic massive unemployment confronted city governments, which responded much as they had in the early nineteenth century. Outdoor relief continued in disfavor and was even abolished entirely in some cities, while temporary work relief became common during emergencies. By the 1880s, private charity in most cities came under the influence of the charity organization societies, whose "scientific philanthropy" seemed little different from the perhaps less sophisticated doctrines advocated by the AICPs and other earlier groups. Social work became a profession during this period, but environmentalism only slowly replaced "social Darwinism" as a prevailing ideology among those who worked with the poor. Not until the Great Depression and the New Deal was social welfare practice—but not social welfare ideology—revolutionized.

The poverty and dependency which characterized the seaport cities in the pre–Civil War period became more widespread and more visible in the larger and more numerous cities of the "age of industrialism." The causes of dependency were not hard to find. Various categories of helpless poor (aged, diseased, crippled, blind, mentally ill) increased along with rising urban populations. The Civil War widowed thousands of army wives in cities and towns in the North and in the South. Orphaned and delinquent children similarly required public attention. A Catholic periodical in New York City estimated 40,000 such vagrant children wandering about the metropolis in 1868. The intensified influx of penniless immigrants—some 25 million of them drawn to the "land of opportunity" between 1860 and 1920—crowded run-down slums and filthy tenements in already burgeoning cities and put new pressures on urban benevolence. In 1901, for example, New York's United Hebrew Charities reported 75,000 to 100,000 local Jews, mostly recent immigrants, in need of assistance.

Other forces also promoted dependency. Three prolonged depressions in the late nineteenth century (1873–78, 1882–86, 1893–97) and several shorter business panics made paupers out of workers. During the depression winter of 1873, about 40,000 laborers in Philadelphia sought relief, while in New York almost 100,000 workers—one quarter of the labor force—went jobless. During the winter of 1893–94, some 20,000 homeless vagrants and tramps sought temporary shelters in New York City police stations, while at least 200,000 additional New Yorkers required some kind of aid. In Chicago more than 100,000 workers had been thrown out of jobs by the depression. In Boston in 1903 over 136,000 persons—more than one-fifth of the city's total population of 606,000—were aided by public relief alone. The national magazines of the late nineteenth century bristled with articles about pauperism, the "tramp problem," the "tenement house problem," and the "lodging-house problem." While intellectuals and the middle class complained about the excesses and the inadequacies of American capitalism, poor immigrants, unorganized workers, and minority groups became its victims.

Low wages, as well as unsteady employment, created dependency. Throughout the period, subsistence living costs consumed the entire wages of underpaid industrial workers unprotected by unions. The United States census of 1890 revealed that of 12.5 million families in the nation, 11 million averaged an annual income of $380. To be sure, many of these families lived on farms, but the statistics seemed alarming nevertheless. About the same time, officials in Massachusetts estimated a subsistence income for a family of five to be $754; in New York City a charity spokesman gave a figure of $624, or $2 a day. As late as 1912, laborers in thirty-nine midwestern steel plants generally averaged 16.7 cents per hour for dangerous, physically exhausting work, and comparable wage scales prevailed in other industries. Jacob Riis, author of the pioneering social investigation, *How the Other Half Lives* (1890), reported earnings of women in the New York garment industry at the turn of the century to be about 30 cents a day. The real wages of workers never improved, and they occasionally declined, even in periods of prosperity in the early twentieth century. Social worker Robert Hunter conservatively estimated 4 million people dependent on public relief alone in 1900 and a total of at least 10 million living in families with below subsistence incomes. One of every eight Americans lived in poverty, Hunter contended, but in New York and other large industrial cities, the proportion rarely fell below one in four.

Urban dependency, then, was not simply a matter of blind, aged, disabled, orphaned, or widowed relief-seekers. Millions of workers and their families lived on the edge of poverty—men, women, and children for whom good times were bad, but for whom hard times were infinitely worse. Compensating for low earnings, workers often put their wives and children to work, took in boarders, and followed patterns of forced underconsumption. That even these techniques often failed is indicated by the startling statistic that 60,463 Manhattan families (14 percent of the borough's population) were evicted for nonpayment of rent in the single year of 1903. Opportunities for upward social and economic mobility for those on the lowest levels remained severely limited. It was Robert Hunter's careful estimate that about 90 percent of industrial workers—even higher in some cities—never became property owners. "Making it" in America remained a rarely achieved idealization. Even more than in pre–Civil War years, pauperism became a persistent characteristic of urban life, one aggravated by the constant arrival of poor immigrants and the uncertain capacity of laborers to find steady work at a living wage.

If anything, general public attitudes toward the poor hardened as evidence of widespread economic distress mounted in industrial cities in the decades following the Civil War. The American gospel of individualism continued to foster the belief that any hard-working, moral man could support his family in independence and dignity. A corollary view, popularized by men like Andrew Carnegie, emphasized poverty as a positive, character-building virtue. The simultaneous emergence of social Darwinism not only promoted acceptance of poverty and economic inequity as part of the natural order of things but cast serious doubt on the utility of public relief and private benevolence. Assistance of any kind weakened character and self-reliance, degraded the "spirit" of the recipient, and promoted the "survival of the unfit." Indiscriminate charity and relief only encouraged more pauperism and greater dependence. Relief, Josephine Shaw Lowell of the New York Charity Organization Society maintained, "should be surrounded by circumstances that shall . . . repel every one, not in extremity, from accepting it." In 1894 philanthropic spokesman Charles Loring Brace, in an address to public relief officials, contended that all charity "should be connected as much as possible with work." But even "relief work," Miss Lowell wrote, to deter habitual pauperism and thus benefit the poor, had to be "continuous, hard, and underpaid." Such deterrents were deemed necessary to prevent "imposters" from being rewarded for their idle and immoral ways. This concern about early welfare cheaters sometimes assumed paranoiac proportions, as when one New York charity official, obviously disturbed by increased pauperism during the depression of 1893, claimed that of every 1,000 beggars roaming city streets each evening, 999 "were frauds who followed this way to make a living, and who, in the day-time, went about well-dressed." For most nonpoor Americans, poverty remained very much an individual rather than a societal defect in these years.

Given these harsh assumptions about poverty and economic insecurity, developments in public relief seem hardly surprising. As antipauperism attitudes hardened and as relief costs rose, hostility to public assistance mounted. The place of outdoor relief especially became a central issue in the welfare debate of the industrial era. All the charges previously catalogued were levied against this form of public aid. And, as if additional arguments were needed, middle-class reformers exposed boss-dominated urban machines which blatantly used relief money for political purposes. Many large cities, beginning with New York in 1874, Brooklyn in 1878, and Philadelphia the following year, abolished outdoor relief entirely. Brooklyn's mayor, Seth Low, contended that these moves placed no additional burdens on the almshouse or private charities, pointedly suggesting that outdoor relief supported worthless idlers and represented an expensive and useless drain on municipal treasuries. By 1900, St. Louis, Baltimore, San Francisco, Washington, Kansas City, New Orleans, and Louisville had also abandoned outdoor aid. Other cities, claiming great savings, severely limited outdoor assistance to those who performed some work. Providence, Rhode Island, for example, spent more than $150,000 on outdoor relief in 1878; with the application of the "work test," the annual cost allegedly had been reduced to $4,700 in 1880. In Cleveland city officials maintained that the work requirement cut a $95,000 relief expense in 1875 to $17,000 in

1880. Thus, outdoor relief, although continued in many large cities, became the *bête noir* of nineteenth century charity "reformers"—a seemingly misguided practice which allegedly worsened the conditions it was designed to alleviate. Only the punitive work requirement made this form of public assistance palatable.

Although outdoor relief fell into disfavor and partial disuse, the place of the almshouse became less controversial during the industrial era because of the increased sophistication of social welfare institutions during the period. The large, central poorhouse, filled with all varieties of dependents, was gradually replaced by a number of specialized institutions for blind, deaf and dumb, mentally ill, and physically handicapped persons, as well as for juvenile delinquents and various categories of medically indigent patients. Increasingly in post–Civil War years, following a trend noticeable in the administration of other urban services, state boards of charities assumed responsibility for these institutions from often inept and sometime corrupt municipal governments. Staffed by professionals, these state boards sought to raise administrative efficiency, to reduce welfare costs, and to treat dependency from a "scientific" point of view. The emerging group of professional public social service officials, as well as leaders from private charities, generally recognized the importance of the categorical institutions for "deserving" cases with special needs. The emphasis on the "worthy" poor, however, limited such facilities to those who conformed to acceptable standards and submitted to an often demeaning institutional discipline.

Private charity confronted massive urban poverty with similar presuppositions, but the old moralism was now buttressed with theoretical underpinnings drawn from social Darwinism, laissez faire capitalism, and the emerging eugenics movement (which blamed heredity for such individual characteristics as alcoholism, insanity, and pauperism). Charity leaders continued to apply moral therapy to the social ills created by urban life and industrial depression.

The "scientific charity" espoused by the charity organization movement typified social welfare in the industrial city. Established in Buffalo in 1877 and modeled on an earlier London group, the first Charity Organization Society (COS) reflected the antipauperism attitudes of the day. The Reverend Samuel Humphreys Gurteen, a transplanted English clergyman and founder of Buffalo's COS, drew upon his experience in the British organization and tried to systematize and rationalize charity in the American city. Within fifteen years, charity leaders in ninety-two cities had established a COS or a group with similar intentions. Moralistic to the core, the COS movement continued to find the roots of dependency in the individual and rejected "soup-kitchen philanthropy." Despite good intentions, Charles D. Kellogg of the New York COS asserted in 1893 that most private charities in the depression years of the late nineteenth century distributed relief indiscriminately to the poor and thus "sank into the sea of common almsgiving." Gurteen, Kellogg, Josephine Shaw Lowell, and other COS leaders sought to counter this kind of charity, which, they argued, only increased the dependency of the poor.

Discarding traditional relief practices entirely, the COS promoted a number of alternative techniques, some of which had been applied earlier by the AICPs. To organize urban charity meant to centralize and coordinate it. Thus, the COS established lines of communication among city charities, used paid agents to investigate all applicants for private aid, and eliminated overlapping philanthropy by keeping master lists of the worthy poor. Employment bureaus were established by every COS to force the poor into jobs where possible. Accepting pauperism as the result of personal defects, COS leaders countenanced charity only as a last resort and even convinced public officials in some cities to abolish outdoor relief. With material aid limited or abandoned, the volunteer "friendly" visitor became central to COS goals. Believing that the dependency of every poor family stemmed from one or two determinable causes (alcoholism, extravagance, aversion to work), COS theorists depended upon visitors to "scientifically" ferret out and eliminate the pauper-producing agents. Much like the district visitors of the preindustrial city, these volunteers (mainly middle-class women) made periodic calls on poor families to observe, investigate, and give advice, encouragement, and support—but not relief. They hoped to end dependency by cultivating proper, middle-class values among the poor —a technique which, given the assumptions of the time, seemed sound but which ignored the obvious (from our perspective) industrial determinants of economic inequity. In the words of one social welfare historian, the COS "emphasized personal failure as the major cause of dependency, believed that no one would work unless goaded by fear of starvation, investigated every aspect of an applicant's life, reduced relief to the lowest possible level, and provided close supervision of any family on its rolls." Reflecting prevailing attitudes, the COS, in short, was nothing less than the old moralism clothed in new "scientific" garb.

Yet ironically, the COS emphasis on personal investigation of poor families led to the eventual formulation of a new view of poverty—at least within the emerging profession of social work. Since about the mid-nineteenth century, an unresolved ambiguity had crept into American social welfare practice. While public officials and private philanthropists almost unanimously traced dependency to individual character failings, the programs they sponsored sometimes denied moralistic assumptions. As early as the 1850s, the New York AICP had sponsored medical dispensaries, had established a juvenile asylum for vagrant children, had built public baths in the slums, had investigated mortality rates among the poor, had urged municipal authorities to create a "sanitary police" for regular health inspections, and had embarked on a significant program for model tenements and housing reform. Similarly, after the great Chicago fire of 1871, when 35,000 people faced immediate starvation and exposure, the Chicago Relief and Aid Society not only assumed the entire burden of municipal relief but financed construction of 8,000 homes for burned-out victims. Programs such as these suggest an unacknowledged, or grudgingly acknowledged, recognition that environment had some relation to dependency. By the end of the nineteenth century, some of those who daily observed the poor and the circumstances of their lives—visitors of the COS, paid agents of other urban charities, residents of settlement houses in immigrant slums, social gospelers and ministers of urban "institutional" churches, professional social workers in state and municipal agencies—could hardly escape the same conclusions.

The emergence of the progressive reform movement in the early decades of the twentieth century, with its emphasis on investigation and facts, also produced evidence to counter traditional assumptions about poverty. Robert Hunter's 1904 social investigation, *Poverty,* perhaps the most careful and objective study to that time, linked dependency to income level rather than to personal morality. The great mass of the poor, Hunter argued, became that way through no fault of their own but because of preventable social and economic evils. Poverty was "bred of miserable and unjust social conditions" which punished the hard-working and industrious laborer as well as the lazy and immoral pauper. The solution lay not in COS-type charity, which Hunter found repressive because its purpose was "making pauperism intolerable" to dependents. Rather, the social and economic causes of poverty had to be eliminated, the urban environment reformed.

Accepting the facts unearthed by Hunter and other investigators, social reformers of the Progressive Era attacked the environmental conditions which fostered not merely pauperism but the more general condition of poverty. While many middle-class, business-oriented progressive politicians emphasized structural reforms—changes in the framework of government to permit greater efficiency and savings—other progressives at every level of government advocated a variety of social reforms to improve the quality of life for most people. Thus, the period witnessed efforts for tenement house reform, industrial safety legislation, improvements in education, public health regulation, minimum wages, maximum hours, elimination of child labor, workmen's compensation, health insurance, unemployment insurance, mothers' pensions, old age insurance, and similar schemes designed to protect the individual from social injustice and economic inequity. The settlement houses, especially, became spearheads for reform and improvement in urban slums. Yet although some partial gains were made, the reformers suffered in the long run from the constraints imposed by a society that was unprepared and indisposed to accept responsibility for those who were unable to survive in a competitive system. For most Americans during this period, pauperism remained the primary problem and relief an evil to be avoided if at all possible.

4

The Great Depression of the 1930s temporarily weakened predominant assumptions about the nature of poverty and the functions of relief. The breakdown of American capitalism affected not only the poor, the unskilled, the underpaid, and ethnic and racial minorities, but the solid middle class as well. Americans brought up to revere the work ethic faced poverty despite willingness to labor. Unprecedented unemployment challenged traditional views that sufficient jobs were available for all. Men who in good times had moralistically condemned relief-seekers now found the "dole" an unpleasant but acceptable alternative to starvation. The inability first of private philanthropy and then of state and local relief to temper the depression crisis forced the nation to consider new measures for economic security.

The magnitude of the depression crisis was most obvious in the nation's cities, where unemployment mounted as the depression deepened after 1929. By October 1931, according to the Illinois Department of Labor, Chicago's unemployed reached 624,000, 40 percent of the work force. Two months later, New York City's jobless totaled more than 800,000. During the same winter, Philadelphia had 250,000 unemployed persons; 223,000 in Detroit went without work. Workers in single-industry cities became especially vulnerable to depression layoffs. In the steel city of Gary, Indiana, 90 percent unemployment hit the city's giant steel mills; 76 percent of the families in Butte, Montana, went on the relief rolls. As foreclosures and evictions rose, the outskirts of every city sprouted "Hoovervilles"—colonies of depression victims, perhaps as many as a million altogether, housed in scrap wood and tar-paper shacks. In New York City people lived in caves in Central Park and on tenement fire escapes with cardboard arranged around the edges. Some estimated as many as 2 million homeless migrants tramping the nation in search of work. Six thousand people sold apples on New York City streets, while hundreds of thousands took odd jobs at any pay, worked only part time at reduced wages, or sent wives and children job hunting. Throughout the nation, city governments went bankrupt, forcing additional thousands of municipal employees into unemployment. When savings and other family resources became exhausted, most victims of the depression turned to public or private assistance for survival.

The persistence of nineteenth century attitudes about poverty and relief prevented speedy action to counter the impact of the depression. President Herbert Hoover personified older laissez faire views, preaching a doctrine of "rugged individualism" as inseparable from American tradition and character. Hoover refused to consider federal action for unemployment relief; he remained convinced that private philanthropy could handle the crisis. If necessary, local relief might be expanded as well, Hoover contended, but the federal government should not be brought into what was essentially a local affair. Federal relief, Hoover said in 1931, would destroy "character," the spirit of "independence," and the "roots of self-government"—an analysis not much different from that popularized by the charity "reformers" of the early nineteenth century. (Yet Hoover's opposition to federal relief stood in stark contrast to his willingness to loan billions to banks, insurance companies, and industry through the Reconstruction Finance Corporation, an agency called a "bread line for big business" by some Hoover critics.) Hoover buttressed the voluntary relief effort by creating an Emergency Committee for Unemployment, which stimulated the organization of relief and unemployment committees at the local level and attempted to coordinate the relief work of state and local officials, industry, social welfare agencies, and other groups. But the president's committee distributed no relief funds and became simply, in the words of one historian of the Hoover period, "an organ of exhortation for the American way." The limited resources of private charity and the antiquated structure of municipal relief proved unequal to the monumental task of rescuing a nation in the throes of depression. The experience of the first few depression winters revealed the total inadequacy—indeed, the complete inhumanity—of the Hoover position.

In the nation's largest cities, where private philanthropy was well organized and well funded, the unemployment crisis quickly exhausted local resources. In New York City, the still-functioning AICP organized a work relief program in 1929, hired more than 1,500 men to work in city parks, spent $200,000, and went broke in a year. The effort was then taken up by the COS, which established an Emergency Work Bureau in conjunction with the city's three other large charities—the AICP, the Jewish Social Service Association, and Catholic Charities. A group of bankers raised $8.5 million in donations for the work campaign, which during the winter of 1930–31 put more than 37,000 persons back to work on a variety of public and nonprofit private projects. But the program came to a forced conclusion when funds ran out after five months. Other cities had similar experiences. In Chicago, with the city government bankrupt and without credit, a Commission on Unemployment and Relief set up in 1930 by the state governor sought to raise private funds for relief. In Philadelphia, where outdoor relief had ended in 1879, community leaders organized a Committee for Unemployment Relief to collect contributions. In Detroit, where heavy layoffs in the automobile industry created massive welfare problems, private charity remained minimal (partially because of Henry Ford's well-publicized opposition to philanthropy as destructive of self-reliance and individual initiative), but public relief was expanded under the leadership of a liberal and humane mayor. In most cities public relief lagged far behind community need, either because it was illegal (as in Philadelphia), because of weak mayoral leadership (as in New York), or because of municipal bankruptcy (as in Chicago). Everywhere the inadequacy of local resources—both public and private—became painfully apparent.

With relief efforts virtually paralyzed in the cities, state governments attempted to take up the burden. While he was governor of New York during the early years of the depression, politically astute Franklin D. Roosevelt recognized the magnitude of the relief crisis and accepted the need for government action. He convinced state legislators to create a Temporary Emergency Relief Administration (TERA) in 1931 to supervise and support home and work relief programs throughout the state. Headed by social worker Harry Hopkins and requiring matching grants from localities, TERA funneled $83 million in borrowed state funds to cities and municipalities within a two-year period. The Roosevelt program in New York State quickly became a model for relief efforts in other places, and by the end of the Hoover presidency, a majority of states had established similar statewide relief agencies. But even state efforts proved inadequate as unemployment mounted. By March 1933, when Roosevelt became president, at least 13 million Americans had no jobs, and when wives and children were counted, the number of needy surpassed that figure several fold.

Roosevelt brought his TERA experience to the presidency and applied it on a national scale. Among numerous measures enacted during the New Deal's "first hundred days," the Federal Emergency Relief Administration (FERA) channeled an immediate half billion dollars in relief money to state and local agencies. Within a single month, FERA administrator Harry Hopkins had more than 19 million people on emergency relief rolls. By 1936, when FERA was abolished, some $3 billion of federal money had been spent for direct relief, and matching state allocations made the total still higher. Numerous other alphabetical agencies supplied jobs and relief during the depths of the depression. The Civilian Conservation Corps (CCC) eventually enrolled 2.5 million young men for conservation and reforestation work. The Civil Works Administration (CWA), a temporary work relief agency created during the winter of 1933–34, employed more than 4 million men and women on a myriad of projects. The Public Works Administration (PWA) put people to work constructing public buildings, schools, hospitals, bridges, naval vessels, airports, public housing, and numerous other projects; the Works Projects Administration (WPA) concentrated on smaller projects. The National Youth Administration (NYA) provided part-time work to more than 2 million high school and college students. Other New Deal programs, although they did not grant relief directly, aided the unemployed by refinancing mortgages, encouraging housing construction, and protecting labor organizations.

Aside from its unprecedented government activism, the New Deal had a marked impact on the direction of American social welfare practice. FERA and WPA programs were merely temporary expedients to temper the depression relief crisis, but the Social Security Act of 1935 had more permanent results. The act established three programs: old-age insurance, to be financed by federal taxes on wages and payrolls; unemployment insurance, to be administered by states and paid for out of payroll taxes; and a series of categorical assistance programs that offered federal aid to states which provided relief to the blind, the crippled, the aged who were not covered by Social Security, and dependent mothers and children. The first two programs, which were somewhat controversial at the time of passage, have since been generally accepted. However, the categorical assistance programs, which caused the least discussion in the 1930s, have permitted the tremendous expansion of welfare in the mid-twentieth century and have become targets of mounting criticism. Although the Social Security Act had little immediate impact on urban relief during the depression, the law eventually changed the entire pattern of public assistance in the United States. As one social welfare historian has argued, "It marked a decisive transfer of welfare functions from voluntary to public institutions, and from the local to the federal level, thus paving the way for contemporary anti-poverty programs."

Yet the old assumptions died hard. Despite the massive joblessness of the depression, there is little evidence that Americans substantially altered their views about the permanently poor—sharecroppers, tenant farmers, migrant workers, female domestic workers, and the millions of unemployables or unskilled, unorganized, and underpaid menial laborers in cities throughout the nation. The economic crisis forced onto relief rolls many normally self-supporting workers and middle-class people, and New Deal agencies emphasized aid to these groups. Few programs were aimed specifically at those who lived in poverty in good times as well as bad times; few relief plans sought to redistribute wealth, to make income levels more equitable, or, in the words of a historian of the era, to extend "the beneficence of government beyond the middle class or drew upon the wealth of the few for the needs of the many." The New Deal, in short, addressed its major relief efforts, first in the form of direct assistance and then through work relief, to depression-induced unemployment. Despite Rooseveltian rhetoric, the New Deal was short on positive efforts to raise the income levels of the permanently poor.

The nineteenth century emphasis on work also continued to shape policy. Any work—even "made work"—seemed better than the "dole" to those administering relief funds. But even WPA-type work programs seemed to contradict the American way, and New Dealers cut back or abandoned these as soon as it was politically feasible. Similarly, the old-age assistance and unemployment insurance provisions of the Social Security Act were tied to previous participation in the work force—a condition which excluded those who needed aid most. The New Deal, although it produced substantial social reforms, treated social welfare problems within the context of an old and essentially conservative ideology. The federal government, to be sure, had taken the initiative from cities and states, but programs emerging from the Social Security Act were work-related and sought only, as historian Roy Lubove has suggested, "to provide some measure of economic security without significantly affecting income redistribution." At the same time, state-established categorical assistance programs retained repressive or deterring eligibility requirements and punitive sanctions against socially unacceptable behavior. Thus, urban social welfare programs retained much of the moralistic fervor and work-enforcing doctrine that had characterized them in the nineteenth century.

5

In the years since the New Deal and World War II, turbulent changes have buffeted American society, particularly the cities, which are beset by crime, congestion, municipal corruption, white flight to the suburbs, shrinking tax resources, racial discord, and air, water, noise, and visual pollution, as well as entrenched poverty and bulging welfare rolls. Technological change and modernization in American agriculture have driven 20 million rural dwellers to the cities since 1940, stimulating social disorganization. More than 20 percent of these rural migrants have been southern blacks; in the five largest metropolitan areas (New York, Los Angeles, Chicago, Philadelphia, and Detroit), black population increases ranged from 39 to 97 percent during the 1950s alone. Like the earlier black migration of World War I and the mass immigration from Europe in the late nineteenth and early twentieth centuries, the recent rural migration has upset the tenuous balance of life and work in the city, has heightened urban tensions, and has revealed the human costs of urban living. Blacks especially have suffered the consequences of job discrimination, segregated housing, substandard education, and inadequate social services, but Puerto Ricans in New York City, Mexican-Americans in the urban Southwest, and American Indians in areas such as Minneapolis, Chicago, and Omaha have also become part of a ghettoized, inferior class. Mostly displaced farm laborers with few marketable skills, the migrants have taken up marginal, often menial, jobs in the city. More often than not, jobs at a living wage are temporary or unobtainable. For men and women such as these, public welfare has become a means of survival.

As noted earlier, city welfare rolls experienced a virtual explosion during the past decade, and the largest increases were in the Aid to Families with Dependent Children program (AFDC), the most controversial aspect of public assistance. For example, although the AFDC case load in New York City rose only 16 percent in the 1950s, the increase measured 300 percent between 1960 and 1969. According to statistics released by the U.S. Department of Health, Education, and Welfare, an average of 10 percent of the population in the nation's twenty largest metropolitan areas drew welfare payments in 1971. Nearly one New Yorker in every six is a welfare recipient; in Boston 15 percent of the population survives on welfare; in mid-1971, Philadelphia welfare recipients totaled more than 306,000, approaching the April 1935 record, when depression relief programs supported 354,000 people. Although some observers (such as former presidential advisor Daniel P. Moynihan) are optimistic that things are improving, few can deny—at least without a twinge of doubt—that mounting welfare rolls and soaring costs reflect a much deeper urban malaise.

One of a number of recent analyses of the past and current state of the welfare system, Piven and Cloward's *Regulating the Poor*, has clearly linked rising welfare rolls to recent developments in urban slums, particularly in black ghettos. The emergence of a militant civil rights movement in the early 1960s sought to counteract the feeling of powerlessness and oppression which pervaded districts like Watts, Harlem, and Chicago's South Side. Black riots and ghetto uprisings moved public officials to loosen welfare restrictions and to increase welfare acceptances as a means of calming urban discontent and restoring weakened social controls. The social programs of the Johnson administration, notably the community action programs, reinforced these trends and stimulated the welfare rights movement. Such organizations printed handbooks to guide applicants through the maze of the welfare bureaucracy, successfully fought arbitrary decision making of administrators whose main concern was saving money, broke down many of the deterrents which formerly kept eligibles off the rolls, and counteracted the sense of powerlessness in the ghetto. The welfare rights movement loosened the welfare structure and made it more responsive to applicant needs. Of course, a tremendous welfare expansion resulted—a purposeful government concession in response to social and political disorder in the 1960s. In the absence of basic economic changes which would redistribute wealth more equitably or bring full employment at decent wages, Piven and Cloward have taken the position that "the current explosion of the rolls is the true relief reform, that it should be defended, and that it should be expanded."

However, expansion of the welfare rolls has reinvigorated the work ethic. Rising relief expenses met mounting criticism from burdened taxpayers and harried politicians, and new efforts have been made to "reform" the welfare system. Yet these proposed changes seem remarkably similar to earlier "reform" efforts. At the federal level, for example, President Richard Nixon advocated a welfare plan primarily designed to force the poor to work. Although it died in Congress, the proposal urged a minimum income for all American families, certainly an advance over earlier practice. But the minimum offered ($1,600 for a family of four in the president's original welfare message, later increased to $2,400) was well below subsistence standards. Basically, the plan sought to induce welfare recipients to join the work force, but without simultaneous governmental reforms to bring about full employment, most of those moving from the welfare rolls would have secured only menial, low-paid, and often meaningless jobs. And by proposing to subsidize marginal wages with relief payments, the administration plan actually would have perpetuated low-wage policies on the part of those who employ the poor. What emerged clearly from the Nixon plan is the idea that work—any work at whatever pay—is important for character and self-esteem and that it is somehow unfair, unethical, and un-American for society to assume responsibility for those who are poor or near starvation because they are unable to compete with the rest of us.

The same attitudes (strangely like those of AICP and COS spokesmen of the nineteenth century) shaped responses to the welfare explosion at the state level. Although partially financed by the federal government under provisions of the Social Security Act, categorical assistance programs like AFDC are administered by the states. Rather than respond to the needs of big cities with huge welfare loads, state governments have instead bowed to the demands of suburban and rural constituencies, have cut welfare appropriations, and have devised new deterrents and exclusionary practices to reduce the rolls. In New York State, for example, legislation established new guidelines which widened the concept of employability, requiring "employable" persons to pick up welfare checks at state employment centers; failure to take assigned jobs resulted in expulsion from the rolls. Despite an earlier Supreme Court decision ruling a residency requirement for welfare unconstitutional, the legislature enacted such a law. To prevent the cashing of forged or stolen welfare checks, the New York legislature required cities to issue photographic identification cards to welfare recipients; in New York City alone, administration of this somewhat paranoid program will cost initially about $2 million (and a subsequent $900,000 annually), all to prevent the loss of about $150,000 each year through fraudulent check cashing. Similarly, investigations were launched to catch welfare cheaters, and administrators used deterrents (such as closing welfare offices early in the day) to reduce the rolls. Many other states also toughened their welfare requirements, trying to reduce the number of recipients and force the poor into jobs. By September 1971, according to a *New York Times* report, such actions had forced a decline in welfare rolls in nineteen states.

Opponents of this sort of welfare "reform" contend that such programs will have little positive benefit. They point to government studies which show that most of those who live below the poverty line are too old, too young, too sick, or too disabled to work or already working at below-subsistence wages. Many others are mothers with dependent children who, in the absence of job training and adequate day-care centers, cannot be expected to be breadwinners. The tough new welfare requirements are hardly relevant for groups such as these. As George A. Wiley, of the National Welfare Rights Organization, has argued, the investigations, the work requirements, and the deterrents are simply "brutalizing the poor."

In many ways, public assistance has always brutalized the poor in the United States. Throughout American history, welfare has attempted only to alleviate the most observable symptoms of poverty. Aid programs merely enabled recipients to subsist in poverty, and even then only after they adopted desired behavior or met acceptable standards imposed by the larger society. Prevailing attitudes prevented any other approach. The competitive society has provided few rewards, few social safeguards, for those who do not or cannot compete. The key variable by which society judges a person poor—inadequate income—has never been squarely confronted. Few government programs have significantly altered the entrenched social and economic conditions which keep 50 million people—mostly city dwellers—below or barely above the poverty line. Until such programs are developed, and until archaic assumptions and attitudes about the poor are changed, poverty in the cities will persist.

Selected Bibliography

Robert H. Bremner's *From the Depths: The Discovery of Poverty in the United States* (New York, 1956) provides an essential overview of the history of urban social welfare. Other useful surveys include Blanche D. Coll, *Perspectives in Public Welfare: A History* (Washington, 1969); Samuel Mencher, *Poor Law to Poverty Program: Economic Security Policy in Britain and the United States* (Pittsburgh, 1967); Robert H. Bremner, *American Philanthropy* (Chicago, 1960); Sidney Lens, *Poverty: America's Enduring Paradox* (New York, 1969); Merle Curti, "Tradition and Innovation in American Philanthropy," *Proceedings of the American Philosophical Society*, 105 (April 1961), 141–56; Ralph E. Pumphrey, "Compassion and Protection: Dual Motivations in Social Welfare," *Social Service Review*, 33 (March 1959), 21–29; and Robert H. Bremner, "The State of Social Welfare History," in Herbert J. Bass, editor, *The State of American History* (Chicago, 1970), 89–98. On social work developments see Ralph E. Pumphrey and Muriel W. Pumphrey, editors, *The Heritage of American Social Work: Readings in Its Philosophical and Institutional Development* (New York, 1961).

Important studies for preindustrial America are David J. Rothman, *The Discovery of the Asylum: Social Order and Disorder in the New Republic* (Boston, 1971); Raymond A. Mohl, *Poverty in New York, 1783–1825* (New York, 1971); John K. Alexander, "The City of Brotherly Fear: The Poor in Late-Eighteenth Century Philadelphia," in Kenneth T. Jackson and Stanley K. Schultz, editors, *Cities in American History* (New York, 1972), 79–97; Stanley K. Schultz, "Breaking the Chains of Poverty: Public Education in Boston, 1800–1860," in *ibid.*, 306–23; Raymond A. Mohl, "Poverty, Pauperism, and Social Order in the Preindustrial American City, 1780–1840," *Social Science Quarterly*, 52 (March 1972), 934–48; Blanche D. Coll," The Baltimore Society for the Prevention of Pauperism, 1820–1822," *American Historical Review*, 56 (October 1955), 77–87; Roy Lubove, "The New York Association for Improving the Condition of the Poor: The Formative Years," *New-York Historical Society Quarterly*, 43 (July 1959), 307–27; and Benjamin J. Klebaner, "Poverty and Its Relief in American Thought, 1815–61," *Social Service Review*, 38 (December 1963), 382–99.

The industrial period of the late nineteenth and early twentieth centuries is covered in Nathan I. Huggins, *Protestants against Poverty: Boston's Charities, 1870–1900* (Westport, Conn., 1971); Roy Lubove, *The Professional Altruist: The Emergence of Social Work As a Career, 1880–1930* (Cambridge, Mass., 1965) and *The Progressives and the Slums: Tenement House Reform in New York City, 1890–1917* (Pittsburgh, 1962); and Robert H. Bremner, "Scientific Philanthropy, 1873–93," *Social Service Review*, 30 (June 1956), 168–73. Key works on urban settlement houses and social workers include Allen F. Davis, *Spearheads for Reform: The Social Settlements and the Progressive Movement* (New York, 1967); Louise C. Wade, *Graham Taylor: Pioneer for Social Justice, 1851–1938* (Chicago, 1964); Daniel Levine, *Jane Addams and the Liberal Tradition* (Madison, Wis., 1971); and Clarke A. Chambers, *Paul U. Kellogg and the Survey: Voices for Social Welfare and Social Justice* (Minneapolis, 1971). Earlier works by charity workers, journalists, and Progressive reformers are indispensable: Josephine Shaw Lowell, *Public Relief and Private Charity* (New York, 1884); Jacob Riis, *How the Other Half Lives* (New York, 1890) and *The Battle with the Slum* (New York, 1902); Robert Hunter, *Poverty: Social Conscience in the Progressive Era*

(New York, 1904); Jane Addams, *Twenty Years at Hull House* (New York, 1910).

A number of studies treat social welfare developments in the twentieth century. Roy Lubove, *The Struggle for Social Security, 1900–1935* (Cambridge, Mass., 1968), contains important background material. Clarke A. Chambers, *Seedtime of Reform: American Social Service and Social Action, 1918–1933* (Minneapolis, 1963), covers the 1920s. Useful in elaborating social welfare problems during the Great Depression are Albert U. Romasco, *The Poverty of Abundance: Hoover, the Nation, the Depression* (New York, 1965); Harry L. Hopkins, *Spending to Save: The Complete Story of Relief* (New York, 1936); Louise V. Armstrong, *We Too Are the People* (Boston, 1938); Josephine C. Brown, *Public Relief, 1929–1939* (New York, 1940); and Bernard Sternsher, editor, *Hitting Home: The Great Depression in Town and Country* (Chicago, 1970).

The rediscovery of poverty in the 1960s began with Michael Harrington's *The Other America: Poverty in the United States* (New York, 1962). Equally effective and important is the recent study by Frances Fox Piven and Richard A. Cloward, *Regulating the Poor: The Functions of Public Welfare* (New York, 1971). Other studies on contemporary urban poverty and welfare include: Richard M. Elman, *The Poorhouse State: The American Way of Life on Public Assistance* (New York, 1966); Daniel P. Moynihan, *Maximum Feasible Misunderstanding: Community Action in the War on Poverty* (New York, 1969); Kenneth B. Clark and Jeannette Hopkins, *A Relevant War against Poverty* (New York, 1968); Anthony Downs, *Who Are the Urban Poor?* (rev. ed., New York, 1970); William Ryan, *Blaming the Victim* (New York, 1971); and Joel F. Handler, *Reforming the Poor* (New York, 1972). For specific case studies see Joseph P. Lyford, *The Airtight Cage: A Study of New York's West Side* (New York, 1966); Todd Gitlin and Nanci Hollander, *Uptown: Poor Whites in Chicago* (New York, 1970); Elliot Liebow, *Tally's Corner: A Study of Negro Streetcorner Men* (Boston, 1967); and Oscar Lewis, *La Vida: A Puerto Rican Family in the Culture of Poverty—San Juan and New York* (New York, 1966). Julius Horowitz, *The Diary of A.N.* (New York, 1970), is a sensitive and effective fictionalized account of life on welfare in New York City. Useful anthologies of articles, essays, and documents on poverty in modern America include Louis A. Ferman, Joyce L. Kornbluh, and Alan Haber, editors, *Poverty in America* (rev. ed., Ann Arbor, Mich., 1968); Daniel P. Moynihan, editor, *On Understanding Poverty* (New York, 1968); Robert E. Will and Harold G. Vatter, editors, *Poverty in Affluence* (2d ed., New York, 1970); and David J. Rothman and Sheila M. Rothman, editors, *On Their Own: The Poor in Modern America* (Reading, Mass., 1972).

Education in the City

Selwyn K. Troen

Like the ancient Greeks who believed that education derives from the totality of experience in the *polis*, contemporary educators are experimenting with programs that take children outside the school, and historians are arguing that the study of education must embrace more than formal schooling. Nevertheless, a scholarship based on such a broad definition of education has not yet appeared, and children are still confined to the classroom; Americans, particularly those living in cities, continue to concentrate the processes of learning in institutions. Such emphasis is the culmination of a tendency that is characteristic of urban-industrial societies in secular nations. Whatever the relationship between formal and informal learning or between schools and other agencies may be, a salient fact of modern societies is the growing reliance on formal schooling as the central instrument for the transmission of culture and for socialization of the young.

Education was differently ordered prior to 1800, although the beginnings of change were visible during the previous two centuries. In the colonial period, traditional agents of socialization—family, church, community, apprenticeship—came under great stress and began to surrender their responsibilities, usually in favor of schools. As homogeneity and stability gave way before the diversity and dynamism of an expanding colonial economy, the easy assurance that religious culture would naturally continue was no longer tenable. Churches suffered from disestablishment, the multiplication of sects, and secularism and came to depend on schools to indoctrinate the young and to train ministers. At the same time, the demand for labor destroyed feudal craft monopolies and weakened the apprenticeship system. The family too lost a measure of control over its young to the temptations, fluidity, and opportunities of colonial society. The personal history of Benjamin Franklin, the archetypal urban American, suggests the changes taking place. Franklin left Puritanism for deism, was self-taught, and made his way in strange communities without benefit or guidance of family; his *Auto-biography* served as a model for generations of self-starters and self-made men. Franklin recognized deficiencies in colonial education and became a leading advocate of societies and schools that would formalize the process of learning.

Colonial Americans were themselves legatees of generations that had experienced profound change. One European historian has linked the Renaissance discovery of childhood as a unique stage of life with the emergence of the family as an increasingly discrete unit in society. As family life became more private, the care of children became a matter of greater attention and concern to parents; the school came to supplement the moral and vocational instruction the family imparted. Thus, the growing importance of the school in the 1500s and beyond was related to a shift of major proportions in the organization of family life and its relation to society.

Colonial child-rearing literature suggests that the family did not willingly give up its children to the school. The debate revolved around the relative merits of educating the child in the home, or "private" education in the English usage, and "public" education—that is, permitting the child to learn outside the home in the company of other children. John Locke, the widely read political and moral philosopher, posed the question directly:

> What shall I do with my son? If I keep him always at home, he will be in danger to be my young master; and if I send him abroad, how is it possible to keep him from the contagion of rudeness and vice? In my house he will perhaps be more innocent, but more ignorant too of the world: wanting there change of company, and being used constantly to the same faces, he will, when he comes abroad, be a sheepish or conceited creature.

Ultimately, Locke judged the hazards to innocence to be greater from servants, fellow students, and even schoolmasters and concluded that "the faults of a private education are infinitely to be preferred."

Both critics and supporters of public schools were sensitive to the role played by the family. Frederick Packard, a leader in the Sunday school movement writing in the 1860s, admitted that schools could "counteract the influence of ill-governed, thriftless and immoral homes" but insisted on the paramount role of home environment in the development of the child. A multitude of experiences, primarily the behavior of parents and neighbors, "made a far deeper impression upon the mind and character [than] a month's, nay, perhaps a year's schooling." Horace Bushnell, a Congregational minister, believed that the child's character is largely formed by the time he is three and that even the "efficacy of preaching and pulpit harangue" pale beside the influence of parents. A leading promoter of public education, Henry Barnard, pointed out that parents had much greater opportunity to give instruction than the schools, since the larger portion of the child's time was spent at home. He viewed the family table, the father's workshop, and the kitchen as major centers of learning.

By the end of the nineteenth century, educators were giving concrete expression to the importance of the family by imitating family experiences in the schools. Courses in sewing and cooking were justified as necessary not only for children with deficient family backgrounds but for all children. In the 1890s, for example, John Dewey incorporated aspects of family life into his laboratory school at the University of Chicago, which catered to middle-class and upper-class children. Symbolically, the cover of Dewey's *The School and Society* featured a typically domestic scene: a girl working at the spinning wheel. While the school endeavored to act *in loco parentis,* it may also be true that the family transformed formal education by modeling the school in its image. Similarly, the introduction of manual training at the turn of the century and now of subjects like computer programming is indicative of the growing shift of responsibilities toward schools and away from traditional methods of vocational preparation.

Leaders in growing colonial communities recognized the importance of schooling early in the seventeenth century. The fundamental educational legislation of Massachusetts stipulated in 1642 that the colony's towns must establish schools to counteract "the great neglect of many parents and masters in training their children in learning and labor." By the end of the century, scholarship and literacy were so widespread in colonial cities that Boston emerged as the second largest (after London) publishing center in the British empire, producing great quantities of religious and practical literature. By the mid-eighteenth century, cities had extensive and varied educational establishments. Philadelphia had perhaps the largest selection: sectarian elementary schools organized by Baptists, Moravians, Lutherans, German Reformed, and Quakers; academies and private institutions that taught mathematics, foreign languages, scientific subjects, and clerical skills; charity schools that instructed the children of the poor; evening schools for working girls that offered a variety of subjects from arithmetic to psalmody; colleges which conducted courses in medicine, law, and higher learning; and numerous societies which offered lectures and provided a forum for discussion and education. Indeed, one historian has characterized colonial Philadelphia as "a literary republic." Such a complex of institutions was necessary not only because of the decline of traditional educational agencies but also because of the demands of urban life. In order to prosper, Philadelphia needed clerks, navigators, surveyors, accountants, and a literate populace. And since it did prosper, it had a market not only for "useful" knowledge but also for the "ornamental."

Developments in nineteenth century America heightened enthusiasm for schooling. Lawrence Cremin, the historian of the common school movement, attributes the growth of that movement to four main factors: (1) the democratization of politics as expressed in the extension of suffrage and increased eligibility for public office; (2) the desire to build an egalitarian society and insure social mobility; (3) the spirit of reform based on a benign view of human nature that stressed the perfectibility of man; and (4) nationalistic currents and the desire to mitigate the dangers inherent in a diverse society by bringing all children, particularly those of Catholic and non-English immigrants, into the common schools. These factors were not exclusively urban, but they had the greatest relevance to urban Americans, for it was in cities that homogenization was most critical, social disparities most evident, and the fear of anarchy most pervasive.

In addition, other imperatives stemmed from the character of urban life. During the nineteenth century, a revolution in education took place in the Western world as industrializing nations established popular instruction as a policy of state. The federal government encouraged education through land grants and created a Bureau of Education in 1869, but its function was to provide information rather than to supervise. State governments limited themselves to providing funds and enabling legislation. Municipalities, then, were the major actors in school management, which resulted in differences of emphasis in philosophy and organizational structure among city systems. Important areas of agreement and conformity were achieved, however, through widespread imitation facilitated by a national discussion on the educational needs of urban Americans in pedagogical journals and official reports. The leading figures in this discussion were state commissioners and city superintendents such as Henry Barnard of Connecticut and Rhode Island, Calvin Stowe of Ohio, Horace Mann of Massachusetts, John Philbrick of Boston, and William Torrey Harris of St. Louis.

Harris, a transplanted Connecticut Yankee and Yale dropout, migrated to St. Louis in the late 1850s to make his fortune; he eventually became one of the most articulate theorizers and practitioners of urban education. Frustrated in business, he turned to teaching and became superintendent of what developed into one of the nation's largest, most innovative, and most imitated systems. Many of Harris's ideas grew in response to the necessity to train children to adapt to urban civilization. His was not an abstract vision; it was the result of personal observation. Like other officials, Harris had witnessed the creation of large numbers of cities of unprecedented size: St. Louis doubled in population every decade between 1830 and 1870; Chicago barely existed in 1830 but reached her first million in 1890; New York surpassed most European capitals by 1860; and spectacular urban booms occurred in virtually every portion of the country. Harris foresaw that the urban movement signaled the beginning of a new epoch in the history of society and concluded that educators must adjust the school to the new social order.

The inculcation of an urban discipline was the primary objective, an emphasis, Harris noted, which distinguished the emerging modern urban school from its rural counterparts, particularly the one-room school-house:

> Wherever any considerable collection of educational material is got together, the broad contrast between the spirit and methods of city schools and those of the country begins to make its appearance. . . . But the most important difference between country and city schools appears in the discipline. In the small community, where individuals are comparatively isolated, discipline is of little significance. In the large community, where each individual is brought into close relation to his fellows, and has to act in combination with them, if he acts at all, discipline is quite essential, and must be carried out with great minuteness. The great lesson of civilization is to learn how to combine with one's fellow-men.

Seven virtues formed the basis of the school's discipline: punctuality, regularity, perseverance, earnestness, justice, truthfulness, and industry. All promoted social conformity and the production of good and functional citizens, but punctuality and regularity received the most emphasis. Harris explained that such concern stemmed from a realization that precise interaction among people was necessary for the viability of an urban-industrial society, and that "in a civilization that is every year becoming more complex and more dependent upon combination of the individual with the whole of society, punctuality becomes a moral issue."

Although attention to the movements of the clock had been of major concern in American culture since at least the time of Poor Richard, the discipline of time took on a new significance in the modern context. Because the uncompromising mechanics of life in the industrial society "fix the times for the minor affairs of life with absolute precision," Harris explained, "in *the age of productive industry* . . . there is one general training requisite for the generations of men who are to act as directors of machinery, and of business, that depends on it—this training is in habits of punctuality and regularity." In contemporary society machines can not wait for men; men must conform to the movements of the machine.

Such concern for discipline often led schoolmen to undesirable excesses. Harris admitted, for example, that it was "a notable fact that the American public schools always lay more stress on discipline than on the speedy acquirement of knowledge." Henry Barnard believed that schools should be concerned "not so much with their children's intellectual culture, as the regulation of the feelings and dispositions, the extirpation of vicious propensities." Barnard foresaw terrible consequences to the child if proper discipline, particularly punctuality, were not strictly enforced: "A disgust to study and the school, follows his loss of self-respect; habits of truancy are acquired, and by and by he is turned out upon society, a pest and a burden, a prepared victim of idleness, vice and crime." As a consequence of this attention to the clock, mid-nineteenth century school reports carried large sections of tables and statistics, often carried out to the second and third place after the decimal point, describing success in the war against tardiness and irregular attendance.

Discipline was not only a desirable moral value but an organizational necessity. Builders of public school systems had an overriding fear of chaos and disorder. The magnitude of the problem can be appreciated by realizing that systems grew proportionately more rapidly than cities, adding thousands of students in a year and tens of thousands in a decade. In addition, over a period of a generation or two, they came to employ hundreds of teachers annually and to manage funds and property valued in the millions of dollars. Aside from such organizations as modern armies and large-scale manufacturing enterprises, there was no precedent for institutions of such size. Moreover, like Harris, "professional" educators were often men of letters with good intentions but with little or no administrative experience. Searching for appropriate models, they turned to the example of the modern factory and the wisdom of contemporary businessmen.

In their drive for efficiency—a key word among nineteenth century schoolmen—they universally rejected the one-room schoolhouse as incompatible with both the organizational needs and the purposes of urban education. Instead, they introduced a graded and standardized curriculum, the district system, normal schools to train professional teachers, and a uniform school architecture.

The district plan, which originally carried no connotations of racism and exclusion, permitted greater control over the size of each school's population, minimized confusion over records, and discouraged pupils from changing schools merely out of disaffection with a particular teacher (the job of keeping track of students was difficult enough without allowing free movement among schools). Efficiency also demanded a graded and standardized curriculum so that educators and parents could predict the nature of instruction in the system's hundreds of schoolrooms. In effect, these reforms aimed at establishing and controlling an educational assembly line that embraced the entire city and which would turn out, according to schedule, a standardized product. One superintendent described the vision: "The program of one school shall be the program of all, the same grade shall recite in the same study at the same hour all over the city."

The metaphor of the factory carried over to the training of teachers, a task which urban systems began to assume during the 1850s. Faced with the prospect of ever-increasing enrollments, city schools could not rely on the haphazard system of supply which characterized rural America. The new curriculum reforms demanded instructors trained to teach approved subject matter in a unique fashion at a particular time. By way of explaining the need for a body of professional teachers, educators constantly alluded to the successful operation of the principle of "division of labor" by the Waltham watchmakers and the Connecticut gunsmiths. To implement educational reforms, as one superintendent put it, well-trained workmen were needed who would enable the schools to function like "some of the large manufacturing establishments where each workman has his allotted work to perform upon the article manufactured, and then hands it over to another and so on until it is finished."

All that was needed to complete the package of efficiency reforms were appropriate facilities. Since many of the classes had been conducted in converted homes, shops, churches, and even bars, it seemed essential to build structures suitable to uniform class size and accepted pedagogic procedures. One popular plan called for four equal classes on a floor equipped for 224 pupils. Thus, schoolhouses could accommodate 224, 448, or 672 students, depending on the number of stories. Interestingly, the new science of school building argued for high ceilings to achieve better ventilation and light since most cities suffered from smoke pollution. In school architecture, form followed function; the standardization of buildings reflected the standardization of the curriculum.

Achieving these reforms demanded tighter control over the system. Beginning in the 1850s, the office of superintendent, another term borrowed directly from the factory experience, was introduced in most cities. It was not always an effective solution, since superintendents shared responsibility with school directors. The directors, comparable to today's school board members, had varying degrees of authority and were responsible either to individual wards, to a citywide constituency, or to the officials who had appointed them. Nevertheless, the long-term trend was toward a centralization of power. John Philbrick of Boston stated the bias of professional educators in a famous survey of American city schools in 1885: "The history of city systems of schools makes it evident that in the matter of administration the tendency is towards greater centralization and permanence of authority and that this tendency is in the direction of progress and improvement." To carry out his beliefs that "there is only one best way" and that "the best is the best everywhere," it was imperative to possess sufficient authority.

St. Louis, according to Philbrick, was exemplary as a system that exercised the necessary controls through a powerful superintendency. In a series of articles published in the *Forum* in 1892, however, the muckraking pediatrician Joseph Mayer Rice exposed the dangers of the excessive supervision and discipline which characterized St. Louis. Rice pointed out that teachers worked under the constant pressure of regular citywide student examinations. The teacher directed instruction to obtain the desired results to insure a good rating for herself. As a consequence, Rice revealed, "the unkindly spirit of the teacher is strikingly apparent; the pupils, being completely subjugated to her will, are silent and motionless; the spiritual atmosphere of the classroom is damp and chilly." "Whenever a pupil volunteered to express an idea suggested to him by the recitation," he continued, "he was cut short by some remark as 'Speak when spoken to,' 'Don't talk but listen,' 'You mustn't raise your hand.' " Despite such repressive regimentation, children did learn how to read, write, and cipher, Rice admitted. The method may have been demeaning, but it was effective. Public educators, in a self-fulfilling prophecy, had created a closed system of values which judged itself by its own criteria.

Indianapolis used a more sympathetic method of supervision to produce a learning environment that accommodated noise and motion. Spontaneity was encouraged by personal discussions between supervisors and teachers and through periodic group meetings. The most important forum was the "principals' club," where on each Tuesday evening during the school year, teachers analyzed pedagogical writings and considered topics like "The Rights of the Child in School," "How to Treat Children," and "How to Manage a School So That Its Administration Shall of Itself Enforce Ethical Laws." The objective of these sessions was to help teachers give "such training as shall make self-active, powerful, helpful, beautiful, happy human beings—what we call in our school law 'good citizens' in the best and true sense." Such experimentation and methodology were rare, however, both because they demanded a unique assembly of people and because they were susceptible to institutionalization and standardization. Indeed, as normal schools took over the responsibility of training teachers, amateurism and spontaneity ended. St. Louis, not Indianapolis, pointed the way to the future.

By World War I, aspiring educational administrators received university training similar in many respects to that given future businessmen; both studied Frederick Taylor's principles of "scientific management" and similar topics. Such training further inhibited administrators from resolving the dilemma of implementing mass instruction while allowing for individual needs. Since the turn of the century, there have been persistent efforts to humanize education. Varieties of progressive schools, Montessori societies, university laboratory schools, and private institutions have endeavored to respond to the unique personalities of children in a conscious, explicit rejection of the urban school's regimentation. The great popularity of such contemporary writers as Paul Goodman, A. S. Neil, John Holt, Charles Silberman, and Jonathan Kozol testifies to the continuing concern with public education's enduring insensitivity to the young. More often than not, however, reform has been successful only in limited and controlled environments outside of city systems.

Because they were actively and energetically seeking to attract the largest possible constituency, builders of public schools ultimately responded to social concerns rather than to individual needs. They viewed the education of urban children as a means of creating a powerful and productive community, pointing particularly to the military and economic triumphs of Prussia after the 1860s and to the extraordinary prominence of resource-poor Massachusetts. This result would be effected by the common school, which would bring together children from all economic, ethnic, religious, and later, racial backgrounds, forging them into a disciplined and literate population.

Despite the abundance of pleading and rhetoric, incessant controversy accompanied the schools' growth—controversy not over the ideal of a successful community but over the means through which it would be achieved. Indeed, the common school has never been realized; substantial segments of urban society have always rejected the vision of commonness and have held alternative philosophies of education and the good society. Moreover, the vision itself was not fixed but in a state of dynamic redefinition. In the antebellum period, the public school was described as a charity institution, and it drew largely preteen children from the lower classes, providing only instruction in the three Rs, some geography and history, and group singing. In response to the needs and demands of different economic, ethnic, and racial groups, existing departments were modified, and new ones were created. For example, from the 1850s to the 1890s, systems added high schools which catered to middle-class students, evening schools that attempted to reach immigrants and illiterate adults, foreign-language instruction in primary grades that attracted immigrant children, kindergartens that sought to redeem children from the slums and prepare them for a life of productive labor, manual training classes and vocational schools that trained future industrial workers, and libraries that served the requirements of various professional and cultural societies and the city at large. In sum, the growth of public school systems in cities was a consequence not merely of adding students but of seeking to accommodate discrete constituencies; as such, the public school was a response to the heterogeneity of the urban community.

The struggle of urban systems to include a vast public was hampered by the prejudices of the people they sought to serve. Initially, the notion that public education was a venture in large-scale charity inhibited the participation of both the poor and rich. Nevertheless, educators recognized that the poor had little choice and that the greater challenge was to persuade the wealthy, who had means and influence, to support public education by enrolling their children. In addition to its other purposes, the high school was deliberately introduced to attract this constituency. While theoretically it was open to all, in practice through the 1890s only those who could afford to withhold their children from the labor market and who had a sense for the value of higher schooling made use of it. The ending of class prejudice against public schools and the democratization of the high school finally occurred at the beginning of the twentieth century.

This victory for the common school idea was short-lived. School systems which depend mainly on local taxation, primarily the property tax, prospered only as long as the middle class was involved. During the past few decades, the political and social fragmentation of the metropolis has resulted in a multitude of school systems with unequal financial capacities. The impoverishment of central-city schools has occurred simultaneously with the establishment of often lavishly maintained suburban systems. For example, between 1940 and 1965 the population of metropolitan Chicago grew from 4.5 to 6.5 million, but only 3 percent of this growth took place in the city. This small increase should have occasioned little difficulty, as the city schools had an extensive plant and a well-established system. But these years also witnessed the exodus of about 600,000 middle-class whites and the influx of 700,000 poor blacks; money and education flowed out of the city as poverty and its culture moved in.

Such population redistribution has resulted in severe educational inequities. Wealthier suburbs spend about $1,000 per child for education; about half that amount is spent in central cities. Moreover, suburban schools may have seventy professionals per thousand students, whereas their counterparts in the slum have difficulty obtaining forty per thousand. Attempts to reduce these inequities are presently proceeding through the courts. In August 1971, in *Serrano* v. *Priest*, the California Supreme Court declared that local taxation as the prime support for public education was unconstitutional, pointing out the inherent discrimination of the traditional system: "Affluent districts have their cake and eat it too; they can provide a high quality education for their children while paying lower taxes. Poor districts, by contrast, have no cake at all." The necessity of finding alternative means of financing has become an urgent urban problem, as the inner-city schools of Philadelphia, Newark, Gary, Independence, and a host of other cities face the possibility of closing their doors.

A further challenge to the common school idea has come from sectarian education, which has grown significantly more influential, particularly in the last generation. This is especially true of Catholic schools, which in 1965 enrolled about 14 percent of the nation's students in 300 institutions of higher learning, 2,500 high schools, and 10,000 elementary schools. Until growth was checked in the late 1960s by the need to pay increasing numbers of lay teachers, Catholic schools expanded continuously in the twentieth century; they counted 5 percent of the nation's precollegiate students in 1900, 7 percent in 1940, and 14 percent in 1965. In cities with a higher percentage of foreign-born residents, the figures have always been higher. At the end of the First World War, for example, Catholic schools enrolled 19 percent of Baltimore's school population, 25 percent of Chicago's, 37 percent of Buffalo's, and 45 percent of the total in Lawrence, Massachusetts. This defection from public schools was especially significant because— unlike that in other countries—it was a voluntary action supported privately rather than by government subsidies. Moreover, if public funds become available, it is possible that parochial schools would continue to increase their share of the nation's students.

Sectarian opposition to public education initially came from Protestants as well as Catholics. The General Convention of the Episcopal Church in 1838 strongly criticized the idea of common education and advocated the establishment of Episcopal parochial schools. Similarly, the Presbyterian General Assembly as early as 1799 took issue with the "vain and pernicious philosophy" of public schools and declared in 1811 that education is "the legitimate business of the church, rather than of the state." Through the 1840s, the New Jersey Synod adopted resolutions demanding support for parochial schools, claiming that denial of funds was "unjust and tyrannical." Not until the 1870s did Episcopalians and Presbyterians give up attempts to secure public support for denominational education.

Of all Protestant groups, the Lutherans provided the most consistent and successful counterattack. During the colonial period they established between 340 and 400 schools, laying the basis for separate systems. In Pennsylvania alone they maintained over 200 schools in the 1820s and were among the major opponents of public education. In the West, the Missouri Synod established in 1840 the rule that *Schulamt* (teaching office) and *Predigtamt* (preaching office) be founded concurrently. This rule was honored, and by 1856 the synod counted 125 congregations and 119 schools.

Had the United States continued as a largely Protestant nation, it is possible that denominational education would have received the support it has in other modern nations. However, the influx of 35 million immigrants between 1820 and 1920, a large proportion of whom were Catholic, placed the debate over state support in a new framework. The result was the unification of most Protestant groups behind public schools and the casting of nonsectarianism in a Protestant mold that aggravated relations with Catholics.

The first major crisis that foreshadowed enduring conflict occurred in New York in 1840. Bishop John Hughes led a fight against the Public School Society, which expended public revenues for "non-sectarian" schools offering instruction in Protestant prayers and songs and the King James Bible; similarly, the Public School Society used textbooks that alluded to "deceitful Catholics" and referred to the Pope as the "man of sin, mystery, of iniquity, son of perdition." Unable to obtain support for Catholic schools, Hughes joined forces with Governor William H. Seward and other liberal Protestants in proposing a bill to make education thoroughly secular. Evidently a majority of Protestants felt that secularism was undesirable, because the proposition lost in an election over the issue in 1841; Protestants celebrated their victory by mobbing Irishmen in the streets and breaking windows in Bishop Hughes's home. In Philadelphia in 1844, the same ancient prejudices occasioned a more violent outbreak. Objecting to the proposed teaching of the Catholic Bible, the Douay Version, Protestant clergymen incited their congregations against Catholics. The consequence was a riot which resulted in twenty dead, about sixty wounded, and the burning of Irish homes. Such outbreaks were characteristic expressions of the nativist sentiment that made the antebellum period one of the most violent in the history of the American city.

Controversy continued after this period, although generally without such violence. In the 1870s, for example, Catholics attempted to establish a voucher plan through which the state would meet the tuition requirements of schools that students selected. In addition, Catholics often led attempts to block increases in the tax rate. Occasionally, a compromise was worked out, as in New York, where the state underwrites limited activities in parochial schools. On the other side, nativist groups tried to discredit parochial institutions and to force Catholics and other foreign-born students into public schools. Thus, at the meetings of the National Education Association in 1890, Archbishop John Ireland had to preface his remarks with the statement that he had never been un-American or an enemy of public education. This tradition of suspicion culminated in a movement during the 1920s to close parochial schools. Such laws were actually passed in a number of states; it required Supreme Court action to overturn the Oregon law in *Pierce* v. *Society of Sisters* (1925) and thus to guarantee the legitimacy of denominational education.

There have also been battles over the propriety of teaching German, Gaelic, Italian, and other foreign languages in public schools. German, for example, was offered in many midwestern cities during the nineteenth century in order to attract or, perhaps, to seduce large German minorities from private systems. This tactic was successful. In St. Louis in 1860 only one in five Germans chose public schools over their own; by 1880, this proportion was reversed as four out of five chose the city system. In Cincinnati a separate public school system served German children. During the First World War, as a result of mass hysteria against Germans and a narrow nationalistic fervor, such concessions ended.

The problem of accommodating ethnic and religious diversity in a society which honors the ideal of pluralism but at the same time is dedicated to assimilation has naturally led to conflict, compromise, and estrangement. Public educators who believed that their mission was to employ the schools as instruments of social order and amalgamation have tended to ignore or criticize those who objected to enforced uniformity. As a consequence of the failure to resolve these tensions, the education of urban children has been a parallel venture between public and private institutions, thus frustrating the hope that public schools would serve to bring together the city's diverse populations.

The unjust treatment of blacks has been another area of continuing failure for public schools. The politics of education generated by pluralistic cities has meant that the apportionment of a system's resources and attention to special requests of particular interests depend on the capacity of individual groups to mobilize favorable community sentiment and apply pressure on school boards. Since blacks suffered from widespread hostility and did not command sufficient weight in community politics, they were relegated to separate, substandard facilities. Except in some northern cities, primarily in Massachusetts, their right to education was not formally acknowledged until the Civil War and Reconstruction era. Even then, only rarely were Negroes provided with equal educational opportunities and integrated schools. In response to discrimination, blacks began a tradition of protest that usually took the form of agitating through petitions and public meetings. Sometimes, as in the case of Alton, Illinois; Springfield, Ohio; East Orange, New Jersey; and a host of other northern cities between the 1890s and 1920s, they organized school boycotts.

With the black exodus to the North in the twentieth century and the growth of large Negro ghettos, the district school plan, originally organizational in purpose, worked to separate black and white children, even in cities where integration was legal. The much-heralded 1954 Supreme Court decision which reversed the separate and equal doctrine could accomplish little in the racially divided metropolis. In fact, the century-old pattern of segregation and attendant inequality reflects not only geographic realities, which can end only through busing or large-scale redistricting, but also attitudes of school boards and of whites in general. As Jonathan Kozol's devastating *Death at an Early Age* reveals, schools systematically destroy the pride and personality of black children. Moreover, since the turn of the century, black writers have questioned the value of good education because black graduates were still denied satisfactory employment. In the face of such persistent degradation and animus both inside and outside the system, many blacks have rejected the promises of common education. Turning to decentralization, they seek to take control of local schools and, in effect, to accomplish within the public school system what other groups have done by maintaining separate institutions.

The problem of dealing justly with blacks points to a fundamental limitation on the schools' capacity to realize their stated mission of building a more democratic and open society. Reflecting the racial, ethnic, religious, and class divisions that aggravate the city, schools cannot by themselves overcome community hostilities. The tensions that shape urban politics also necessarily form educational policy. As the recent spate of teacher strikes, student unrest, and struggles of dissidents for control suggest, the schools are part of the social problem, not the answer to it.

Educational reform, therefore, has traditionally been part of broader programs of social and political action. In the antebellum period, for example, many proponents of the common school idea participated in the temperance movement, in rehabilitation efforts aimed at juveniles and prisoners, in abolitionism, and in local and national politics. During the Progressive period, the same people who fought for controls on rampant capitalism, to secure the rights of labor, and to create a better environment for the urban poor advocated changes in the curriculum and management of the system to produce a more humane and democratic society. Similarly, the struggle for control over local boards and redirection of the curriculum, particularly through the introduction of minority studies, is part of a program of contemporary radicalism which recognizes both the significance of education and its role in reforming the whole of society. From Plato, Thomas More, and Rousseau to nineteenth and mid-twentieth century communitarians, education has been an integral part of utopian planning.

Education can be used not only as an instrument of reform but as a means of maintaining the status quo. From the 1830s through the present, some have feared that an untutored citizenry or a citizenry schooled in alien and wrong ideas could be dangerous to public order. Through laws which provided that English could be the only language of instruction, through the introduction of classes in civics, American government, and history to inculcate faith in the American system, through the prohibition against teaching Darwinian biology, and through the exclusion of "dirty" books and radical literature, many conservatives have tried since the 1830s to use the schools to instill confidence and trust in established institutions and mores.

Therefore, throughout the history of public education, men of different vision and interest have contended for control over the established system or for power to change it. In antebellum New York, for example, a small group of wealthy directors, operating out of a sense of noblesse oblige, arrogated to themselves the task of educating the poor through the Public School Society, the forerunner of the city's present system. They maintained class education both in organization and in content. Among the complaints leveled against the society were its unresponsiveness to the mass of citizens, to religious differences, and to parental wishes and prerogatives and its tendency to blunt the aspirations of the lower class for social mobility. Class antagonisms and religious resentment united working-class groups and Catholics, who proposed alternatives ranging from overturning the leadership of the society to decentralizing decision making and asserting the principle of local control. The question of who governs has always been enmeshed in the struggle over structure because of the recognition that bureaucratic forms are not neutral. Opposing factions have frequently argued the issues of local control versus centralization as well as the relative weight of professional judgments and of community preferences. In addition to pressures from outside the schools, teachers and administrators have become resistant to change because they fear loss of privileges and job security.

The persistence of conflict not only reflects antagonisms within the urban community but the significance Americans attach to education. Schools are worth fighting over. Having assumed enormous importance, they consume vast amounts of money and demand an ever-increasing involvement from the young. Whereas in the nineteenth century the average city child attended school from three to six years, in the mid-twentieth century twelve or more years of attendance is common. This growing commitment results from the recognition that in modern societies schools are the chief agents of socialization and the most important avenue to upward mobility. The individual and society depend on formal education in a way that was not imagined only a few generations ago and look to it as a means of improving the quality of life and attaining wealth. With so much at stake, education necessarily continues as a matter of paramount concern. As Americans assess their institutions, they can learn from the exaggerated hopes of the past and the jeremiads of the present. Schools can accomplish a great deal. City schools, public and private, made urban America one of the first universally literate societies in history and assisted in adjusting millions of individuals to modern life. If they are to do more, particularly in the area of social relations, widespread support of change is required. Schools can serve us well, but they can only lead where we are willing to go.

Selected Bibliography

The study of urban education is an emerging area of research that draws on the work of historians of American education as well as on conventional scholarship. A good beginning for the colonial period is Lawrence A. Cremin, *American Education: The Colonial Experience, 1607–1783* (New York, 1970). Studies which develop the changing relationship between schooling and other institutions during this period are Bernard Bailyn, *Education in the Forming of American Society* (Chapel Hill, N.C., 1960), and Philippe Ariès, *Centuries of Childhood: A Social History of Family Life* (New York, 1965). Good syntheses on the dynamics of public education in the nineteenth century are Lawrence A. Cremin, *The American Common School: An Historic Conception* (New York, 1951); Michael B. Katz, *The Irony of Early School Reform: Educational Innovation in Mid-Nineteenth Century Massachusetts* (Cambridge, 1968); and Rush Welter, *Popular Education and Democratic Thought in America* (New York, 1962).

Studies by and about leading educators should be consulted, especially John S. Brubacher, editor, *Henry Barnard on Education* (New York, 1931); Kurt F. Leidecker, *Yankee Teacher: The Life Story of William Torrey Harris* (New York, 1946); and Merle Curti, *The Social Ideas of American Educators* (Paterson, N.J., 1959).

Of special value are contemporaneous histories and analyses such as John D. Philbrick, *City School Systems in the United States* (Washington, D.C., 1885); Joseph Mayer Rice, *The Public School System of the United States* (New York, 1893); and Nicholas M. Butler, editor, *Education in the United States: A Series of Monographs Prepared for the United States Exhibit at the Paris Exposition 1900* (2 vols., Albany, N.Y., 1900).

Two important studies of the Progressive period and Progressive education are Sol Cohen, *Progressives and Urban School Reform: The Public Education Association of New York City, 1895–1954* (New York, 1964), and Lawrence A. Cremin, *The Transformation of the School: Progressivism in American Education, 1876–1957* (New York, 1961).

The problems of public education in a pluralistic society have received considerable attention. Two provocative essays are David B. Tyack, "Onward Christian Soldiers: Religion in the American Common School," in Paul Nash, editor, *History and Education: The Educational Uses of the Past* (New York, 1970), and Timothy Smith, "Protestant Schooling and American Nationality, 1800–1850," *Journal of American History*, 53 (March 1967), 679–95.

For studies on religious groups consult Andrew Greeley and Peter Rossi, *The Education of Catholic Americans* (Garden City, N.Y., 1968), and Walter H. Bek, *Lutheran Elementary Schools in the United States: A History of the Development of Parochial Schools and Synodical Educational Practices and Programs* (St. Louis, 1939).

Although there is not yet a satisfactory treatment of black education in the North, there is much good work on blacks in the South, especially Horace Mann Bond, *The Education of the Negro in the American Social Order* (New York, 1966), and Henry A. Bullock, *A History of Negro Education in the South: From 1619 to the Present* (New York, 1970). A popular study of the problems of contemporary black children in northern ghettos is Jonathan Kozol, *Death at an Early Age* (Boston, 1967).

An excellent study of the bureaucratization of schools is Raymond E. Callahan, *Education and the Cult of Efficiency: A Study of the Social Forces That Have Shaped the Administration of the Public Schools* (Chicago, 1962), and for a political perspective on many of the same problems see Michael B. Katz, *Class, Bureaucracy, and Schools: The Illusion of Educational Change in America* (New York, 1971).

Useful studies on inequalities in contemporary education are James B. Conant, *Slums and Suburbs* (New York, 1951), and Arthur Wise, *Rich Schools, Poor Schools: The Promise of Equal Educational Opportunity* (Chicago, 1967). There is a growing popular literature of criticism on present education, among which are David Rogers, *110 Livingston Street* (New York, 1968), and Charles E. Silberman, *Crisis in the Classroom: The Remaking of American Education* (New York, 1968). For an excellent anthology on the crisis in urban education see Alvin Toffler, editor, *The Schoolhouse in the City* (New York, 1968).

Scholarly articles on education can be found in most historical and educational journals, especially the *American Quarterly* and the *History of Education Quarterly*. In addition, the *Saturday Review of Education* contains good reviews on current literature and articles on present problems.

Religion and the City

Jacob H. Dorn

An old and influential assumption in America holds that "the city" is inherently inimical to religion. This assumption is related to strains of anti-urbanism that have run through numerous facets of American culture, and it can be traced in the thought of both Protestant and Catholic churchmen. Even those who have sought to arouse the churches to undertake singularly urban ministries have often done so with a rhetoric of crisis that reflected fear of the city. No better example of this fear within Protestantism can be offered than *Our Country* (1885), written by Josiah Strong, pastor of the Central Congregational Church of Cincinnati. Strong's book, which catapulted him into national Protestant leadership as general secretary of the ecumenical Evangelical Alliance, sought to awaken the churches to seven great "perils" facing the nation. The first six of these "perils" were immigration, Romanism, Mormonism, intemperance, socialism, and wealth, and most of these converged in the city, the seventh and, in Strong's view, most serious "peril" of all. In a later book, *The New Era, or The Coming Kingdom* (1893), Strong exhibited ambivalence toward the city: "The first city was built by the first murderer, and crime and wretchedness have dwelt in the city ever since, but the city is to be redeemed."

Although occasional voices in the churches have called for a celebration of urban life—for example, Harvey Cox's *The Secular City* (1965)—virtually all segments of Protestantism, at least since the mid-nineteenth century, have viewed the city as a hostile force. As church historian Robert T. Handy puts it, "One of the reasons that city churches long have had difficulties is a stubborn tradition that religion is at home in the country but alien in the city, and that the patterns of the rural church are normative for the religious life." The same point is made by Truman B. Douglass, a denominational executive long active in urban church planning. Deploring "an anti-urban bias which has become almost a point of dogma," Douglass writes that "many leading Protestants genuinely feel that a permanent and deadly hostility exists between urban man and those who are loyal to the Christian faith and ethic; that village ways of life are somehow more acceptable to God than city ways."

The reasons for such a view are complex, but a few salient factors provide a partial explanation. One factor, to which both Handy and Douglass point, is the early success of Protestantism in rural America, especially at a formative stage of development in the early nineteenth century. After the American Revolution, Protestantism faced serious problems—the disruptions of war, the rise of Unitarianism and deism, separation of church and state, and the opening of the trans-Appalachian West—but experienced a marked resurgence. This renaissance was nowhere as remarkable as on the western frontier, where a revivalistic method of recruitment and an individualistic ethos carried the day. This success story in a predominantly rural culture came to stand in sharp contrast to the difficulties encountered in late nineteenth century industrial cities.

In addition, because of the close affinities that this resurgence fostered between Protestant churches and rural culture, Protestantism became infused with many of the personal and social ideals of the countryside. A rural-based pietistic moral code, emphasizing simplicity, sobriety, thrift, and similar virtues, become part of Protestantism's cultural "baggage" as it came to face urbanization. The association between Protestantism and such manifestations of moral coercion as prohibition and Sunday "blue laws" exemplifies religious and cultural values shaped largely in a rural setting. Similarly, Protestantism carried over into the city rural models of social homogeneity, both ethnic and racial, and of personal familiarity, which obstructed the growth of rapport between the churches and city life, with its greater diversity and anonymity. Douglass contends that rural antipathy to urban ways has continued to shape Protestant reactions to the city well into the twentieth century. Pointing to one sample of 1,709 ministerial students, of which only 36 percent came from cities of more than 250,000 population, he concludes that "because of their rural and small-town origins, many ministers bring to their work in a city church a distaste for city ways—a distaste which is the more disabling because it is largely unconscious."

Because Catholicism in America has been preponderantly urban for most of its history, it may be surprising to find Catholic spokesmen expressing fears of the city similar to those of Protestants. We must remember, however, that despite their urban concentration in America, the Irish and German Catholics who poured into the nation in the 1840s and 1850s and many of the "new immigrant" nationalities of the late nineteenth and early twentieth centuries often came from rural societies in Europe; moreover, many priests came from rural homes and were trained in rural seminaries.

To a great extent, the nineteenth century movement to colonize Catholic immigrants in the countryside sought to prevent an erosion of their faith in the cities and to create a rural Catholic population that could continually reinvigorate and supply leadership for the American church. Although he was not altogether negative in his assessment of urban life, Bishop John Lancaster Spalding of Peoria, Illinois, supported colonization on the ground that rural life was more conducive to social stability and Catholic piety. A similar preference for the countryside over the city runs through the thought of such men as Father Edwin V. O'Hara, founder in 1923 of the National Catholic Rural Life Conference, and Monsignor John A. Ryan, one of the Church's most conspicuous advocates of industrial justice and a steady supporter of urban liberalism. Even well into the twentieth century, according to one historian, many churchmen have tended "to concentrate upon resisting the city's impact on the Church, instead of upon developing the Church's impact on the city."

Organized religion has indeed encountered in cities obstacles that are not present, or at least are not as pronounced, in rural areas or small towns. Other institutions have provided greater competition—that is, religious associations have been less able to monopolize social life in the more complex and more specialized urban institutional matrix. The extreme heterogeneity of ethnic, racial, and social class groupings in the cities has also created problems not commonly found in rural areas; in particular, urban residential mobility has made it difficult for congregations based on neighborhood constituencies to survive when the ethnic, racial, or social class character of their neighborhoods has changed radically. In addition, the multifarious social and human needs of urban people have imposed demands on urban religious institutions that go far beyond any such demands on rural religious institutions.

On the other hand, urban religion has enjoyed advantages and exceptional resources. Comparisons made at different times have generally shown that urban churches far outstrip rural ones in income, average size of membership, size and training of professional staff, number and frequency of religious services, physical plant, and number and variety of auxiliary organizations. Moreover, because of the presence of a wide variety of other social institutions in the cities, religious institutions have been able to specialize their functions and to rationalize their operations in ways not usually possible for rural churches. There is also considerable evidence that rural churches, at least Protestant ones, have not been as healthy as the myth of rural religiosity would lead one to expect. Comparatively speaking, urban churches have supplied most of the vitality, innovation, and leadership in American religion since the late nineteenth century. Religious institutions, through major adjustment and accommodation, have been able to sustain a viable existence in the cities.

1

In the colonial period, the church was the central social institution of each of the five villages that became cities by the time of the Revolution. In three of these villages, legally established churches held at least theoretical monopoly of religious life: in Boston, Congregationalist Puritanism; in New Amsterdam, the Dutch Reformed Church; and in Charles Town, the Church of England. In the other two villages, Newport and Philadelphia, no single denomination was legally established, but by virtue of numbers and influence, Quakers predominated. Although apparently only a small minority of the villagers were church members, the churches had extensive influence over the whole village population, an influence that was enhanced by the compactness of the settlements, by the intimate relations between religion and public affairs (especially the churches' functions as custodians of public order), and by the absence of significant competition from other social institutions.

As the villages grew into towns and then, in the eighteenth century, into small cities, two developments of long-range significance increasingly affected religious life. First, through a process which varied in pace and extent from city to city, the monopolies of founding groups broke down, and the cities accepted a variety of religious groups. For example, in Boston, which initially was most strongly committed to religious uniformity, Congregationalists tolerated Anglican, Baptist, and Quaker congregations well before the end of the seventeenth century. Religious competition was not unique to colonial cities—it occurred throughout the colonies, including frontier zones—but in the cities, competing religious groups were closer to each other than elsewhere. Urban religious diversity certainly impeded the perpetuation of social control as envisioned by the founders; it probably also contributed to the eventual disestablishment of legally privileged groups. Yet by bringing various Protestant groups into mutual observation and contact, the urban experience had the seemingly contradictory effect of encouraging early forms of ecumenicity such as the sharing of buildings, union prayer services, and pulpit exchanges.

The second development that affected urban religion was the formation in the eighteenth century of an increasingly variegated institutional network, especially a host of new societies devoted to philanthropy and civic betterment. Some scholars have interpreted this development as an aspect of the secularization that urbanization supposedly fosters. From this perspective, the growth of these societies represented a loss or surrender by the churches of functions they had formerly claimed—in effect, a narrowing of the religious purview through a steady decline in influence over public affairs. In addition, colonial historian Carl Bridenbaugh argues that these new urban institutions represented secularization in the sense of "enticing people to other considerations than the health of their souls." "Breathless absorption with tremendous theological speculations occupied the minds of very few burghers in the eighteenth century," he writes, as these urbanites turned toward nonreligious associations to achieve purely worldly ends.

These interpretations should not be accepted uncritically. Sociologists of religion have devoted considerable attention recently to the concept of secularization, and a number of them (often influenced by Talcott Parsons' work on religion and society) have expressed dissatisfaction with past usage of this concept because of its careless and ambiguous definitions and its frequently normative connotations. In the light of recent sociological literature on secularization theories, it is possible to view the emergence of institutional structures outside of church control as part of the processes of specialization and differentiation in modern societies rather than in terms of a value-loaded word such as *secularization.* The undifferentiated functions that churches performed in rural and village societies naturally came to be shared with new institutions that were called into being for specific ends in the more complex cities, but this does not necessarily mean that churches were narrowing their purview or that new institutions were untouched by religious values. In fact, many philanthropic societies were organized and led by churchmen, and some had denominational origins or backing. A direct stimulus to their founding came from the Great Awakening in the second quarter of the eighteenth century, especially through the intercolonial preaching tours in 1739–40 of the English evangelist George Whitefield, who found large and responsive urban audiences from Charles Town to Boston.

2

In the period from the Revolution to the Civil War, the United States experienced its most extensive territorial growth. And although the churches confronted fundamental issues of internal readjustment under separation of church and state and of external adaptation to rapid social change, their preeminent concern was the Christianization of the West. Eastern urban clergymen such as Lyman Beecher and Horace Bushnell pleaded eloquently for home missionary enterprises to counteract the potential "barbarizing" of western people by their environment. Much of Protestant success in the early nineteenth century West was due to the establishment of stable church life and educational and cultural institutions, but revivalism supplied much of the energy and many of the motifs of this Protestant resurgence.

We misunderstand the nature of revivalism, however, if we equate it solely with frontier camp meetings. Early nineteenth century revivals, sometimes described as a Second Great Awakening, occurred along the settled eastern seaboard as well as in the interior. Their urban phase was more sedate and polished than the frontier phase, but the two phases shared common goals and similar modes of operation. The essential unity of urban and rural revivalism as the accepted strategy for recruitment and revitalization within Protestantism is exemplified by the career of Charles G. Finney. A lawyer who after a dramatic conversion in 1821 devoted his life to preaching and leading evangelical enterprises, Finney began his revivalistic career in the towns of the "burnt-over district" in western New York. In the late 1820s he made a successful transition to larger urban centers, settling for a time in the 1830s in New York City, where a group of prosperous merchants and financiers erected a permanent tabernacle for him.

After the 1830s a great deal of the leadership of Protestant revivalism, and of the moral crusades and benevolent enterprises that revivalism nourished, came from urban pastors and prosperous urban laymen. Other urban pastors supplemented Finney's ventures into the large eastern cities, notably Edward Norris Kirk, who founded the Mt. Vernon Congregational Church in Boston in 1842 and made it into a revival center, and Albert Barnes, pastor for forty years of the First Presbyterian Church of Philadelphia. Especially distinctive of urban revivalism was the system of "new measures," a coherent methodology for mass evangelism worked out by Finney. These "new measures" included the use of vivid colloquial language and a dramatic style of exhortatory preaching, the holding of services at "unseasonable hours" and the occasional practice of "protracting" them for several days or even weeks so that an audience might be "broken down," the inclusion of laymen in prayers or testimony, and the famous "anxious bench" for counseling with seekers. Some of these techniques were also used in rural revivalism, but as a total, integrated system, the "new measures" were essentially urban.

Some urban Protestants were initially suspicious of this form of evangelistic outreach, partly because of the association of revivalism with the excesses of frontier camp meetings at the outset of this Second Great Awakening. By the eve of the Civil War, however, revivalism had been widely accepted in eastern cities and was a more or less continuous feature of Protestant urban activity. The major revivalists were by then predominantly based in cities; urban revivals were more elaborately planned and more efficiently conducted along the lines of business enterprises; and much of the opposition to revivals came from rural and parochial backwaters of the Protestant denominations. The urban orientation of revivalism was underscored by the religious outburst of 1857–58, which began in a series of prayer meetings in New York's financial district and spread quickly through citywide interdenominational meetings in such cities as Brooklyn, Hartford, Boston, Buffalo, and Detroit.

Although there is inadequate statistical evidence to indicate which segments of the mushrooming urban populace were evangelized by revivalism in this period, impressionistic evidence suggests that then as later, revivalists were most successful in reaching native-born Americans of Protestant background, often recent rural migrants to the cities. Revivalism has never been conspicuously effective as a means of winning non-Protestant immigrants, in this instance Irish and German Catholics who were arriving in large numbers in the 1840s and 1850s.

Revivalism was not only a strategy for winning men's souls; it was also a means of indirect social control, in both its urban and frontier phases. In the cities, its strongest lay support came from professional and mercantile groups. Despite their radicalism on issues like slavery, urban revivalists held thoroughly conservative positions on economic issues and on matters of public morality. The essential thrust of their preaching was to encourage conformity to prevailing urban social class arrangements and economic institutions. They might aid urban workers to improve their moral and social positions, largely through the inculcation of individualistic virtues, but they feared class consciousness and particular reform objectives that sprang from the working class itself.

These urban Protestant leaders stopped short of tackling urban social and economic issues that called for more than moral solutions, yet they felt the need to facilitate social control over urban groups that were generally unsusceptible to revivalistic appeals. They thus created an interlocking network of voluntary societies to achieve specific purposes. These societies were frequently led by the same men who sponsored the revivals and were an integral part of the so-called Benevolent Empire of humanitarian agencies that also encompassed movements for antislavery and world peace. Fear of urban disorder partly motivated the founders of the American Bible Society (1816), the American Sunday School Union (1824), the American Tract Society (1825), and the American Temperance Society (1826), each of which grew out of local societies in Boston, New York, or Philadelphia. In their thinking, the propagation of evangelical literature and the institutionalization of moral uplift might prevent lower-class and immigrant disruption.

In some cities, the methods of local societies were innovative and systematic. For example, by 1829 the New York City Tract Society had divided the city's fourteen wards into districts of about sixty families each and had appointed tract distributors to make the rounds of each district once a month. Religious literature was often published in foreign languages and distributed by *colporteurs* who spoke these languages. Protestant philanthropists sometimes went beyond religious indoctrination to create houses of refuge for juveniles, societies to counteract the inroads of a convivial "continental" sabbath, penitent-females' refuges and Magdalen asylums, and facilities to aid the poor. The YMCA was similarly designed to provide wholesome religious influences for the urban newcomer, but it was more enduring as a vehicle of Protestant urban ministry. A British innovation, the first U.S. YMCA was begun in Boston in 1851. Its greatest work was to come after the Civil War, but by the late 1850s it had spread to most large cities, serving as a carrier of the revival of 1857–58.

3

In the late nineteenth century the rise of industrial cities evoked a fascinating and almost incredible variety of patterns of religious life. Since then, virtually every conceivable kind of religious impulse, ideology, and form of organization has appeared in various urban environments. Existing urban churches perceived the nature of their mission in diverse ways and shaped their programs accordingly. New and indigenously urban religions, such as Christian Science and the Salvation Army, appeared on the urban scene. And immigrants to the cities, both native and foreign born, brought distinctive faiths that added to the complexity and richness of urban religious life. Although new religious movements and innovations in religious work have continued to emerge, many of the basic contours of modern urban religion had taken shape by the 1920s. Indeed, many of the trends that appeared between the 1870s and the 1920s are still operative. Because of their generally decentralized structure, the usual absence of hierarchical restraints, and a tradition of lay initiative, Protestant churches exhibited the widest disparities of urban religious activity. For this and other reasons, historians have given a seemingly disproportionate share of attention to Protestantism during the industrial period.

Before the Civil War, Protestant leaders viewed cities with moderate alarm and directed the energies generated by revivalism into selected forms of moral uplift and service to the urban poor without becoming over-whelmed by the massiveness of urban change. In the late nineteenth and early twentieth centuries, the rapid industrialization of the cities, their pro-liferation across the continent and pell-mell physical growth, and their ever greater heterogeneity because of rural in-migration, foreign immigration, and class differentiation combined to produce shock. Although the wealth and leadership of Protestantism became increasingly based in the cities, Protestant churches in this period lost their earlier hegemony over the reli-gious loyalties of urban people. Non-Protestant foreign immigration typi-cally found its locus in eastern and midwestern cities and brought about a fundamental realignment in the religious configuration of the nation. From the beginning of their large-scale immigration in the nineteenth century, Jews and Catholics were much more highly urbanized than Protestants as a whole. But the decline of Protestant hegemony was due also to a serious "leakage" from the major denominations of much of their own native-born constituency. Although late nineteenth century Protestant spokesmen sometimes were more alarmist than they need have been about future pros-pects in the cities, considerable estrangement occurred among both urban-born and rural-born working-class people of Protestant background, who found the elegant worship, the refined preaching, the system of pew rentals, the emphasis on stylish dress and outward decorum, and the impersonality of many urban churches uncongenial. In their analyses of the problems of urban Protestantism, late nineteenth century churchmen often lamented the social class breach that was appearing because of the socioeconomic upgrading of numerous congregations.

Several distinctive religious patterns emerged in industrial cities. One of the most important responses to urbanization and associated problems since the Civil War has been movement from areas of unwanted change. A variety of ecological changes have contributed to removal, or flight, but the most common factor has been radical alteration in the racial, ethnic, or so-cial class composition of the immediate neighborhood. The urban exodus began in the late nineteenth century among Protestants, who recoiled from the influx of southern and eastern European Catholics and of eastern Euro-pean Jews. It has continued in the twentieth century and has broadened to include Catholics and Jews who have moved upward into the middle and upper classes; since the ending of mass immigration from Europe in the 1920s, the most disruptive factor has been residential neighborhood change caused by in-migration of rural whites and blacks.

Examples from the first stages of removal in the nineteenth century in-dicate a desire to preserve the congregation as a socially and economically exclusive entity. In 1860 the Broome Street Reformed Church followed its members northward out of its original neighborhood in New York City; inasmuch as the City Missionary Society began almost immediately to work in the area just abandoned, removal was not because the neighborhood had ceased to merit Protestant attention. Sixteen years later the Washington Square Dutch Reformed Church in New York City voted to disband, in the words of its own records, "owing to the moving away of the class of population in this quarter whose needs are met by such a church."

In the early 1890s, Josiah Strong, one of the earliest Protestant leaders to examine urban religious life with the tools of social science, attempted to measure Protestant strength in cities and found Protestant churches failing to keep pace with urban population growth. A central factor in his explanation was the search for a homogenous style of religious life. He had no high regard for the immigrants' religions, contending in *The New Era* "that a majority of immigrants believe either in a perverted and superstitious form of Christianity or in none at all." Yet he deplored the fact that while in the twenty years before 1888 nearly 200,000 people had moved into New York City below Fourteenth Street, seventeen Protestant churches had moved out, and only one synagogue and two Catholic churches had been built to take their place. Too many Protestants, he wrote, were "under the impression that the church is a kind of religious coterie or 'steepled club,' existing expressly for 'our sort of folks.' " In short, as Strong saw it, the exodus of Protestant churches occurred "not because there are no perishing men all around them, but because the class for which they exist has moved uptown; showing unmistakably that they are class churches."

The desire to maintain congregational (or parish) life along homogeneous socioeconomic lines has not been unique among Protestants, although Protestant churches have been more prone to collapse quickly following the departure of important groups of members. The typical Protestant church's reliance on a high degree of lay participation and dependence on its own financial resources have probably made it more vulnerable to neighborhood membership losses than the Catholic parish. But if sociologist Kenneth Underwood's *Protestant and Catholic* (1957), a study of Holyoke, Massachusetts, in the 1940s, is representative of Catholicism in other cities and in earlier decades, the Catholic parish system has also conformed to a great extent to homogeneous socioeconomic lines. According to Underwood, the Catholic clergy in Holyoke accepted the "one-class parish" as a natural "adaptation of the church to the social structure in the city," and instead of trying to bring different social classes into contact, they sought to minister to men "within their various stations in life." Whatever minor differences may stem from variations in religious policies, the voluntary nature of American religious institutions has tended to bring about the movement of these institutions in accordance with the migratory patterns of their constituents.

Many churchmen in the twentieth century, like Strong in the nineteenth, have been sharply critical of this pattern of removal from the center of the city, sometimes because they have seen it as an escape from the "urban crisis," to which the churches should have contributed their full resources, and sometimes because they have seen it as a betrayal of some normative model of congregational inclusiveness or universality. One of the most strident judgments on the middle-class white Protestant withdrawal has come from religious sociologist Gibson Winter in *The Suburban Captivity of the Church* (1961). In Winter's judgment, flight represents a quest for "insulation" in homogeneous groups following the nineteenth century breakdown of the "communal fabric" of local neighborhoods. His historical analysis is perceptive, except for his somewhat nostalgic evocation of an earlier "communal fabric." It is altogether possible that social homogeneity in congregational life—in short, exclusiveness—has a longer history than Winter acknowledges.

While many congregations have reacted to the modern industrial city by fleeing from it, others have continued to find in the diverse components of the urban population a clientele and resources adequate to a viable existence with only the most modest adaptations to the needs of their neighborhoods, or even no adaptation at all. Thus, a second kind of institutional response, typical of churches in reasonably stable residential or downtown neighborhoods, has been to retain a rather homogeneous constituency, sometimes from the immediate neighborhood and sometimes from both the immediate neighborhood and a broader geographic area, through a strongly traditional program. In the 1920s the interdenominational Institute of Social and Religious Research sponsored a series of studies of urban churches under the supervision of H. Paul Douglass, a churchman and sociologist of religion who utilized a heavily statistical methodology to measure degrees of adaptation to urban influences. In probably the most significant work in this series, *1000 City Churches: Phases of Adaptation to Urban Environments* (1926), Douglass contended that the typical urban church was an elaboration of the rural church. The vast majority of churches in his sample of 1,044 stayed in cities but made little conscious effort to develop a coherent strategy for urban mission. Many churches that made innovations in their programs remained "unconscious of any new principle" of urban ministry, Douglass believed. Essentially, the study showed that sizable segments of major religious bodies have perpetuated themselves without either fleeing cities or fundamentally reconstructing their institutional activities

A third kind of response to industrial cities came from churches that remained in profoundly altered neighborhoods and found a viable existence through means other than essentially traditional programs. The majority, but not all, of these churches have been located in radically transformed downtown areas. As historian Robert D. Cross puts it, they suddenly found themselves "with a conspicuous location, an equally conspicuous loss of neighborhood membership, and consequently a pressing need to redefine their mode of preaching to the community." They determined to stay where they were despite the outward movement of their original constituencies, often from a sense of historical tradition and prestige or of corporate responsibility to the community. These downtown churches usually chose one of two options for survival, options not necessarily mutually exclusive.

One option was to seek the continued allegiance of a highly stratified segment of the metropolitan community, usually a business and professional elite; churches did so by becoming "cathedrals" of their respective denominations, distinguished for elegant music, elaborate worship, and eminent clergymen. As "Old First" churches, they enjoyed sufficient financial and leadership resources to prosper in the face of profound changes in their immediate environments. As H. Paul Douglass saw it, they substituted a "new and distinctly urban basis of human association," one based on the accessibility provided by urban transportation, for "that of the original church group based on proximity." Sometimes these churches experimented with new ways of reaching urban people, either by drawing them to the downtown church itself or, more commonly, through mission chapels. Because of a strain of paternalism running through such endeavors, the chapels have not been very successful among the wage earners to whom they have been directed.

A second option taken up by some strategically located churches has been to sponsor specialized ministries to disadvantaged urban groups. In the late nineteenth and early twentieth centuries, such ventures were commonly called *institutional churches*. Douglass identified them as "socially adapted" churches, and Cross has called them "reintegrations." For Douglass, what distinguished them from other forms of urban adaptation was that they sought to serve "peculiar constituencies, frequently those laboring under social handicaps." Their programs might include kindergartens or day nurseries, clinics and dispensaries, English and civics classes, employment agencies, and the like; in fact, some had such elaborate plants and services that they were almost indistinguishable from the social settlements of progressive reformers. St. George's Episcopal (New York City), Grace Baptist Temple (Philadelphia), Congregationalist Berkeley Temple (Boston), and Fourth Church (Hartford) stood out in the 1890s for their charismatic pastoral leadership and dramatic numerical growth. Found in all the major denominations, institutional churches seemed to hold the answers for Protestant work in the cities.

Institutional churches were often inspired by the Social Gospel movement that flourished before the First World War, a movement which church historians generally consider the most concerted effort in American Protestantism to deal realistically with the growth of industrial cities. Many spokesmen for the Social Gospel moved beyond the moralistic and individualistic outlook of pre–Civil War Protestants to accept an environmentalist interpretation of urban ills. Through their institutional churches and similar forms of ministry, advocates of the Social Gospel sought out the urban poor for service rather than simply for social control, thus drawing together the poles of the urban social class spectrum. A man such as Washington Gladden, pastor from 1882 to 1918 of the First Congregational Church of Columbus, introduced institutional programs in his own church, started a settlement house, served a term on his city council, supported the trade union movement, and advocated public welfare and unemployment programs. Much of the Social Gospel's concern about urban life became institutionalized early in the twentieth century in denominational and interdenominational agencies created to handle urban ministries and related kinds of social service.

Institutional churches have not become the panacea for Protestant urban ministry that many expected at the turn of the century. Their cost of operation was one obstacle to widespread imitation. In addition, and perhaps of crucial importance, they typically reflected ambiguities growing out of ministry to dual constituencies. The original constituency, made up of parishioners with strong loyalties to a historically distinguished church and with money to support social services, rarely became integrated socially with the needy to whom services were offered. As Cross notes, usually the "transformed" downtown church, which appealed to an urban elite through sophisticated worship and preaching, undertook "reintegration" through institutional services to a fundamentally altered neighborhood population. It would have been unlikely for these services to become more than appendages to established activities of such churches.

A fourth kind of response to the industrial city, and an infinitely diverse one, was the attempt of newcomers to the city to recreate familiar patterns of religious life they had known in the country. In his classification of "modes of churchly response" to urban environments, Cross speaks of "transplantations," by which he means both the "ethnic churches" of foreign immigrants and the "village churches" of rural in-migrants. These "transplanted" churches merit special attention because of the light they shed upon the intriguing relations between religion and urbanization.

For European immigrants—whether Jews, Catholics, Lutherans, or others—religious institutions not only filled spiritual needs but also served as custodians and preservers of the language, customs, and general cultural heritage of the ethnic group. This latter function was clearly at stake for German and Scandinavian Lutherans, who insisted on setting up separate nationality synods in America. It was also at stake for the German, Polish, Italian, and other Catholic immigrants who resisted the parochial leadership of the Irish-dominated (and hence English-speaking) American clergy. Some of the most serious internal struggles in late nineteenth century Catholic history pitted recently arrived immigrant groups against an Americanized clergy that was alien to ethnic cultures. Although the Catholic hierarchy never abandoned as normative the principle of the territorial parish in favor of national parishes, patterns of immigrant settlement often produced ethnically unified parishes in which Old Country patterns could be reestablished. For Jews, the tensions between eastern European Orthodox immigrants and the highly Americanized German Reform leadership of Jewish institutions represented the desire to reproduce intact not only religious patterns but also a traditional Yiddish culture that had grown out of the ghettos of Poland and Russia.

For rural, native-born Protestants, the twentieth century proliferation of urban sects and cults and the rapid growth of Pentecostalism, "holiness" churches, and varieties of Fundamentalism can be understood, at least in part, as a reaction to their inability to find a remembered kind of fellowship in the adapted denominational churches of the cities. Although historians have shown that some of these movements have not been restricted in their appeal to rural-born people, much of their continuing dynamism certainly seems to rest on the movement from country to city. In an essay in Isabel Leighton's *The Aspirin Age, 1919–1941* (1949), journalist Carey McWilliams tells of visiting the Angelus Temple of Los Angeles in 1938 to hear the dazzling founder of the Four-Square Gospel movement, Aimee Semple McPherson. When Sister Aimee "asked the audience how many had ever lived on a farm," he recalls, "the entire audience stood up." When he returned to Muncie, Indiana, in the mid-1930s to write *Middletown in Transition* (1937), sociologist Robert S. Lynd found that two-thirds of the new churches added since 1925 were "Spiritualist, Holiness, Apostolic Faith Assembly, and so on"; he attributed this growth to the arrival of large numbers of casual workers from the southern mountains.

Scattered studies of urban sects seem to confirm the suggestion of Robert Lee, a sociologist of religion, that membership in sects may be a means by which new migrants to cities, experiencing "culture shock" in unfamiliar environments, attempt to "recover a sense of security and find supportive group relationships." In short, sects may be forms of initial social reorganization for in-migrants. In his study "Store-Front Religion," G. Norman Eddy, a professor of human relations, found that such groups provide "(1) a sense of status to the member, (2) assurance of spiritual healing, (3) opportunity for emotion expression," and that they "appeal to those classes and castes of our population which are socially and economically insecure."

And Father Renato Poblete and sociologist Thomas F. O'Dea, after studying ex-Catholic Puerto Rican participants in ten store-front churches in New York City, concluded that sect membership represented a "quest for community in the face of the loss of more traditional social structures and the impersonalization of modern American urban society." This quest was reflected in the typical statement of one participant: "I used to go to the Catholic Church, there nobody knew me. . . . Now in my church they call me sister."

Interpreters of black urban sects, cults, and store-front churches have stressed similar themes. For blacks, who are overwhelmingly Baptist and Methodist in the rural South, the formation of divergent groups has been almost entirely an urban phenomenon and one whose roots can be traced to the mass migrations since the First World War. According to the pioneering students of black churches, Benjamin E. Mays and Joseph W. Nicholson, established black city churches, which represented the adaptation to the city of rural Baptist and Methodist traditions transplanted earlier under less disruptive conditions, were unable to meet the religious and social needs of newcomers, who were seeking warmth, personal attention, and an opportunity for free expression. Building on the work of Mays and Nicholson, Arthur H. Fauset contends in *Black Gods of the Metropolis* (1944), a study of five northern urban cults, that the growth of cults among northern urban blacks was a response to psychological needs created by the adjustment of blacks to urban modes of life and unfamiliar racial mores. For rural-oriented blacks living in cities under more "complicated and nerve-racking pressures," Fauset argues, the cult offered assurance that "they will be aided not only in their efforts to support their customary burdens, but that in addition they will be equipped to measure arms with the white man." More recently, the distinguished black sociologist, E. Franklin Frazier, writes in *The Negro Church in America* (1964) that "the 'storefront' church represents an attempt on the part of the migrants . . . to re-establish a type of church in the urban environment to which they were accustomed."

Transplanted religious movements experienced radical alterations in outlook when urbanization facilitated the socioeconomic and educational upgrading of their constituents and thrust them into contact with a pluralistic religious situation. Val B. Clear, the historian of the Church of God (Anderson, Indiana), has traced several remarkable changes in one of the "holiness" denominations born among rural people in the late nineteenth century. Urbanization undermined this denomination's opposition to coffee, tobacco, and alcohol, altered its strategy of "grab-him-by-the-lapel" evangelism, softened its criticism of other Christian groups, and stimulated a search for respectability through more sophisticated worship. Under the impact of urbanization, Clear writes, the church "puts robes on the choir and candles on the altar, divides the chancel, replaces folding chairs with oaken pews, and calls a college-trained minister."

A similar process has occurred in some urban sectors of the Church of the Nazarene, among southern Baptists who have migrated to northern cities in large numbers since the Second World War, and in a variety of Fundamentalist churches of rural origins. Mays and Nicholson also found that as early as 1933, a significant proportion of urban black churches had more elaborate worship, a more variegated program "of the social and community-serving type," a better educated clergy, a more bureaucratized administration, and a higher incidence of "this-worldly" sermons than their rural counterparts. The same forces have lessened previously intense local and ethnic differences among Jews and Catholics. These internal changes have certainly been due in part to the greater educational and socioeconomic opportunities available to at least some rural in-migrants in the cities.

4

Although religion in the cities has continued to manifest several of the patterns described above since the Second World War, some features of the contemporary scene merit separate discussion. As many core cities became increasingly black and poor white in composition, the middle-class components of Protestantism, Catholicism, and Judaism declined within city limits. But the overall strength of the three major faiths within total metropolitan areas remained stable until the 1960s, when a marked slump in membership and attendance occurred. Statistics of church and synagogue membership are quite unreliable, and they say little about the quality or intensity of personal religious belief, but most religious statisticians agree that membership as a percentage of the total population was higher in the 1950s than ever before in American history. All three faiths prospered in the suburbs, especially during the so-called religious revival of the 1950s. Moreover, although both Protestantism and Catholicism in the core cities lost much of their middle-class clientele to burgeoning suburbs, lower-class Protestants from the countryside were arriving in large numbers, and Catholicism was finding new ways of drawing blacks and poor whites.

Rabbi Albert I. Gordon concludes in *Jews in Suburbia* (1959) that among Jews, the most suburbanized of the three major groups, "the synagogue remains the strongest and most important Jewish institution in suburbia." Although noting that suburban Jews have become largely non-Orthodox in their religious ideas and practices (for example, sabbath observance and fidelity to dietary laws), he suggests that *"more* Jews today are turning to the synagogue in search of religious values than has been true since the 1930s." Committed to affirming their Jewishness, they select from their Judaic heritage ceremonies and rituals that strengthen their families and their ethnic identity.

Similar studies of Protestantism and Catholicism in metropolitan areas indicate that urbanization has affected religious values and the functions of religious institutions, but without sounding the death knell for religion as a source of values and identity. Father Joseph H. Fichter's *Social Relations in the Urban Parish* (1954), a study of three urban Catholic parishes in the South, shows that as many as 30 percent of the infants baptized in a normal parish may become "dormant" or lapsed Catholics; of those who do function as parishioners, about 20 percent are "marginal," 70 percent "modal" or "middling," and only 10 percent "nuclear." However, he concludes that "urban Catholic spirituality, while different, is not of a lower grade than its predecessor." Moreover, although for the "modal" parishioners the church is not a "solidaristic social group" cutting across racial, occupational, and class lines, many parish groups "exemplify a high degree of social solidarity."

Gerhard Lenski's sociological study of religion in Detroit, *The Religious Factor* (1961), provides further evidence that urbanization is not obliterating religious loyalties. Not only are religious organizations still vigorous; it is also clear, he argues, "that religion in various ways is constantly influencing the daily lives of the masses of men and women in the modern American metropolis" and through them, "all the other institutional systems of the community." Lenski stresses the function of religious subcommunities in intensifying loyalties, indoctrinating the young, and providing primary personal relationships in "the religiously divided modern metropolis, where individuals are exposed to so many influences which are alien to the spirit of their church."

It is also pertinent to observe a significant change that has occurred, most notably since the 1950s, in the ways that some churchmen seek to deal with the larger issues of urban society. Harvey Cox notes the emergence in all three major faiths of a "new breed" of clergymen who have adopted a style of action different from that of the earlier Social Gospel and its Catholic and Jewish counterparts. He uses urban poverty to illustrate this change. The earlier response to the poor was primarily to dispense a needed service, a humanitarian but somewhat paternalistic approach. In contrast, the new breed, conditioned partly by the churches' loss of social service functions to government, has organized the poor to bring pressure to bear on the institutions that affect them. This might mean organizing a boycott of merchants, a rent strike, or a picket line in front of a welfare office. The new breed, which represents a more activist involvement with the whole gamut of urban political and economic structures, may point to a major reorientation of religious institutions in the cities that would rank in significance with early nineteenth century experiments with revivalism and benevolent social control and with turn-of-the-century social service patterns. Whatever the new activism of our own day means for the future, it is another sign of the ongoing process of revitalization and innovation that has marked American religion in the cities throughout the past.

5

In conclusion, it is apparent that the urban experience has profoundly affected religious forces. Unfortunately, neither historians nor sociologists have explored with sufficient conceptual clarity the precise nature of the impact of urbanization (as distinct from such factors as social class, ethnicity, and race) on religion. However, it is possible to suggest some relationships that deserve further exploration. First, as this essay has contended, it does not appear that urban life has been the threat to religious institutions that churchmen have commonly believed it to be. It is at least questionable that the concept of secularization, whether applied to the narrowing functions of religious institutions or to basic human orientations toward life, is an adequate analytical device for understanding urban influences on religion.

Second, it seems likely that a number of interrelated changes in the mechanics and structure of religious institutions, parallel to changes in other institutions, have resulted from forces in urban society. These changes, which may be described by such terms as *professionalization* and *bureaucratization,* have appeared both in settled congregational life and in such supracongregational religious movements as revivalism. Students of Protestantism, Catholicism, and Judaism have observed a common trend toward specialized training for urban clergymen; toward multiple staffs of persons with well-differentiated functions, organized according to bureaucratic models; and toward significant increases in the proportion of time given by urban clergymen to administrative duties. A similar trend, geared to urban demands for efficiency and functional rationality, has marked the history of revivalism since Charles G. Finney. The heirs to Finney's mantle, Dwight L. Moody in the late nineteenth century, Billy Sunday in the early twentieth century, and Billy Graham in the mid-twentieth century, have moved relentlessly toward complete systematization of the mechanics of revivals, the use of a large staff of experts, and virtually complete control of the elements considered essential for a favorable response to the revivalist's message.

A third conclusion that the literature on urban religion seems to support is that partly because of the heterogeneity of cities, urban religious institutions draw more highly stratified constituencies than rural religious institutions. Comparative studies that demonstrate this difference conclusively are needed, but it is clear that large cities contain a broad range of religious institutions that appeal to particularistic segments of the community. Much of this stratification is along social class lines, but some of it appears to follow more subtle lines such as taste, psychological needs, cultural values, personal and family exigencies, and the like. Urban populations, because of their size and diversity, can create religious communities of like-minded persons.

Finally, urbanization has promoted ecumenicity. The proximity of rival religious groups in the cities, together with political, economic, and cultural factors, has led to interfaith conflict, as in the outbursts of anti-Catholicism during the heyday of the Know-Nothing movement before the Civil War and again with the rise of the nativistic American Protective Association in the late 1880s and 1890s. Yet urbanization has fostered better understanding and cooperation. Urban pluralism has facilitated first-hand acquaintance and has lowered age-old barriers between religious groups. The complexity of urban life, especially its multiplicity of organizations, has also pressed home the need for coordination among religious groups. This latter factor was particularly important in the creation in 1894 of the Open and Institutional Church League and in the formation around the turn of the century of the earliest urban church federations or councils; both movements gave impetus to the birth in 1908 of the Federal Council of Churches, whose initial orientation was preeminently toward urban issues. In recent years, joint Protestant-Catholic-Jewish action in the cities has carried the imprint of mutual trust and the sense of the need for united resources stimulated by the urban experience.

American cities have challenged, altered, and sometimes extinguished religious organizations; American religious organizations, for their part, have helped to humanize the cities. The relationship has been mutually stimulating. This essay has focused primarily on the ways in which the cities have touched religious life; someone might profitably write another to explore the ways in which religion has affected city life.

Selected Bibliography

In addition to the works cited above in the essay, there are numerous historical and sociological studies of particular churches and synagogues, and many histories of individual cities contain sections on religion. By and large, however, the subject of religion and the city badly needs synthesis and sharper conceptualization of uniquely urban influences on religious life. Two anthologies, Robert Lee, *Cities and Churches: Readings on the Urban Church* (Philadelphia, 1962), and Kendig B. Cully and F. Nile Harper, *Will the Church Lose the City?* (New York, 1969), contain useful if sometimes preliminary explorations into the relationships between religion and urbanization by historians, sociologists, and theologians. The former contains essays by Truman B. Douglass, H. Paul Douglass, G. Norman Eddy, Renato Poblete and Thomas F. O'Dea, and Val B. Clear that are used in this essay; the latter contains Robert T. Handy's succinct "The City and the Church: Historical Interlockings."

The following works are sufficiently broad in scope to merit the general reader's attention. The relationship between urbanization and revivalism in the early nineteenth century receives analysis that helps to correct a traditional frontier interpretation of the revivals in Timothy L. Smith, *Revivalism and Social Reform: American Protestantism on the Eve of the Civil War* (New York, 1957). Two important works, Henry F. May, *Protestant Churches and Industrial America* (New York, 1949), and Charles H. Hopkins, *The Rise of the Social Gospel in American Protestantism, 1865–1915* (New Haven, Conn., 1940), cover Protestant responses to a wide range of post–Civil War social issues, many of which arose from urbanization and industrialization. Hopkins's *History of the Y.M.C.A. in North America* (New York, 1951) is a useful case study of an institution that has reflected many of the changes in Protestant conceptions of urban ministry over the last century. Aaron I. Abell's *American Catholicism and Social Action* (New York, 1960) and his introduction to the documents in *American Catholic Thought on Social Questions* (Indianapolis, 1968), like the works by May and Hopkins, range beyond strictly urban influences on religion; his *The Urban Impact on American Protestantism, 1865–1900* (Cambridge, Mass., 1943) focuses more explicitly on religious responses to urbanization. Robert D. Cross, "The Changing Image of the City Among American Catholics," *Catholic Historical Review*, 47 (April 1962), 33–52, surveys Catholic thought on the meaning of urbanization for that religious body. The studies of urban religious adaptations sponsored by the Institute of Social and Religious Research—especially H. Paul Douglass, *1000 City Churches* (New York, 1926), *The Springfield Church Survey* (New York, 1926), and *The St. Louis Church Survey* (New York, 1924), and Mays and Nicholson, *The Negro's Church* (New York, 1933)—are still useful sources of data on patterns of congregational life, although they are somewhat dated in methodology and conceptualization. Robert D. Cross has recently offered a provocative typology of religious responses to urban environments in his introduction to the historical documents in *The Church and the City, 1865–1910* (Indianapolis, 1967).

The Police in the City: A History

James F. Richardson

In recent years, scholars, public officials, and citizens have become increasingly aware of the pivotal importance of the police in urban society. No longer can society take the men in blue for granted; no longer can it assume that only criminals reject police authority or the legitimacy of their role. In an age when all institutions and all forms of authority seemingly are suspect, the police have become one of the most controversial and studied public services.

Much of the discussion has been critical—attacks on police corruption, incivility, and insensitivity to civilians, especially black and Spanish-speaking people, occasional undue and excessive use of force, and indifference or hostility toward civil liberties and constitutional guarantees of due process. The police have defenders—even critics of police performance recognize the importance of many of the services they perform—and politicians play on and respond to the public's fear of crime. While all scholars in the field lament the inadequacies and inaccuracies of crime statistics, almost all believe that the incidence of criminal acts and the prospect of being victimized have indeed risen in recent years. People who are fearful of robbery resent attempts to "handcuff" the police and limit their effectiveness in fighting crime. But whether adding more men or equipment is the best method of controlling crime is a moot question, and policemen should not be considered solely as crime fighters.

Considerable confusion and disagreement currently exist about the proper role of the police in urban society—conflict which has grown out of the checkered history of American police institutions and public attitudes toward them. Those who wish to understand the present must look to the past, but they should not expect to find satisfactory models or answers to current dilemmas.

During the colonial period, Boston, New York, and Philadelphia, like

English cities, relied on citizen initiative to deal with crime and disorder. The cities employed constables to look out for vagrants who might become public charges and to keep men from working on Sunday; they also followed English precedent by establishing night watches to alert citizens to possible fire or riot. For the most part, however, citizens relied on each other to prevent crime and preserve order. Economic and political dislocations, such as those associated with the American Revolution, subjected the social fabric to considerable strain and made such voluntary policing less effective.

The available alternatives were even less attractive. Relations between the British Army and American civilians before and during the Revolution were never good; even Loyalists complained about the behavior of the British soldiers who were occupying New York during the War for Independence. In the political thought of the American revolutionaries, a standing army connoted tyranny, and only the most nervous individuals wanted military garrisons stationed in the cities to preserve order. To many Americans and Englishmen of the eighteenth century, the word *police* raised specters either of a quasi standing army or of a body of snoops and informers that would be every bit as dangerous to liberty as a regiment of fusileers. Freedom and any kind of organized police seemed incompatible.

In London in the eighteenth and early nineteenth centuries, police officers did not receive salaries from the public treasury; rather, they offered their services to victims of crime for a stipulated sum or a percentage of stolen property recovered. Officers received £40 for the arrest of those guilty of serious crimes and often let young criminals go until they had reached their "weight"—that is, until they committed a £40 crime. To earn rewards for the recovery of stolen property, officers cultivated criminals and frequently conspired with them. In short, officers were not public servants; any work they did advanced private interests, their own and those of the civilians who hired them. The elites who set public policy assumed that if all involved pursued their private interest diligently, the public interest would benefit. American cities of the eighteenth and early nineteenth century relied on similar police and watch instruments.

In the decades after 1780, these police arrangements became increasingly unacceptable to articulate Englishmen. British reformers such as Patrick Colquhoun, Jeremy Bentham, Edwin Chadwick, and Sir Robert Peel wanted a public agency that (1) would provide a professional but civilian force for the prevention and suppression of riot and civil disorder; (2) would act to prevent crime as well as to catch criminals and recover property after the event; and (3) would reform and regulate the morals of the people by repressing unacceptable behavior such as public drunkenness. These reformers, aided by military officers who did not want the army involved in suppressing civil disorders, overcame traditional resistance to an organized police, and the London Metropolitan Police Act was passed in 1829. By 1856, Parliament had extended financial aid to police forces who met specified standards in other parts of the nation. England was now a policed society in that it possessed a group of salaried professionals who devoted their working hours to the prevention and detection of crime, the maintenance of order, and the control of unseemly behavior in public places.

These English developments had great influence upon municipal police practice in the United States. American cities experienced rapid and disorderly growth in the 1830s and 1840s. During these decades, the citizens of Boston, New York, Philadelphia, and other cities felt themselves engulfed by a rising tide of theft, robbery, riot, prostitution, and drunkenness. Many diverse groups resorted to violence in the 1830s. Rioting by the unemployed and the hungry and rampaging by restless youth were traditional, but in the 1830s "gentlemen of property and standing" who feared that abolitionist ideas and tactics would subvert established social relationships organized and directed antiabolition mobs. Religious and racial clashes periodically disrupted urban life as the social controls of a stable, essentially deferential society broke down in the face of rapid population growth, the immigration of culturally diverse people, and changing status relationships caused by economic growth and the increasing concentration of wealth.

By the middle of the nineteenth century, the major American cities were large and heterogeneous. Men who worried about the disintegration of deference and social control founded Bible and tract societies, Sunday schools, and benevolent institutions to uplift as well as to relieve the poor. They hoped to restore the social and religious uniformity and the acceptance of the existing order that was characteristic of the homogeneous town. These institutions reached only a limited number of the poor and had apparently even less success in effecting the kind of changes intended.

In this context, the traditional aversion to police seemed outmoded. If crime, disorder, and vice continued to increase despite the best efforts of church, school, and benevolent society, then more formal instruments of social control would be necessary. Thus, propertied and conservative men hoped that organized police forces might restore social cohesion and control in a society that appeared increasingly anarchic. The London Police Act of 1829 provided a model of a preventive police, although in subsequent years there was much talk but little precision in American cities about the meaning of *preventive*. In general, the founders of organized forces expected that by their presence the police would deter people from committing criminal acts, that they would foster the moral reformation of drunkards, and that they would keep street disturbances from becoming major riots.

In practice, American police departments varied considerably from the London Metropolitan Police. American officers were armed early in their history because a society that was committed to widespread ownership and use of guns could not be policed by a group of unarmed civilians in uniform, which was the way the English conceived of their police. The home secretary appointed and supervised the chief administrators of the London force, who in turn maintained a careful check on the exercise of authority by their subordinates. In the United States, the national government would not be involved in the administration of the police department of any city other than Washington, D.C., nor would American conditions and political culture support a bureaucratic police, isolated from the community and political party organizations, as was the case in England. English policemen sought to encourage and enforce moral conformity among all segments of the population; they were not subjected to manipulation by popular control. In London, the commissioners recruited from the countryside, preferring farm boys to native Londoners, who might be too wise in the ways of the city and not so willing to be molded in the image of the "bobby," strong, reserved, and watchful.

Americans relied on popular control rather than careful administrative direction to limit abuse of authority by police. The statutes and ordinances creating American police forces guaranteed that departments would be enmeshed in the partisan politics of their cities. Recruits usually had to be residents of the city for a stipulated length of time before appointment; in New York, policemen had to live in the ward in which they served. Appointments were often for limited terms, with the prospects of a high turnover if the opposition party won the next election. Local politicians intervened frequently and successfully on such matters as appointments, assignments, and promotions. Such cities as San Francisco, Chicago, Cleveland, and Brooklyn had elected heads of police in the mid-nineteenth century as a way of assuring popular control.

In the early years of organized forces, the city council usually governed the police, making policy and controlling all appointments, promotions, and assignments, an administrative pattern which helped keep the police heavily involved in local politics. Beginning in the 1850s, however, New York and other cities established boards to govern the police. The boards varied from separately chosen bodies whose sole function was to oversee the force to ad hoc collections of officials who conducted police affairs in addition to other responsibilities. New York's board from 1853 to 1857 consisted of the mayor and two judges. This movement reflected the greater complexity of urban government and the removal of executive functions from city councils, which became more exclusively legislative bodies. To some extent, the boards increased police professionalism and efficiency by reducing, but not eliminating, democratic control of the police. Another innovation designed to increase police efficiency, authority, and visibility was to put the patrol force in uniform. The New York board introduced the uniform, over policemen's objections, in 1853.

Despite the changes, police behavior followed the dictates of the major political powers in the community rather than the formal dictates of the law. Moralists wished the police to act energetically against prostitutes, gamblers, and saloonkeepers who violated sabbath restrictions, but for the most part, these laws were ignored in cities, which had a large number of transient and cosmopolitan people who did not share the values of rural Protestant America. Rural and small-town Protestants made up a majority of voters of the states and dominated state legislatures. Individuals of similar background also constituted a substantial portion of the urban population, but Catholics and those who were indifferent to religion formed a greater percentage of large cities' population than they did of other areas, and these groups did not subscribe to the Puritan sabbath.

The very social diversity that made conservatives pine for uniformity inhibited any agreement on police functions. Precisely because cities were heterogeneous and therefore seemingly in need of more formal instruments of social control, their governments had difficulty reaching agreement about the proper scope and performance of the police function. If the police acted to suppress Sunday drinking, they cut themselves off from immigrant and working-class populations. If they ignored the law, temperance and sabbatarian forces attacked them as unfaithful to their responsibilities as law enforcers. Different interest groups in the cities fought hard to force the police to operate according to their views and principles.

The inability to agree on policy has left it to the police themselves to determine how they will exercise their discretionary authority. Administrators avoid discussion and the establishment of policy to minimize public controversy and criticism. The result is that individual patrolmen are left to their own devices, and in this vacuum, tradition and the values of the police subculture have long been the major controls over the exercise of authority.

Control of the force was vital to political organizations. The police supervised the conduct of elections, regulated many legitimate as well as illegal enterprises, and constituted a valuable source of patronage in their own right. Throughout the nineteenth century and well into the twentieth, most urban police departments functioned as adjuncts of political organizations rather than as independent agencies. Even when policemen secured good behavior tenure and so were no longer subject to removal after an election, political leaders still determined their occupational futures. Desirable assignments, promotions, and protection against disciplinary action depended more on good relations with local political powers than on impartial and efficient performance of a patrolman's responsibilities. These local political powers were often heavily involved in such activities as liquor dealing and gambling. Police action against bookmakers, faro dealers, and saloonkeepers often served to regulate unwanted competition and to assure prompt payment of required operating fees. Statutes were enforced selectively to serve ends other than upholding the law.

In a number of instances, states took control of local police forces to prevent such corruption and indifference toward vice legislation and to weaken the power of local organizations and local values in police affairs. In New York, for example, the state created a special police district in 1857 to neutralize Mayor Fernando Wood's blatantly partisan and personal use of the police. This action also strengthened the Republican minority in New York City by giving it a preponderant voice in police patronage and affairs. In Chicago during the middle of the century, control of the police shifted dramatically, depending on whether the Republicans or Democrats controlled the state legislature. State governments also controlled police forces for various periods in Boston, Cleveland, Detroit, Kansas City, St. Louis, Baltimore, and New Orleans. States could intervene in such a manner because the cities were the legal creatures of the states and had only those governing powers that state legislatures saw fit to grant. Therefore, it was possible for a state legislature to make fundamental changes in a city's charter or its police department without consulting either the officials or the voters of the city.

At the end of the nineteenth century, reformers demanded an end to excessive state interference, arguing that only if the cities secured the ability to control their own government could they avoid corruption and fix responsibility. State legislatures, dominated by rural interests, lacked sympathy and knowledge of urban conditions, whereas voters of a city under home rule could write a charter appropriate to the needs of the city and thus exercise the kind of watchfulness that would assure honest and efficient conduct of public business. New York State adopted a limited home rule provision in 1894, and Ohio passed one in 1912. Although cities still faced severe restrictions in such areas as taxation and borrowing power, most cities regained control over their police departments. (One of the exceptions was Boston, whose police commissioner was appointed by the governor of Massachusetts until 1962; the governor of New York retains the power to remove the police commissioner of New York City.)

Whether under state or local control, police departments faced difficult problems which can be organized under three main headings: (1) preventing and detecting crime; (2) keeping the peace and preserving order; and (3) providing aid to people in trouble. The first problem, crime control, is difficult even to describe accurately because statistics are notoriously unreliable. In addition, the recent President's Commission on Law Enforcement and the Administration of Justice found that a large number of crimes go unreported because the people involved see no point in reporting burglaries that they know from experience the police will not be able to solve. There is no doubt that the rate of crime—reported and unreported—is rising, although there are some indications that the rate has not always increased. In Massachusetts, available statistics indicate that felonies dropped from 1835 until the end of the century; the high point of criminal activity in Buffalo came in the 1870s, with the rate moving downward for the next few decades.

Scholars do not agree on the sociological and psychological roots of criminal behavior, but there are significant statistical correlations. Crime rates are traditionally highest in decayed inner-city areas that are marked by high rates of poverty, overcrowding, family instability, and transiency. This pattern holds whether the area was populated by Irish immigrants a hundred years ago, by Italians and Poles sixty years ago, or by blacks and Spanish-speaking people today. Criminal behavior, at least the kind that makes the police blotter and FBI crime reports, is closely associated with social disorganization and economic deprivation. (This statement of course does not include the enormous impact of corporate violations of antitrust and other statutes—"white-collar" crimes that damage the economy far more than burglary and robbery.)

The police cannot control the conditions which seem to generate crime, nor can they prevent individual criminal acts. Therefore, the easiest way for a chief or precinct commander to show a good clearance rate—the ratio of crimes cleared by arrest relative to crimes reported—has been and is to falsify the figures in some way, either by discouraging victims from signing complaints where no solution is possible or by purposely underreporting the number of known crimes. Adding more men to the force has long been the response of administrators to newspaper campaigns about "crime waves" or citizen fears of assault and violence from strangers. Yet there is little evidence that adding more policemen makes the streets any safer.

For most civilians, and probably for most policemen as well, detective work is "real police work," and detective has always been a high-prestige position. Patrolmen yearn for the "good pinch," an arrest which will bring publicity, prestige, and possible promotion to the detective bureau. The news media emphasize the role of the police as crime fighters and law enforcers, and the public long has tended to judge the police by their success in clearing spectacular crimes involving respectable people. For example,

Thomas Byrnes, New York's famous chief of detectives in the late nineteenth century, made his reputation by solving several major robberies. Departments must go all out to solve homicides of children or leading citizens to convince their communities that the police are efficient, alert, and worthy of public support.

Although the media play up these aspects of the police role, most policemen spend most of their active time on duty dealing with noncriminal matters. From the beginning of organized forces, policemen have been called upon in a limitless variety of situations, from stray horses and lost children to disputes between husbands and wives or between landlords and tenants. In these situations policemen had to rely on their common sense; they could call only on their experience or their general know-how in coping with these problems. The beat patrolman was expected to know his route and the people on it, and to keep the peace as best he could. Whatever formal training policemen received concentrated on law enforcement rather than on the sensitive areas of settling disputes without resorting to formal legal mechanisms. Training programs have emphasized such matters as the criminal code, rules of evidence, and modes of criminal investigation, rather than the most effective ways of "cooling off" disputants.

While most peace keeping requires individual police intervention to stop a Saturday night drunk from beating his wife or to settle a dispute between immigrant parents and an adolescent son over the disposition of his earnings, maintaining order occasionally demands that police act as an organized body to cope with strikes, parades, or riots. Maintaining order has usually meant preserving the status quo, with the defenders of order as a primary value opposed to those who wanted to raise a little hell or to effect social and economic change. For example, throughout the nineteenth century—indeed, to the 1930s—police intervened in labor disputes more often on behalf of employers than on behalf of strikers; the best strikers could hope for was the neutrality of the police, which generally only occurred when the local leadership favored a strike. When the political powers opposed a particular strike, the police intervened to facilitate strikebreaking. The police were not equally available to all segments of the community; they protected the interests of the powerful against those who threatened such interests.

In cities such as Chicago and New York, police often acted with scant regard for civil liberties and sometimes with great brutality toward strikers, anarchists, and communists. By habit and occupational interest, policemen wanted orderly and predictable behavior. They had little sympathy for those who questioned established values or the distribution of political and economic power.

As organized labor acquired some strength and political legitimacy in the 1930s, the situation began to change. In New York City the La Guardia administrations followed a policy of neutrality in labor disputes, although in 1937 the Chicago police killed ten civilians, most of whom were shot in the back while trying to escape the rampaging bluecoats in the infamous Memorial Day massacre outside the Republic Steel plant in South Chicago. Since World War II, police neutrality has been easier to achieve because industrial management has realized that in most instances the costs of continued operation in the face of a strike outweigh possible benefits.

In recent years, the most difficult problems in the maintenance of order have come from racial, political, and student protest. Again, the police are usually found on the side of the status quo. Although the police themselves have become more militant in pressing for satisfaction of their own salary demands, they have limited tolerance for black rioters and political and student demonstrators. In some situations departments have acted with superb professional aplomb in grappling with difficult problems; they have maintained order while protecting the rights of the demonstrators. In other instances, such as at Columbia University in New York City in 1968, the police have used far more force than anyone had anticipated. In the case of student protests, it may be that police, who are recruited largely from working-class and lower-middle-class backgrounds, resented the students for apparently scorning opportunities for education, material possessions, and security that represented the American dream to the men in uniform.

Racial violence is an old and ugly story in American cities. Until recent years, the characteristic pattern was white aggression against blacks, followed by black retaliatory violence, to which whites responded with overwhelming force. In major riots such as in East St. Louis, Illinois, in 1917 and in Chicago in 1919, the police joined white civilians in action against blacks. In contrast, the riots of the 1960s were black assaults on white-owned property and institutions. Police practices stood high on the list of grievances of black rioters; often the precipitating incident in major upheavals, such as Harlem in 1964, Watts in 1965, and Detroit and Newark in 1967, involved a police-civilian encounter. These riots put the police under severe strain, and in the most serious cases the National Guard and the United States Army had to intervene.

The riot, the demonstration, and the possible police "bust" are sometime things—major American cities have gone for years without a significant occurrence of this kind—but police problems associated with unseemly behavior in public places are constants. Every day the police must deal with drunks, prostitutes, numbers runners, and narcotics addicts and pushers. It is in this area of "crimes without victims" that the police have had the most difficulty arriving at a viable, stable understanding with all the elements of their diverse constituency. Not surprisingly, most problems of police corruption arise in the same sphere. There is a large market for the services of bookmakers, numbers bankers, and prostitutes, which means that entrepreneurs can well afford to corrupt policemen in order to do business. A significant portion of the public simply does not want vice laws enforced and prefers that the police force concentrate on maintaining order.

The police are caught between the customers and purveyors of desired but illegal products and services and those who want the department to clean up the city. One of the great controversies in this area in the nineteenth century concerned Sunday liquor sales. Sabbatarians wanted the police to enforce Sunday closing laws and to keep the saloon doors, both front and back, locked on Sundays. Saloonkeepers were prepared to lock the front door and draw the blinds as long as customers could enter through the rear. Paying five dollars a month or so to the man on the beat and more to his superiors obviously made good business sense. A policeman who liked to drink himself could easily see this as clean money. What legitimate interest suffered if the bars did stay open during prohibited hours?

Much the same was true of gambling. Men who grew up in a culture where playing the horses and numbers was part of life were prepared to take a little money to let people do what, in their eyes, was perfectly acceptable. Prostitutes serviced a significant portion of the urban population, and police officers sometimes made considerable money from the "fancy houses." In New York in the 1890s, houses paid $500 to open or reopen after a raid or when a new captain came into the precinct. The monthly rate varied from $50 to $75 or more, depending on the price structure and the number of girls.

Periodic scandals exposing police protection of organized crime have erupted almost from the beginning of organized departments. In many instances, such scandals have generated "reform" political movements whose thrust was to sever protection-for-pay relationships existing among policemen, politicians, and what used to be known as the underworld, now variously styled the Mafia, the Cosa Nostra, or the syndicate of whatever local variety or ethnic composition. Usually these reform movements, such as that led by Seth Low in New York City in 1901, lasted only one term. The voters might not like corruption, but they liked reform even less if it meant interference with their gambling and drinking habits.

The most serious gap between popular behavior and the criminal statutes came with the triumph of prohibition in the Eighteenth Amendment and the Volstead Act. The strength of prohibitionist sentiment lay among evangelical Protestants, especially Methodists and Baptists, who were most numerous in rural areas and in small towns and cities. Within the nation's urban giants, the prohibitionist minority consisted of middle-class residents of peripheral areas and suburbs. Inner-city residents, often of foreign birth or parentage, were overwhelmingly wet. If they could not prevent the adoption of prohibition, they could certainly limit its enforcement. In such cities as New York, Chicago, Cleveland, and Detroit, police departments connived at widespread violations of the law. In Chicago, police sometimes convoyed shipments of illegal alcohol to keep rival gangsters from hijacking them. In Cleveland, the police shut down some speakeasies and bootleggers to give others a monopoly of a particular market.

Prohibition opened a new and very profitable venture for organized criminals, who previously had concentrated on gambling, prostitution, the provision of labor goons, and narcotics. Al Capone presented himself as a public benefactor who kept thirsty Chicagoans supplied with beer and whisky; that his methods of marketing ranged from bribery to murder represented an unfortunate by-product of a misguided criminal law. Capone eventually went to prison for income tax evasion, but his less flamboyant and talkative associates managed to survive the end of prohibition, and they continued to flourish in both illegal and legal enterprises. Gambling, loan sharking, and narcotics generate enormous amounts of money, some of which goes to corrupt police officers to allow numbers bankers and others to function.

The closest contemporary counterpart to prohibition is the drug laws, especially those relating to marijuana. The use of marijuana is widespread, particularly among the young, creating the same gap between behavior and criminal law which existed with prohibition. The cases are far from identical, however—police and legal authorities are more antagonistic to drug users than they were to beer drinkers in the 1920s. Prohibition era policemen and drinkers were part of the same social world; they shared values and neighborhoods and often had their feet on the same bar rail. Although the use of marijuana and other drugs has spread among "straight" youth, most nonusers probably still perceive drug users as members of a counter-culture that rejects the values of patriotism, order, stability, and competitiveness which are dear to most policemen. Young people who by their dress, hair styles, and behavior proclaim themselves as "hippies" or "street people" or those who live in high-crime areas are likely to receive considerable unsolicited attention from police on drug laws.

Most marijuana arrests result from searches of persons or vehicles. In order for such a search to be valid, the policemen must either have a warrant, which is rare, or have prior probable cause that a crime has been committed. It is possible that officers conduct a constitutionally invalid search in many cases and only take to court those cases in which they have turned up evidence of a crime. The policeman must then perjure himself about the existence of prior probable cause. The nub of the difficulty is that the law cannot be enforced and constitutional guarantees observed at the same time. Unfortunately, officers seem to be more outraged at the constitutional limitations than at the impossible task they have been set.

Whereas in most situations the police intervene only after being called by citizens, controlling such activities as gambling, prostitution, and drug usage requires that the police take the initiative. In cases of "crimes without victims," no one involved is going to call headquarters and demand action; the police must use undercover agents, wiretaps, and their own testimony in order to make a case. A department that is committed to enforcement must resort to such measures and must accept the testimony of its own members. The laws against these practices therefore encourage various kinds of malpractice from the accepting of bribes to violations of civil liberties. Moreover, they contribute to the existence of a police subculture which permits other forms of malpractice.

Sociologist Albert Reiss, Jr., and his associates conducted a large-scale study of police operations in which observers rode in police cars on patrol in four cities. The researchers found one in five of the officers, *who knew they were under observation,* guilty of illegal transactions. (These cases did not include any systematic payoffs from organized crime.) Apparently, the illegal acceptance of money or goods is so ingrained in the police subculture that the men involved did not care whether or not they were under observation. The Reiss study also found that about four of ten officers observed seriously violated departmental rules, such as by sleeping or drinking on duty; in one out of nine encounters with citizens, policemen were hostile, authoritarian, or derisive toward civilians.

The problems of police corruption, poor performance, violations of civil liberties, and hostility to citizens are most serious in lower-class areas populated by racial and ethnic minorities. Numbers runners and prostitutes flourish openly in such areas, and children quickly learn what these activities are all about and that policemen must be suborned for the numbers game to operate. Blacks perceive officers as corrupt much more often than whites. Residents of high-crime areas also complain that the police do not protect them against the chaotic and violent conditions of their environment. The Civil Rights Commission found that in Cleveland in 1966 the department took four times longer to respond to calls from black areas than it took to respond to comparable calls from white areas. In addition, the poor use the police much more frequently as a general service agency than do middle-class residents. When the poor are in trouble (and their lives are filled with trouble), they call the police for help. If officers respond to such calls with incivility or condescension, they further impress the poor with their powerlessness and increase their sense of oppression.

Police brutality, in the sense of the physical abuse of suspects or other civilians, is probably less common than it was forty years ago, when the

Wickersham Commission appointed by President Herbert Hoover showed the widespread use of third-degree tactics in cities such as Buffalo, Cleveland, and Chicago. When citizens complain of brutality today, they usually refer to verbal abuse or incivility. One serious problem today is the ineffectiveness of citizens' complaints about the police. When accusations against a member of an agency must be made to that agency rather than to an independent body, there is little likelihood that the complaint will receive satisfaction unless a gross violation has occurred. But proposals for grievance mechanisms outside police departments have had rough sledding, often because middle-class and stable working-class people do not have much sympathy with proponents of civilian review boards for complaints against police officers. Policemen usually treat such people civilly, if not respectfully, and those citizens cannot understand why others want to control the police and therefore "handcuff" them and coddle criminals. In 1966, for example, an independent review board was defeated by a two-to-one vote in a referendum in New York City.

Indeed, most citizens do not appreciate the extent to which police behavior varies toward different social groups. The police respect the political power and the access to the media of the more prosperous and therefore treat them civilly, and for the most part these people and the police have parallel interests except on traffic violations. The situation is different with lower-class people. The police insist on respect, even deference from these groups, whose young male members especially look on policemen as enemies. In some neighborhoods it is rare for a young man to reach the age of twenty-one without a police record, and these juveniles know that it is the policeman who makes the key decision about their fate, when he decides whether to invoke the criminal justice system or to deal with a situation informally. Officers frequently make these decisions on the basis of a boy's family, his dress, and his demeanor. If he fails the attitude test and impresses the policemen as a "fresh punk," he may spend a year in jail for an offense for which another boy might only receive a "chewing out."

Lower-class juveniles know that officers possess this discretionary power, but they are not deferential as a result. Often they take perverse delight in demonstrating contempt for the police. Black youth are especially hard on black officers, whom they regard as traitors. This escalating hostility between lower-class youth and the police is one of the most serious impediments to the development of a truly civil society in cities. And it is not only the youth—older inner-city residents also have grievances against the police for being incivil and indifferent; in extreme cases they see the department as an alien army of occupation rather than as an agency devoted to protecting and serving the people of the community.

There has always been some separation between police and community in American cities. In the nineteenth century, officers, their wives, and police reporters noted that civilians distrusted policemen and that department work schedules tended to limit officer's social associations to other members of the department and their families. The very nature of the job made policemen both an occupational and a social group.

In the twentieth century, a number of developments have widened the gap between policemen and civilians. In an effort to curb the influence of political organizations, civil service reformers promoted the bureaucratization of police departments and other public agencies. Entry and advancement would now be by fixed, formal standards rather than by personal and political clout. This system has limited the power of political organizations to a considerable extent, but at the cost of allowing the bureaucracy to resist outside pressure for change as "political interference." The police have sought, and increasingly they have obtained, autonomy—the ability to do their jobs and run their organization as they see fit. In many instances this has led them to protect their interests, their "turf," more vigorously than they have served the public. Although this concern for the maintenance of traditional practices and prerogatives at the expense of the constituency can be found in many public and private institutions, it seems particularly strong among police departments.

After the debacle of prohibition and the revelations of the Wickersham Commission, police administrators became increasingly interested in professionalism. Outsiders had stressed the necessity for more professional police administration in the 1920s; in the 1930s officers themselves promoted this trend, and the climate of the depression, which made police work a desirable job for young men with good educations, also helped. Professionalism has gained ground slowly in major departments, although slum precincts have been least affected by the emphasis on the social and behavioral sciences and the movement away from the traditional "tough cop" approach. Like slum schools, slum precincts get the rejects of the system, those men who have failed elsewhere or have displeased their superiors. New York's Harlem long served as a dumping ground for incompetent or erring policemen, who were the least likely to be sensitive to minority cultures and the most prone to express racial hostility and to act accordingly.

The model of professionalism most often discussed is that of the officer as the dedicated, incorruptible, and highly trained crime fighter—the image of Joe Friday on the television program "Dragnet." In real life, however, the police officer is only rarely a crime fighter; his role—and it is a professional occupation in that it demands a high level of discretion over areas of vital concern to the people involved—is more frequently that of restoring order and providing service for people in trouble. Indeed, European policemen often think of themselves as akin to social workers, a job description that most American officers would sneer at. If officers are encouraged and rewarded for being aggressive, impartial enforcers of the law, they will not give primary attention to their peace-keeping role. Moreover, professional law enforcers almost by definition must be remote from the community; the techniques of "aggressive preventive patrol," considered by professionals to be the best way to curb crime, raise tensions within a community and further increase hostility between policemen and the civilians among whom they work. Of course, it may not be possible to curb crime in any way that is consistent with a free society that permits a high degree of income inequality. The law enforcement model promises what the police cannot deliver, and any organization charged with unattainable goals is sure to have morale problems.

The police can keep the peace. Over the years they have been one of the reasons why American cities could have so many diverse and potentially conflicting groups living together without undue violence, if not always in peace and harmony. They have not always succeeded, of course, as witnessed by the race riots of 1917–19 and those of the 1960s. If the police are to perform this role in an era that is marked by racial conflict and economic decay in cities, they will have to develop a conception of professionalism that stresses peace-keeping and general service.

Departments probably will also have to change their pattern of recruiting. Traditionally, the police have served as a security haven for white working-class and lower-middle-class youth, who join the force because it provides a steady job and a good pension system. The police have not attracted men of middle-class background and education, except in extraordinary situations like the Great Depression. The bureaucratic practice that allows entry only at the lowest level, with substantial time required for promotion to senior ranks, has not been attractive to those who are able and ambitious, nor have most departments sought such recruits. In addition, most departments have not secured a substantial number of black and Spanish-speaking members.

Policemen themselves oppose lowering entrance requirements to recruit more minority-group members. Ignoring minor arrests records or easing test requirements threatens the status of the job. Policemen, like many other people, want to raise the prestige of their occupation; any attempt to lower standards (and modifying them in any way can be construed as lowering) is resisted as selling out to minority groups and giving them an advantage others did not have. If we could meet the requirements, why can't they? is the police response. The very terms *we* and *they* indicate the racial feelings involved.

Technology and changing residential patterns in metropolitan areas have also increased the sense of separation of police from community. The foot patrolman is a rarity in most American cities. Now officers ride in radio cars, which increase their capability of responding to citizens' calls for service but reduce nonadversary contact with civilians. Men in cars cannot pass the time of day with the people on their routes; they interact with citizens only in specific service situations, many of which involve conflicts between two or more people which policemen must try to resolve. In such circumstances, the hostility of one or more of the parties can become focused on the officer who intervenes. If the policeman is uncivil or condescending, the problem can be compounded.

In contrast to the nineteenth century, when policemen had to live in the city (and in the case of New York, in the ward in which they served), many big-city policemen now commute from the suburbs. Like other people in their income brackets, they seek newer housing and more pleasant surroundings in the outer reaches of the metropolitan area. The city, especially its high-crime areas, is the jungle, where men on duty warily cope with social and personal disorganization, endemic violence, aggression, alcoholism and drug abuse, and people in trouble who lack the resources to deal with that trouble effectively. In too many instances, policemen who have isolated their own families from the uncertainties of the urban environment see the people among whom they work as "animals" or "assholes."

Policemen tend to develop cynical views of man and society, and they have long had an affinity for extremist political movements such as the American Protective Association of the 1890s, the Ku Klux Klan of the 1920s, and the John Birch Society. In recent years, police-community relations have deteriorated even further; assaults and ambushes of policemen have risen dramatically—in New York City alone ten policemen were killed in 1971—and officers want a shotgun in the car as well as a pistol and club. If cities are to be at all viable, there must be less violence and more civility; surely one important index of the extent of civility in society is the state of police-community relations. If policemen conceive of their role as making it possible for people of diverse backgrounds and interests to live together peaceably, and if society gives them the resources to keep the peace without violence, the quality of life in cities should improve. Otherwise, a frightening cycle of intensified rhetorical and physical violence may hasten the decay of our urban cores.

Selected Bibliography

As with most other urban topics, sociologists and political scientists became interested in the police before historians. In recent years, however, scholars have made up for past neglect. Roger Lane, *Policing the City: Boston, 1822–1885* (Cambridge, Mass., 1967), and James F. Richardson, *The New York Police: Colonial Times to 1901* (New York, 1970), trace the origins and development of police agencies in the nineteenth century. A number of dissertations on police history in other cities are also being written. English developments are covered in great detail in Leon Radzinowicz, *A History of English Criminal Law and Its Administration from 1750* (4 vols., London, 1948–68). Sam B. Warner, Jr., *The Private City: Philadelphia in Three Periods of Its Growth* (Philadelphia, 1968), contains considerable material about the forces that created disorder between 1830 and 1860 and the political steps taken to restore order. Two useful older works by Raymond Fosdick embodying historical perspectives are *European Police Systems* (New York, 1914) and *American Police Systems* (New York, 1920).

Sociologists who have studied the police include Michael Banton, *The Policeman in the Community* (London, 1964), which is based on field investigations of both British and American forces; David J. Bordua, editor, *The Police: Six Sociological Essays* (New York, 1967), which contains an excellent essay by Allan Silver; Harlan Hahn, editor, *Police in Urban Society* (Beverly Hills, Calif., 1971), a collection of recent pieces; Arthur Niederhoffer, *Behind the Shield: The Police in Urban Society* (Garden City, N.Y., 1967) (before he became an academic sociologist, Niederhoffer spent more than twenty years as a member of the New York Police Department); Albert Reiss, Jr., *The Police and the Public* (New Haven, Conn., 1971), a major study of police interaction with citizens; Jerome H. Skolnick, *Justice without Trial: Law Enforcement in Democratic Society* (New York, 1966), which emphasizes the contrast between a rule of law and the maintenance of order through bureaucratic means; William A. Westley, *Violence and the Police: A Sociological Study of Law, Custom, and Morality* (Cambridge, Mass., 1970), which is a brilliant examination of the police subculture.

Political and legal studies of police include Paul Chevigny, *Police Power: Police Abuses in New York City* (New York, 1969), a study of lying and other abuses on the part of police by an attorney for the New York Civil Liberties Union; Jameson Doig, editor, "A Symposium: The Police in a Democratic Society," *Public Administration Review*, 28 (September, October 1968), 393–430, which contains essays by Herman Goldstein, James Q. Wilson, and others; John A. Gardiner, "Police Enforcement of Traffic Laws: A Comparative Analysis," in James Q. Wilson, editor, *City Politics and Public Policy* (New York, 1968), 151–172, which shows the extent to which traffic enforcement varies from one community to another; John Kaplan, *Marijuana: The New Prohibition* (Cleveland and New York, 1970), an eloquent plea for the legalization of marijuana use on the grounds that the present laws cannot be enforced without destroying the constitution and young people's faith in the legal system; Wallace S. Sayre and Herbert Kaufman, *Governing New York City: Politics in the Metropolis* (New York, 1960), which includes considerable material on the police, emphasizing the power of the organized bureaucracy; Thorsten Sellin, editor, "The Police and the Crime Problem," *Annals of the American Academy of Political and So-*

cial Science, 146 (November 1929), a good index to academic thinking on crime and police in the late 1920s; and James Q. Wilson, *Varieties of Police Behavior: The Management of Law and Order in Eight Communities* (Cambridge, Mass., 1968), which differentiates various styles of policing.

Government reports have devoted considerable attention to police in recent years. The *Report of the National Advisory Commission on Civil Disorders* [Kerner Commission] (New York, 1968) emphasizes the contribution of the poor state of police-community relations to the ghetto riots of the 1960s; The President's Commission on Law Enforcement and Administration of Justice, *The Challenge of Crime in a Free Society* (New York, 1968), and *Task Force Report: The Police* (Washington, 1967), contain valuable material on many aspects of the police, from recruiting to corruption.

Specialists in police administration and police officers have contributed important books. Among them is William H. Parker, *Parker on Police*, O. W. Wilson, editor (Springfield, Ill., 1957), a collection of speeches by the long-term Los Angeles Chief of Police, emphasizing police as law enforcers and crime fighters. Bruce Smith, *Police Systems in the United States*, was published in three editions (New York, 1940; New York, 1949; and New York, 1960), the last of which bore his son's name, Bruce Smith, Jr. Smith, the outstanding independent expert in police administration of his time, directed many surveys of police agencies. August Vollmer, *The Police and Modern Society* (Berkeley, Calif., 1936), presents the mature reflections of a man who served as chief of the Berkeley, California, department before becoming an academic specialist in police administration. *The New Centurions* (Boston, 1970), by Joseph Wambaugh, is a best-selling novel by a Los Angeles detective sergeant which presents a vivid picture of the cop's view of the world. Arthur Woods, *Policeman and Public* (New Haven, Conn., 1919), is an insightful little book by the reform police commissioner of New York who served under Mayor John Purroy Mitchel between 1913 and 1917.

Urban Bosses and Reform

Bruce M. Stave

Philosophizing at the turn of the century, the Tammany Hall ward boss, George Washington Plunkitt, remarked, "Ignorant people are always talkin' against party bosses, but just wait till the bosses are gone! Then, and not until then, will they get the right sort of epitaphs." Discussion of urban bosses and reformers has often been framed in the context of corruption: bosses were corrupt and the corrupters of others; reformers consistently established efficient "good government"; cities suffered under boss rule, but were saved by reform movements. If one is to avoid such oversimplification, other factors than the unequivocal goodness of reform and the unquestionable evil of bossism must be considered.

Concepts such as the functions of the political machine, the physical and demographic development of America's cities, the social backgrounds of bosses and reformers, the structural forms of city government, and the recent relationship of municipal to federal government are all relevant to the understanding of urban decision making. For it is decision making which one must discuss when considering urban bossism and reform. Who makes the important decisions related to city development and government—and why? Which groups benefit from such decisions and which do not? Is a city's image, growth, and development determined in the politicians' smoke-filled rooms, in posh board rooms occupied by corporate executives, around polished coffee tables in middle-class homes, or in the offices of bureaucrats in the state or national capital? How have the focuses of power changed over time? Why did the boss become an American institution? For what reasons was he so often challenged by reformers? Moreover, how does the growth of a city affect decision making within it? For growth, of both geographical boundaries and population, is a key to the understanding of urban bossism and reform.

The roots of the political machine appeared long before the shift of the American city from the pedestrian city to the larger, more dispersed metropolis of modern times, but this change called forth the rise of the classic urban political machine. The prototype Tammany, for instance, has existed in one form or another since 1787. Beginning as a nonpolitical fraternal order, it gradually evolved into the political center of the Jeffersonian Republican party (later the Democratic party) of New York County, and as early as 1809, it faced charges of corruption in conjunction with the building of a memorial dedicated to American prisoners of war who had died during the Revolution. Nevertheless, it was the subsequent growth of New York City and the concomitant fragmentation of power and breakdown in communications which called forth the need of a Boss Tweed and his Tammany Hall. Just as the men who were dominant in the integrated, homogeneous, walking city of the early nineteenth century—lawyers, bankers, commission merchants—controlled its urban political leadership, so the boss and the political machine rose later in the century to cope with the problems faced by cities that were feeling the effects of industrialization, immigration, and the general process of massive urbanization.

Between 1820 and 1870, New York City's population increased by more than 800,000, bringing the city close to the one million mark. In the latter year, the height of the Tweed Ring's activities, nearly half the population were immigrants, mainly from Ireland or Germany. The city was growing without direction, and the strains on streets, buildings, transportation, and welfare services increased daily. New York had outgrown its official government. Moreover, political power was fragmented, which made it increasingly difficult for the government to confront the city's problems. As one observer commented in 1866, "It occurred to us that perhaps the best way of beginning an investigation of the city government would be to go down to the City Hall and look at it. It proved not to be there. To keep the whole city from falling a prey to the monster, it has been gradually cut to pieces, and scattered over the island. Was there ever such a hodgepodge of a government before in the world?"

The social and political disorder New York witnessed immediately before and after the Civil War was also felt in cities as diverse from New York as Cincinnati during the middle 1880s and early 1890s. There, not only did lynch mobs, election violence, and labor unrest lead many to believe that there was a breakdown in law and order but the explosion of urban growth quickly outmoded the services of the walking city. With no significant increase in the fire department in over ten years, in 1886 the city's fire marshall predicted that if two large fires occurred at once, it would mean disaster for Cincinnati; in the summer of 1890, the city's water supply ran short, which raised the danger of a "water famine" for the rest of the decade. Lack of sewers created a health hazard, and municipal services generally fell into decay.

Thus, in cities across the country arose a crying need to create order out of urban chaos. If official government institutions of a city could not meet the demands of emerging metropolises, extragovernment institutions like the bosses and their political machines would. Not only did they attempt to unify the nation's cities but in so doing the bosses served the needs of the swelling immigrant populations and met the demands of business, both licit and illicit, which arose as a result of urban expansion.

The American urban marketplace would offer something for everyone; the quid pro quo was measured by what the traffic would bear. In return for a patronage job, a turkey at Christmas, coal for heating during winter, the immigrant would gratefully pledge his political allegiance—his vote and those of his family. In return for his cooperation in obtaining a franchise to build a new street railway, the "legitimate" businessman might pay the boss a bribe. In return for not interfering with gambling establishments or brothels, the "illegitimate" businessman (the gambler or racketeer) might pay "protection money" to the political machine. The political machines, then, provided services the legitimate government could not or would not supply.

Sociologists refer to such services as the *latent functions* of the political machine. A boss such as Tweed instinctively satisfied these functions. His ward captains arranged jobs, loans, and other favors for needy families. At Christmas 1870, he himself donated $50,000 to the poor of New York's seventh ward. Nor were business interests ignored. For example, Tweed interceded with New York's judges on behalf of financier Jay Gould. The result was a change—in Gould's favor—in the manner of electing the Erie Railroad's board of directors. The Erie won concessions for the transportation of westward-bound immigrants from the Castle Garden reception center in New York City. Tweed, in return, was not only elected to the railroad's Board of Directors but was aided politically by Gould in counties along the railroad's route. Moreover, catering to the underworld, Tweed's city employed public officials such as George Hill, better known as the gambler "Cooley Keys," and Jim "Maneater" Cusick, a frequent inmate of Sing Sing who served as clerk to a city court and also held a position in the sheriff's office.

By standards of normal morality—by the commonly accepted criterion of "good" and "evil"—the machines sank low. Political patronage violated choice on the basis of ability; bossism challenged the concept that a vote should represent a rational, intelligent decision and not allegiance to a new type of feudal lord; bribery or, conversely, what came to be known as "honest graft" offended proprieties with respect to the sanctity of private property; protection for crimes violated the generally accepted concept of law and order. Thus, it was relatively easy for the *New York Times* and Thomas Nast of *Harper's Weekly* to play upon this sense of morality and lead the crusade against the Tweed Ring. Nast hated the immigrant Catholics who supported Tweed. His poison-pen portraits unmercifully lampooned the nearly six-foot, almost 300-pound boss with the reddish brown mustache and chin whiskers, to the point that the slovenly, bewhiskered Tweed of the cartoons became the symbol of boss politics. Realizing the power of the pen, Tweed remarked, "I don't care a straw for your newspaper articles, my constituents don't know how to read, but they can't help seeing them damned pictures."

Was it, however, simply a matter of an outraged sense of morality over the issue of corruption which led reformers to crusade against the Tweed Ring? It would seem that it was not. The controversy over corruption often clouded the more significant issue of how a city should develop physically. In New York, Tweed and his associates argued for unlimited expansion and far-ranging public expenditures; his opponents advocated restrained growth and a careful regard to costs. When the municipal indebtedness of New York City rose from $30,000,000 in 1867 to $90,000,000 in 1871, with two-thirds of the increase coming between January 1, 1869, and September 16, 1871, the opponents of rapid city growth seized upon the corruption involved in this spending to mobilize opposition against the boss and his machine. However, the real disagreement revolved around Tweed's policies and what they meant for the development of New York City rather than the issue of morality. Undoubtedly, there was moral outrage at the fact that the corruption-ridden courthouse Tweed built behind New York's City Hall cost nearly twice as much as the whole of Alaska, but the broader issue of the day was one between the old and the new New York City—whether it should expand beyond lower Manhattan or not.

A similar situation arose in as unlikely a place as nonindustrial Washington, D.C. After the Civil War, the nation's capital was more of a swampy mudhole than a monumental city; conditions were so bad that moving the capital to the Midwest and abandoning the city entirely was considered. However, in the early 1870s Congress authorized a massive building program, and Alexander Shepherd, a member of the Board of Public Works, emerged as its leader and ultimately came to be called "Boss" Shepherd by his opponents. Controlling a huge payroll and lucrative construction contracts used to the advantage of the national Republican party, Shepherd's patronage and graft system resembled that of Tweed. More important, however, was the fact that Shepherd's conception of urban growth was also similar to the New York boss's.

Shepherd urged rapid expansion of the city and launched a comprehensive effort to improve street paving, lighting, and sewage facilities. Such a program was expensive and was opposed especially by those who lived in Washington during only part of the year and owned property in that city as well as in their home areas; those who came to play at government in the nation's capital were not interested in paying for the improvement of two cities. Thus, many large taxpayers advocated restricted growth. Nevertheless, Shepherd engineered the passage of a massive bond issue, which in the space of three years, made the district's debt larger than that of all but seven states and concomitantly helped put money into the pockets of real estate speculators such as Shepherd. It also served as a catalyst to the growth of a modern and more efficient and livable Washington.

If the developmental philosophy of men such as Tweed and Shepherd ultimately won the war over how cities would expand, in the short run, they personally lost their battles. Shepherd's economy-minded enemies launched congressional investigations into his activities in 1872 and 1874, and by 1876, shorn of his position and fortune, Shepherd fled with his family to Mexico. Meanwhile, in 1871 the Tweed Ring had fallen from power, and the boss entered prison. Upon his arrival to begin serving his sentence, Tweed answered the warden's question about what his profession was by loudly proclaiming "Statesman!" In April 1878 he died of pneumonia at New York's Ludlow Street jail, a structure built on his authorization.

Tweed's successor, "Honest" John Kelly, was the first in a long line of Irish bosses of Tammany Hall, an early example of the general Irish success in American urban politics. While Tweed was of middle-class, third-generation, Scottish Protestant stock and Shepherd was a native Washingtonian of "respectable" family background, one study of twenty municipal bosses found that fifteen were either immigrants or the children of immigrants. For many newcomers to America or their children, machine politics was one of the few avenues of social mobility open to them. This was especially true of the Irish, who began arriving in America in large numbers during the 1840s and 1850s and were greeted by nativist "Irish Need Not Apply" signs when they sought employment. Blocked from easy entry into American society, they took to politics and spawned bosses like Kelly's Tammany successors in New York, Richard Croker and Charles Francis Murphy, Jim and Tom Pendergast in Kansas City, Boston's James Michael Curley, and Ed Kelly of Chicago. As the fictional Irish boss Frank Skeffington, hero of Edwin O'Connor's *The Last Hurrah*, remarked, "I had no education to speak of, a good many roads were closed to our people, and politics seemed the easiest way out."

Some other newcomers made their way up the American social escalator by means of activities such as sports and the rackets, but the Irish seemed especially well suited for politics. Because English was their native tongue, they had an immediate advantage over other immigrant groups. Moreover, by uniting rural Irish custom with urban politics, they were well prepared for machine government. Their indifference to Yankee proprieties gave them little concern about stealing elections, a practice which reflected eighteenth century Irish politics. Their tradition of regarding English formal government as illegitimate and informal Irish government as legitimate allowed them to easily operate within the *informal* machine government of America's cities, which existed side by side with the often inefficient or inflexible *official* city governments. Moreover, many Irish immigrants had previous political experience, and the narrow boundaries of peasant Ireland prepared them for work in small precinct confines. Finally, the social structure of the Irish village, ruled by a stern oligarchy of elders, in which a person's position was likely to improve with time, mirrored the essentials of a Tammany Hall. In several cities, the maturity of an ethnic group was measured by when it wrested control of politics from the Irish; when Carmine DeSapio became the boss of Tammany Hall in the middle of the twentieth century, many felt that the Italians had come of age in New York.

The fact that most urban politicians and bosses rose from humble and immigrant origins, often with Catholic or other nonpietistic religious backgrounds, has been offered as another explanation for "corrupt" city politics. Allegedly, their social origins explained why the bosses and their followers regarded politics as a business; as "political entrepreneurs," they peddled their influence, passed laws, and sold franchises for personal and party gain. They looked upon politics as a vehicle for advancement and not one for reform because they believed, as did George Washington Plunkitt, "that when a man works in politics, he should get something out of it." Their deprived economic backgrounds impressed upon them the need to secure a return for their efforts—a need elite reformers did not feel. Moreover, the reformers allegedly conceived of politics in the framework of Yankee-Protestant morality, which viewed governing as a means of reforming public morals and serving the rather amorphous "public good." Such an explanation with no further elaboration, although it introduces the significant social variables of ethnicity, religion, and economic origins, falls short of considering the boss-reformer relationship in the context of city growth.

An explanation which considers the impact of urbanization on bossism and reform places the two in the framework of conflict between the periphery of the city and its center. Recent historians have applied this analysis particularly to urban politics during the Progressive Era. During the last part of the nineteenth century, the revolution in urban mass transportation, especially the development of the electric street railway, extended the boundaries of many cities. In Boston, for example, the outer boundary of dense settlement in 1873 stood approximately two and one half miles from its city hall, whereas by the 1890s, with the advent of the electric street railway, the outer border of settlement ranged at least six miles. Cincinnati's physical boundaries increased from six square miles in 1850 to fifty square miles in 1910, and by 1912 the city had 222 miles of streetcar track. Because the new technology permitted them to cover increasingly long distances in relatively short periods of time, many people chose to leave the central city for new outlying areas. In contrast to recent trends, however, which show individuals leaving central cities for independent suburbs, annexations at the end of the nineteenth century brought many newly settled areas within city boundaries. Thus, those who fled the central core were still city residents; they could not abandon the city as would many of their post–World War II counterparts.

Residents of nineteenth century middle- and upper-class streetcar suburbs attempted to leave behind the problems of the central city. They sought escape from the new industry and concomitant environmental problems, from overcrowding and the large influx of Catholic and Jewish European immigrants, and from what appeared to be increasing crime. They were the old city dwellers, often white Anglo-Saxon Protestants, who could afford to move to newer areas but who still had a stake in urban development. These residents of pleasant and spacious suburban neighborhoods often became the spearheads for urban reform, and they saw the inner city as the bastion of the boss and his immigrant following. As a result, the urban reform movement during the Progressive Era became a struggle between periphery and center to determine which group would shape city life and development.

However, one should not overlook the fact that although many of the reformers might have lived in peripheral neighborhoods, they were still tied to the center of the city by their jobs. If nineteenth century technology served as a catalyst to residential dispersal, it also allowed for commercial centralization. Geographical distance could serve as an easy indicator of social distinction between the classes, but those who lived in outlying neighborhoods often had close professional and business links to the central city. The skyscraper helped to centralize business in the downtown areas, and the increasing use of the telephone and street railways tied suburban residents to the center. Thus, rather than a conflict between periphery and center, the dispute between urban bosses and reformers might be seen in terms of a contest between the center-as-residence (for the bosses and their immigrant following) and the center-as-place-of-business (for the reformers).

Contrary to the contemporary Progressive view (most prominently espoused by muckraker Lincoln Steffens) that reform was often an uprising against business, business frequently advocated reform in American cities of that period. However, it was a limited type of reform. If we consider that

Progressive reform was of three types—economic, social, and structural—on the municipal level, the businessmen of the era were generally most interested in the last type. Structural reform aimed at changing the structure of government so that it would be more efficient; it separated politics from administration, made use of experts, and fashioned itself in the image of the corporation, which was the model for municipal government preferred by many businessmen reformers. Although Progressive rhetoric was usually framed in terms of broadening democracy, structural reformers often centralized decision making.

They achieved centralization by instituting city manager and commission forms of government and by changing from ward-based to citywide elections for city councils and school boards. Whereas the former elections gave influence to various city areas and allowed a voice to immigrant neighborhoods, which were often united by the political machine, the latter shifted control to those with a geographically larger public perspective—namely, residents of streetcar suburbs whose occupational and professional interests tied them to the center of the city. As chambers of commerce, civic clubs, voters leagues, and other reform organizations succeeded in instituting changes in municipal government, they simultaneously brought a different type of person to public office.

In Pittsburgh, for example, before the introduction of citywide elections in 1911, representation on the council and school boards was essentially in the hands of the lower and middle classes. The great majority of officeholders were small businessmen such as saloonkeepers (a popular occupation for politicians because the saloon provided a social gathering place for residents of ethnic neighborhoods), grocers, and druggists, white-collar workers such as clerks and bookkeepers, and skilled and unskilled craftsmen. After electoral changes were instituted, the occupational and class structure of decision makers changed so that the majority were upper-class corporate managers, big businessmen, and professionals, whose conception of desirable public policy differed from that of previous officeholders. They hoped to take formal power from the lower and middle classes, to replace the ward and block focus of earlier politicians with concern for the city as a whole, and thus to rationalize the administration of their city.

In general, it was easier for the elite to institute changes such as the city manager system in smaller municipalities, which they could more easily dominate, than in larger, more heterogeneous cities. However, structural reform was not the only type of reform to win support during the Progressive Era. Social reformers such as Hazen S. Pingree, Tom Johnson, and "Golden Rule" Jones, the mayors of Detroit, Cleveland, and Toledo, respectively, fought for lower electric, gas, telephone, and street railway rates and sometimes for municipal ownership of utilities. They advocated the expansion of parks and educational facilities, free public baths, and an incipient form of public relief. Moreover, they made little effort to control working-class morals by acting against Sunday drinking, gambling, and prostitution or by calling for restrictive blue laws, as did some other reformers. Their attempts to achieve greater social and economic equality frequently alienated any upper-class and business support they might have had and forced them to rely on a lower-class base.

Paradoxically, their effectiveness, especially in the case of Pingree, was due in large part to the creation of a well-disciplined political machine. Although Pingree's machine was devoid of the graft and corruption associated with many of the bosses, its structure and methods were no different from those of any of the bosses. The reform mayor hand picked other candidates, made certain that the public payroll worked for and was loyal to him ("If a man does not want to sympathize with the principles of the administration let him get a new job"), and generally ran a tight ship. Similarly, in recent years, the reform mayor of New York City, John V. Lindsay, has been assisted by the John V. Lindsay Association, an organization characterized as comparable to the clubhouses of Tammany Hall days. The city's $35,000-a-year highway commissioner, a member of the association, remarked, "What can I produce? Two hundred-and-fifty experienced doorbell ringers. People who know what it's all about, who know how to pull out a vote, and who know how to identify a vote." Just as the old political machines were feudal hierarchies, with "The Boss" at the top of the pyramid and the precinct captain at the bottom, it is also apparent that reformers must have their machines as well; one might wonder when is a "machine" an "organization" and a "boss" a "leader"?

The distinction between boss and reformer is further clouded by the fact that some bosses actually supported reform. Many observers came to agree with George B. Cox, the late nineteenth century boss of Cincinnati, who claimed that "a boss [was] not necessarily a public enemy." As he tried to bring order to his city in disorder, Cox midwifed the birth of several important reforms. At the peak of his control, the city initiated housing regulations, lowered municipal tax rates, streamlined its government, supported the growth of the University of Cincinnati, and professionalized the police force.

The same is true for no less a boss than Tammany's Charles Francis Murphy, whose influence extended beyond New York City and into the halls of the state legislature in Albany; if Progressive legislation was to be passed in New York, it needed at least the support of, if not initiation by, Murphy. Although the Democratic state legislature under Murphy's control passed a flood of patronage and "ripper" bills, which created new positions and removed Republicans from lucrative appointive posts to make room for "deserving" Democrats, it also enacted significant reform legislation with the boss's blessing. Not only did Tammanyites support a host of social and labor legislation, which included laws establishing workmen's compensation, public employment agencies, and factory safety standards, but they also championed political reforms such as woman suffrage, direct election of senators, and the direct primary system of nomination—measures which some authorities claimed un-civic-minded political machines opposed. Even if these reforms originated with reform associations, they could not have become law without the support of Tammany-controlled legislators and political leaders, whose progressivism was in large part a manifestation of the machine's self-defense tactics. Tammany realized that its constituents desired such reform; hence, to remain in power, it supported progressive legislation.

It is ironic that one of the young New York State Democratic legislators who opposed Tammany during the Progressive Era because of its old image of bossism (and regardless of its support of reform) was Franklin D. Roosevelt. For although the Progressive Era was filled with crusades against bossism (even if they were perhaps misguided), Roosevelt's New Deal cooperated with and depended on big-city bosses. Many of them remembered his Progressive years and originally opposed FDR's nomination for President in 1932, but once the nomination was won, Roosevelt successfully courted their support; for instance, one of his main foes, Frank Hague, boss of Jersey City and a supporter of Al Smith's candidacy, was immediately asked to join the Roosevelt camp. During FDR's four national campaigns, the big-city machines could be counted on by the New Deal leader, and they could depend on him.

If it is ironic that the previously antimachine Roosevelt became both benefactor to and beneficiary of the political machines, the irony increases if one agrees with the view that the New Deal ultimately debilitated the bosses and their machines. One popular interpretation holds that the New Deal's welfare program undid the necessity of the machines' service function. In this instance, growth, in the context of the expanding role of the federal government, allegedly had a profound effect on urban politics. As a character in *The Last Hurrah* remarked,

> He [FDR] destroyed the old-time boss. He destroyed him by taking away his source of power. . . . All over the country the bosses have been dying for the past 20 years, thanks to Roosevelt. . . . The old boss was strong simply because he held all the cards. If anybody wanted anything—jobs, favors, cash— he could only go to the boss, the local leaders. What Roosevelt did was take the handouts out of local hands. A few things like social security, unemployment insurance, and the like—that's what shifted the gears, sport. No need

now to depend on the boss for everything; the Federal government was getting
into the act. Otherwise known as social revolution.

Moreover, other factors such as the alleged assimilation of ethnic groups,
the affluence of American society during post–World War II years, a better
educated population, and the extension of the merit system, which decreased the pool of available patronage jobs, all supposedly weakened the
old-line political machine, causing its demise.

Yet intuitively, Americans of the 1970s, who are familiar with the Daley
Democratic machine of Chicago, still powerful despite losses in the 1972
election, and with the fact that the Hudson County (Jersey City) organization did not fall until 1971, must realize that the death knell for the bosses
and their machines was sounded much too early in the development of
American urban history. But if boss politics did not wither away in the
wake of the New Deal, what happened? Was a new boss tradition created?

In several cities, such as Pittsburgh and Kansas City, the New Deal actually aided the machine rather than enfeebling it. In Pittsburgh, an impotent pre–New Deal Democratic party was transformed into a powerful political machine, grounded in the new-style patronage made available by
Roosevelt's federal government. New Deal work relief programs especially
served the needs of David L. Lawrence's Pittsburgh organization and attracted personnel to serve as precinct committeemen.

The motivation of the new converts to Democratic activism during the
1930s was perhaps best summed up by the committeeman who remarked, "I
needed a job. The depression was on; I got a job. I started in politics in
1930 as a Republican, but switched when Roosevelt came in. The Democrats had emergency programs like CWA, WPA [Civil Works Administration, Work Progress Administration]." Committeemen such as this one
moved from the work relief payroll to the public payroll and maintained
city, county, or state jobs after the New Deal ended; indebted to the machine for their livelihood, they worked to bring out the vote for their party.
In this sense, the internal structure of urban politics had changed little from
the late nineteenth century, when Lord James Bryce wrote in his *American
Commonwealth*, "Those who in great cities form the committees and work
the machine are persons whose chief aim in life is to make a living by
office."

As the federal government took on an increasing role as guardian of the
individual American's welfare, local politicians benefited from the federal
government's largess. In 1965, after the New Deal had long since passed
from the scene, Chicago's Mayor Daley commented, "There's nothing
wrong with politics if it does some good. . . . What's wrong with ward com-

mitteemen sending capable men or women for jobs in the poverty program?" Moreover, when jobs were not available, the new bosses could provide an information function for their constituents by telling them where to go and whom to see for quick service or special advantage with respect to welfare, unemployment compensation, and public housing apartments. These remained especially valuable in ghetto neighborhoods, where poverty had not disappeared, in contrast to the alleged increased affluence of American society. In Chicago's black wards, for instance, welfare checks are sometimes delivered not by mail but by precinct captains.

As mayor and chairman of the Central Committee of the Cook County Democratic Organization, Daley also controls about 34,000 city and county "temporary appointment" patronage jobs; few appointments are made in Chicago without the knowledge of the mayor's office. In addition to using patronage and providing a service function not unlike that of the classic machines of the late nineteenth and early twentieth centuries, modern Boss Daley has important links to leading businessmen. Just as in post–World War II Pittsburgh, where Lawrence's Democratic machine worked closely with businessmen reformers to produce the Pittsburgh Renaissance and to rebuild the city's downtown area, Daley quickly aligned with the Windy City's business leaders. After his first election in 1955, he immediately began to revitalize the downtown area and to serve the interests of the financial community. By the end of his first term, the businessmen, most of them suburbanites who had economic ties within Chicago but who, unlike the businessmen of the Progressive Era, resided outside the city's boundaries, supported the mayor's bid for reelection, and they have continued to do so in succeeding campaigns. For them, Daley was a builder, a man who governed an efficient city, a boss who brought order to Chicago when other cities seemed plunged into urban disorder. Daley's concrete expressways speed commuter and commercial traffic in and out of Chicago; the city's airport is the busiest in the world; city streets are well swept and well lighted; the downtown area is in the midst of a building boom; and as an added attraction, the city's five largest banks at the beginning of the 1970s were grossly underassessed, and contributors to Daley's cause who happened to be real estate speculators were granted millions of dollars in tax breaks.

In 1971, one of Daley's wealthy backers remarked, "If a businessman went to [Daley's predecessor] for something he needed, like changing zoning to get a parking facility for his plant so he wouldn't have to move out to the suburbs, . . . he didn't deliver." Daley did deliver. He did just what Tammany boss Richard Croker, almost seventy years earlier, said a boss should do. As Croker remarked to Lincoln Steffens, "A businessman wants to do business with one man and one who is always there to remember to carry out the business." Daley was always there.

Thus, in contemporary Chicago, as in Pittsburgh, the political machine in post–New Deal America worked to establish what one observer has called "the reverse welfare state." That is, government resources under two Democratic mayors, themselves bosses of their own machines, were used to the advantage of usually Republican corporate interests. In the process, the cities' commercial areas thrived and the new bosses, like their prototypes, assumed what appeared on the surface to be a broad view of urban expansion and development.

However, although the city under such a process is physically renewed and downtown areas benefit, social renewal frequently rates a poor second; new skyscrapers glisten, but housing and schooling suffer. In Daley's Chicago, the urban renewal program tore down three times as much housing as it replaced; plywood covers the windows of schools in a system considered one of the weakest in the nation. Thus, while the machine provided some basic services to the urban poor, primarily blacks, and cheaply kept the ghetto wards—at least until 1972—within its voting columns, the recent in-migrants to urban America apparently benefit considerably less from the largess of the political machine than did the "new" European immigrants who began coming to America in such large numbers almost a century ago.

One result of this dissatisfaction in many cities has been the movement for decentralization of urban decision making. The calls for neighborhood control of schools and politics are responses to the same kind of centralization which characterized the Progressive Era. However, this time, in a city such as Chicago, the political machine represents not those who desire neighborhood control but those who advocate consolidation of power at the center. In other areas, the establishment of metropolitan government is seen as a vehicle for maintaining urban control by those who have fled the city for the suburbs. The process of urban decision making has moved into a new stage in the cycle of centralization and decentralization of power, a cycle in which bosses, reformers, immigrants, and businessmen have played leading roles. And they are yet to completely disappear from the American urban landscape.

Selected Bibliography

Although there is no recent general synthesis of bossism and reform, several books have concentrated on individual bosses and concomitantly on the reformers who opposed them. New York City's Tweed machine has been studied in Seymour Mandelbaum, *Boss Tweed's New York* (New York, 1965), and Alexander B. Callow, Jr., *The Tweed Ring* (New York, 1966); the roots of Tammany Hall are investigated in Jerome Mushkat, *Tammany: The Evolution of a Political Machine, 1789–1865* (Syracuse, 1971). In *A Study in Boss Politics: William Lorimer of Chicago* (Urbana, Ill., 1971), Joel A. Tarr offers an ethnocultural interpretation of the political boss in urban politics; he focuses on the clash between elite municipal reformers and the immigrant-based machine. An interpretation which contends that residence rather than ethnicity was the key factor in this clash of bosses and reformers can be found in Zane Miller, *Boss Cox's Cincinnati: Urban Politics in the Progressive Era* (New York, 1968), which follows the model of the periphery versus the center.

A study which concentrates on a reformer rather than a boss is Melvin G. Holli, *Reform in Detroit: Hazen S. Pingree and Urban Politics* (New York, 1969). Holli distinguishes between social and structural reformers and places Pingree in the former category. The relationship between businessmen and urban structural reform is considered in James Weinstein, *The Corporate Ideal in the Liberal State, 1900–1918* (Boston, 1969), and Samuel P. Hays, "The Politics of Reform in Municipal Government in the Progressive Era," *Pacific Northwest Quarterly*, 55 (October 1964), 157–69. The impact of business-inspired reform in recent America is discussed by Roy Lubove in *Twentieth Century Pittsburgh: Government, Business, and Environmental Change* (New York, 1969); the early view that reform was generally an uprising against business is clearly expressed in muckraker Lincoln Steffens' *The Shame of the Cities* (New York, 1904).

The effect of the New Deal on the urban political machine is investigated by Bruce M. Stave in *The New Deal and the Last Hurrah: Pittsburgh Machine Politics* (Pittsburgh, 1970) and is mentioned in Chapter 8 of Lyle W. Dorsett's *The Pendergast Machine* (New York, 1968), both of which see the New Deal as benefiting the political machines that the authors study. On the other hand, the essays in the May 1964 issue of *The Annals*, "City Bosses and Political Machines," maintain that the New Deal weakened the machines, leading to their demise. A critical popular study of a contemporary boss is Mike Royko, *Boss: Richard J. Daley of Chicago* (New York, 1971).

The latent functions of the machine are discussed by Robert K. Merton in *Social Theory and Social Structure* (New York, 1957); an old Tammany ward boss delightfully presents his point of view in William L. Riordon, *Plunkitt of Tammany Hall* (New York, 1905). A discussion of the centralization and decentralization of urban decision making which influenced this essay can be found in Samuel P. Hays, "The Changing Political Structure of the City in Industrial America," an essay yet unpublished in the United States. Two anthologies of readings concerned with the topic of this essay is Bruce M. Stave, editor, *Urban Bosses, Machines, and Progressive Reformers* (Lexington, Mass., 1972), and Blaine A. Brownell and Warren E. Stickle, editors, *Bosses and Reformers* (Boston, 1973).

The Crabgrass Frontier: 150 Years of Suburban Growth in America

Kenneth T. Jackson

Hundreds and thousands, formerly obliged to live in the crowded streets of cities, now find themselves able to enjoy a country cottage, several miles distant, the old notions of time and space being half annihilated; and these suburban cottages enable the busy citizen to breathe freely, and keep alive his love for nature, till the time shall come when he shall have wrung out of the nervous hand of commerce enough means to enable him to realize his ideal of the "retired life" of an American landed proprietor. (*Andrew Jackson Downing, 1848*)

Relentlessly, almost unconsciously, the United States has become a suburban nation. In 1970, the Census Bureau announced that the suburbs contained 76 million people, or 12 million more than the cities which spawned them. Even the 8 million citizens of New York City found themselves outnumbered by the 9 million outsiders who lived within sixty miles of Times Square. And predictions for the late 1970s uniformly assert that suburbanites will not only remain the largest single element of the American population but they will increase their proportion of the total. By 1980, millions of acres of brush, scrub oak, pine, and prairie will have given way to crabgrass and concrete, and corporate offices, factories, and big-league stadiums will be more commonplace on the urban periphery.

Suburbia, of course, represents different things to different people. The concept is broad and confusing; the word alone is enough to unleash myths. The typical stereotype is one of station wagons, shopping centers, single-family houses, and curvilinear streets, all liberally sprinkled with children on bicycles and young couples giddy from martinis. Uniformity supposedly prevails. In 1967, an Ohio housewife expressed this homogeneous view: "Suburbs are small, controlled communities where for the most part everyone has the same living standards, the same weeds, the same number of garbage cans, the same house plan, and the same level in their septic tanks."

Actually, there is no such thing as the "typical" suburb or suburbanite any more than there is a "typical" city or urban resident. Even the most casual investigation will establish that American suburbs come in every conceivable type, shape, and size; from industrial Hoboken to posh Winnetka, from black Robbins to lily-white Cicero; from Polish Hamtramck to Waspish Darien; from colonial Cambridge to innovative Reston. In the face of such a conglomeration, scholars have been unable to agree on the definition of *suburban.* Economists assign suburban status on the basis of the functional relationship between the neighborhood and the larger metropolitan area, ecologists on the basis of residential density, political scientists on the basis of separate legal and corporate identity, and sociologists on the basis of "a way of life." In this essay, I shall regard suburbs as low-density, residential areas (1,500 to 10,000 residents per square mile) at the edge of the built-up portion of large cities.

The Earliest Suburbs

The term *suburb* (or *burgus, suburbium,* or *faubourg*) has had a versatile two-thousand-year history and has been employed to describe such diverse agglomerations as the estates surrounding the Sumerian city of Ur, the villas ringing Imperial Rome, the housing clusters outside the walls of medieval Toulouse, and the pubs at the Bowery and Astor Place in eighteenth century New York City. John Wycliffe used the word *suburbis* in 1380, and Geoffrey Chaucer introduced the term in a dialogue in *The Canterbury Tales.* By 1500, Fleet Street and the extramural parishes were designated as London suburbs, and by the seventeenth century the adjective *suburban* was being used in England to signify both the place and the resident. On this side of the Atlantic, residential settlements existed outside Philadelphia and New York long before the thirteen English colonies won their independence from King George III. In New Orleans, following the French tradition, communities just outside the legal city were known variously as Faubourg Ste. Marie, Faubourg Marigny, and Faubourg Solet.

Thus in one sense, suburbs are about as old as cities. But *suburbanization,* the systematic and regular growth of fringe areas at a pace more rapid than that of central areas, probably occurred first in the United States, where it can be dated from the second quarter of the nineteenth century. Since that time the process has been heavily influenced by developments in transportation technology, by the institutionalization of the low-interest, long-term, home loan, and by the desire of generations of families to seek their own house on their own piece of land. The historical dimension of the suburban trend is important because the urban structure we have inherited has been largely shaped by the decisions and impulses of a half century and more ago.

In 1825, American cities, like those elsewhere, were essentially "walking cities." Commercial and residential districts were ill defined and overlapping, and the rich and the poor often lived near each other. Despite the availability of inexpensive land on the urban periphery, city inhabitants crowded together. Streets were narrow, lot sizes small, and houses close to the curb. Tiny Elfreth's Alley in Philadelphia survives as an example of the compact nature of urban life two centuries ago. The easiest, cheapest, and most common method of getting about was by foot. Few people could afford the expense or nuisance of maintaining a horse and carriage; thus, there was a significant advantage in living within easy walking distance of the city's stores and businesses. Not surprisingly, the most fashionable and respectable residential addresses were close to the center of town, and neighborhoods generally deteriorated as one moved farther from the core. Indeed, the suburbs of the first quarter of the nineteenth century and before were little better than slums. Building regulations were designed to protect the city, not the periphery; thus, slaughterhouses, tanneries, and brothels were located beyond the city limits, where the air was often rancid from stagnant water, dead animals, and garbage. As late as 1849, one observer noted: "Nine-tenths of those whose rascalities have made Philadelphia so unjustly notorious live in the dens and shanties of the suburbs."

The Emergence
of the "North American" Pattern

Between 1825 and 1910, America's large cities underwent a dramatic spatial transformation. In effect, they were turned inside out, as a new pattern of peripheral affluence and central despair emerged. The shift was not sudden, but it was no less profound for its gradual character. In Philadelphia, a dozen suburban areas were consistently outgrowing the central city in population by 1850, as bankers, merchants, and physicians moved out to West Philadelphia or Germantown "for all the beauties of the country, within an easy and cheap communication with the city." In the first decade after the Gold Rush, wealthy San Francisco families exited from the downtown area to the heights of Fern (Nob) and Russian hills or to "steamboat suburbs" such as Oakland and Alameda. In Chicago, the number of suburbs contiguous to the city exceeded fifty even in 1875, and North Shore realtors were busy advertising "qualities of which the city is in a large degree bereft, namely its pure air, peacefulness, quietude, and natural scenery." And in Cincinnati, Sidney D. Maxwell wrote in 1870:

In whichever direction the beholder turns, he sees suburban places. The city is surrounded with hills that are already blossoming like a rose. Beautiful cottages, stately residences, and princely mansions are springing up as by magic. Villages are multiplying along the great thoroughfares. Tasteful suburban homes are each year, in increased number, skirting the waters of the Ohio or peering through the foliage that fringes the summits of the surrounding highlands.

Some of the nation's earliest, most extensive, and most famous suburban areas grew up around New York City. As early as 1823, Hezekiah Pierrepont advertised land in Brooklyn Heights, then undeveloped, as

situated directly opposite the southeast part of the city, and being the nearest country retreat, and easiest of access from the center of business that now remains unoccupied; the distance not exceeding an average fifteen to twenty-five minute walk, including the passage of the river; the ground elevated and perfectly healthy at all seasons; as a place of residence all the advantages of the country with most of the conveniences of the city.

Gentlemen whose business or profession require daily attendance into the city, cannot better, or with less expense, secure the health and comfort of their families than by uniting in such an association.

With its tree-shaded streets, pleasant homes, proximity to Manhattan, and general middle-class ambience, Brooklyn quickly developed many characteristics of the modern suburb. Regular ferry service across the East River to Fulton Street began in 1814; by 1830, Brooklyn's growth rate regularly exceeded that of its giant neighbor, and by 1850, New York newspapers had begun to express concern over "the desertion of the city by its men of wealth." In 1870, work began on the Brooklyn Bridge; thirteen years later the span was completed amid speculation that it was the eighth wonder of the world and the greatest construction achievement in history. Majestic in the sweep of its great cables, the bridge was wide enough for two rail lines, two double carriage lanes, and a footpath. By 1898, when it became one of the five boroughs of New York City, Brooklyn had well over a million residents.

The metropolis was also growing west toward New Jersey and north toward Westchester County. In 1861, a New Jersey booster admitted that "Newark and its vicinity—including the cities of Jersey City, Hoboken, Hudson, and Elizabeth, as well as the villages of Belleville, Orange, and Bloomfield,—has become but a suburb of the great city of New York." On May 6, 1871, a supplement to *Harper's Weekly* included a pictoral map of New York from the vantage point of a balloon. The caption explained:

On the right, the city of Brooklyn, and the towns lying eastward as far as Ja-
maica and Hempstead, and northward as far as New Rochelle, with the railroads that make the suburbs of New York, and the islands and headlands of
the Sound. On the left he will see Staten Island, with its picturesque villas, Jersey City, Newark and all the pleasant suburban villages and towns of New Jersey as far south as Perth Amboy, westward to West Orange, and northward to
Caldwell and Paterson.

Noting such sprawl, the United States Census Bureau announced in
1880 that for certain purposes it would consider New York, Brooklyn,
Jersey City, Newark, and Hoboken as "one great metropolitan community."

Suburbanization in New York became especially pronounced after
1860. Although Manhattan Island would not "fill up" until 1910, its decen-
nial growth rate lagged behind its suburbs in every census after 1840. As
early as 1825, some parts of the old city were losing population on an absolute as well as on a relative basis; by 1860, as houses and apartments gave
way to factories and offices, the area of absolute decline included everything south of Houston Street. A few neighborhoods, notably the Lower
East Side and Harlem, were becoming more congested as late as 1900, but
the suburban trend for the region was by then unmistakably strong. Even
Harlem was thought to be "the country."

The deconcentration process in New York differed in scale but not in
substance from that experienced by Boston, Philadelphia, Baltimore, and
other large cities. Four mutually reinforcing developments resulted in the
physical spreading of the city and the exodus of the middle and upper
classes: (1) the growth of the total urban population, especially the urban
poor population, on an unprecedented scale; (2) the creation of larger, more
impersonal, and more aesthetically obnoxious manufacturing and work organizations, coupled with an increase in urban nuisances; (3) the introduction and expansion of mass transportation systems; and (4) the articulation
and popularization of a "suburban ideal."

In part, suburbanization was and is a function of urban growth. In
1840, less than 11 percent of the nation's populace lived in cities; by 1910,
the proportion was more than 45 percent. The number of persons in cities
of 100,000 or more rose from less than 1 million in 1840 to more than 27
million in 1910; the number of such cities grew from four to forty-four. At
the same time, large cities were receiving a disproportionate share of impoverished immigrants from eastern and southern Europe. At a time when less
than one-half the national population was urban, more than five-sixths of
all first-generation Russian-Americans and Irish-Americans lived in cities.
Among immigrants from Italy and Hungary, the proportion was more than

three-fourths. This urban concentration was especially marked in the twenty-eight largest cities, which in 1890 contained less than 13 percent of the native-born and more than 33 percent of the foreign-born population of the United States.

But why did the poor newcomers settle at the center rather than at the edges of the city? In large part, the answer is simply that the upper and middle classes came to prefer the suburbs, and they abandoned their old neighborhoods to the less advantaged. And in part, the answer is related to the expansion of the central business district. Greater population concentration led to increasing demand for office and residential space, which caused land prices to rise. The greatest pressure was at the center, but it was difficult to determine just when and in which directions the central business districts (CBD) would expand. Anticipating windfall profits, speculators bought residential properties on the commercial fringe. But years, sometimes decades or longer, intervened between the purchase of these properties and their conversion to business use. Meanwhile, landlords who hoped that their houses or apartments would be demolished to make way for offices had little incentive to keep their holdings in proper repair or to listen to the complaints of tenants. Downtown residential areas, once the most prestigious in the city, deteriorated.

The expansion of central business districts was accompanied by an increase in the average size of factories. In the early years of the nineteenth century, before moving assembly lines or interchangeable parts were commonplace, most urban residents labored individually or in work groups of fewer than a half dozen persons. Typically, they lived and worked in proximity, often next door or in the same building. A journey to work of more than half a mile was unusual. As industrialization proceeded, the average size of factories, stores, and offices increased. In Philadelphia, for example, the number of people working in factories of more than 100 employees increased more than fiftyfold between 1860 and 1930, although the total population increased less than four times. Many of these larger organizations—refineries, machine tool industries, iron and steel mills, and chemical plants—created offensive odors or noises. Nearby neighborhoods lost status, particularly among professional and business people. The close relationship between home and employment weakened, and tendencies toward separation of work and residence increased.

Not every big factory was located in or near the center of the city. Urban congestion, prices, and traffic drove factories as well as individuals to the suburbs. Central area land was scarce and expensive, taxes were high, and municipal regulations were annoying. In 1898, Adna F. Weber noted that "statistical data regarding the location of factories in suburbs are not available, but the strong tendency in that direction is familiar to all Americans." Every city offered examples. Philadelphia's mammoth Baldwin Locomotive Works moved three times in the nineteenth century, each time farther out. In 1880, George M. Pullman began developing a model industrial town eight miles south of Chicago, where he hoped to capitalize on the Windy City's incomparable railroad connections while avoiding its legendary saloons, brothels, and gambling dens. Finally, in 1915, Graham R. Taylor made a study of the industrial suburbs of Chicago, St. Louis, Cincinnati, and Birmingham. "The suburbanite," he wrote, "who leaves business behind at nightfall for the cool green rim of the city would think the world had gone topsy-turvy if at 5:30 he rushed out of a factory set in a landscape of open fields and wooded hillsides, scrambled for a seat in a streetcar or grimy train and clattered back to the region of brick and pavement, of soot and noise and jostle." But, said Taylor, this was the situation being created by the "shifting of factories one by one to the edge of the city." Regardless of location, the increasing size of factories contributed to increasing differentiation of urban neighborhoods. With the passage of every year after about 1850, cities became less "mixed up" and more segregated by function, race, and income.

Advances in transportation technology also led directly to new patterns of urban settlement. In 1825, not even a rudimentary mass transit system existed anywhere in the United States. The first omnibuses (wagons with large wheels) appeared on Broadway in New York in the late 1820s. These crude, twelve-passenger contraptions were uncomfortable, slow, and relatively expensive, but they established the essential conditions for an urban transportation system: operation along a fixed route, according to a regular schedule, for a single fare. Placing the wagons on rails (horsecars) in the late 1850s gave them increased efficiency, comfort, and speed. The popularity of the vehicles rose proportionately; in New York City, the number of transit patrons increased from less than 7 million in 1853 to more than 36 million in 1860.

Meanwhile, ferries, steam railroads, and cable cars provided additional alternatives for the journey to work. Ferries were especially important on the East and Hudson rivers in New York, whereas cable cars found their most extensive use in San Francisco and Chicago. Steam railroads were also important in a number of areas. As early as 1860, for example, the seven railroads serving Boston had introduced season tickets and family rates for commuters and had experimented with free Sunday excursions for persons interested in buying property on the edges of the metropolitan region. The result was that by the time of the Civil War, the Boston railroads had persuaded 10 percent of the city's work force to use the rails and had converted such quiet villages as Dedham, Quincy, Brighton, and Medford into "railroad suburbs." And writing of the relationship between New York and Newark in 1878, an observer asserted:

> When, forty years ago, it took nearly two hours to span the distance between the two cities, the population of Newark was about 20,000. Now, when the distance is reduced to half an hours travel, Newark being joined to New York by no less than 198 trains daily over four lines of railroad, the population is more than six times greater.

But in terms of suburban development, the most important of the nineteenth century transit innovations was the electric streetcar, popularly known as the trolley. In 1888, in a large-scale experiment in Richmond, Frank Sprague demonstrated the feasibility of the new method. Thereafter, the transition from horse to mechanical power was rapid, and by 1902, more than 96 percent of track mileage had been electrified. Moreover, by raising the speed of the cars to 15 or 18 miles per hour, electrification made practical the extension of tracks into undeveloped areas. Farmland as far as ten miles from the downtown district was subdivided for house lots, often by men with substantial investments in the transit companies. The results were "streetcar suburbs"—like Dorchester and Roxbury in Boston—on the fringes of every major city by 1900. Most of the residents of the new communities were middle-class workers or professional people who could afford ten to twenty cents per day for transit fares and whose jobs allowed them sufficient flexibility to commute for perhaps five to ten hours per week. The lower half of society could afford neither the money nor the time.

Although early mass transportation was relatively expensive, it was not inevitable that the middle and upper classes would gravitate to the urban edges. Many European cities have until recently offered a contrary pattern, as many communities continue to do all over the world. In the Union of South Africa, for example, the privileged white minority occupies the central areas of Johannesburg and Durban, whereas the disadvantaged and oppressed black population must struggle daily with crowded commuter trains. In Calcutta, Santiago, Lima, and Buenos Aires, the most degrading slums are to be found in the miserable quarters on the outskirts, where sanitary facilities, running water, and police and fire protection are practically unknown. In Caracas, the richest city in South America, the magnificent mountains surrounding the metropolis are dotted with the shacks of the very poor; the wealthy live lower in the valley.

In North America, on the other hand, the residents of large cities who could afford to live anywhere had usually decided by 1900 that the good life could best be found on the edges rather than near the centers of cities. This general pattern owes much to the antiurban heritage and agrarian tradition of the United States. Thomas Jefferson, Alexis de Tocqueville, Ignatius Donnelly, and William Jennings Bryan, among others, frequently articulated their distrust of the city and their faith in a people with close ties to the soil. One of the first men to translate the rural ideal into a "suburban ideal" was landscape architect Andrew Jackson Downing. Before the Civil War, he reached a large and predominantly well-to-do audience through a monthly journal of rural art and rural taste known as the *Horticulturist.* The Newburgh, New York, native seldom referred directly to suburbia, but he accepted the romantic concept of the superiority of rural existence over urban life. "In the United States," Downing wrote in 1848, "nature and domestic life are better than society and the manners of towns. Hence all sensible men gladly escape, earlier or later, and partially or wholly, from the turmoil of cities." Downing built secluded estates for the wealthy as concrete examples of the way a satisfying life style could be achieved and also designed the innovative residential community of Llewellyn Park, New Jersey, in the late 1850s.

Another important nineteenth century exponent of suburbia was Frederick Law Olmsted. Best known for his prize-winning design for Central Park in New York in 1857, Olmsted became the nation's most prolific and influential landscape architect in the generation after the Civil War. Unlike Downing, Olmsted saw the suburb not as an escape from the city but as a delicate synthesis of town and wilderness. With his partner, Calvert Vaux, Olmsted laid out suburbs in several American cities, the most famous of which is Riverside, which opened on the west side of Chicago in 1869. Meticulously planned in every detail, Riverside offered generous lots, curved roadways, and a parklike setting. Such communities, Olmsted thought, were "the most attractive, the most refined and the most soundly wholesome forms of domestic life, and the best application of the arts of civilization to which mankind has yet attained." And he made a prediction: "No great town can long exist without great suburbs."

Downing and Olmsted were the forerunners of even more vocal advocates of the naturalness and desirability of suburban living. As the nineteenth century drew to a close, a number of periodicals—*Countryside, House Beautiful, Country Life in America,* and *Suburban Life*—began to cater to the new suburbanites or to those city dwellers who longed to swap their cramped apartments for a house with a garden. As described by Sidney J. Low in 1891, it seemed so healthy and satisfying to be a suburban dweller: "His horizon is not limited by walls of brick and stone. If he does not live in the fields, he may have the fields at his door; he may be able to stretch his limbs by a walk over a breezy common, and get the smoke of the city out of his lungs by a ramble down a country lane."

One way to make the spacious fields and restful shade available to the city resident while adding a few social amenities to suburban life was to organize a "country club." The first of the genus in America was apparently the Country Club of Brookline, which was established in 1882 on a hundred picturesque acres about six miles from the State House in Boston. Within the next dozen years, such venerable institutions as the Westchester Country Club, the Larchmont Yacht Club, the Essex Country Club of New Jersey, and the Philadelphia Country Club had been established. Most found their raison d'être in the encouragement of outdoor sports in the company of social equals, but they soon developed more elaborate activities for women only or for whole families to go along with the golf, polo, tennis, and yachting.

For the wealthy, the country club added important benefits to suburban living that previously had been unattainable. For others, the suburban routine was considerably less exciting. Like their namesakes of the present day, many nineteenth century suburbs were "women's towns" during the week. Writing from Brooklyn before the Civil War, Walt Whitman often commented on the matriarchal and middle-class character of his town. And William Dean Howells, another early suburban resident, in 1870 described a typical weekday morning in his community:

> A sober tranquility reigns upon the dust and nodding weeds of Benicia Street. At that hour (11 a.m.) the organ-grinder and I are the only persons of our sex in the whole suburban population; all other husbands and fathers having eaten their breakfasts at seven o'clock, and stood up in the early horse-cars to Boston, whence they will return, with aching backs and quivering calves, half-pendant by leather straps from the roofs of the same luxurious conveyances, in the evening.

Then, as now, the towns to which the men returned had their share of problems. Soon after his maid quit because of the inconvenience of getting to work, Howells reflected upon the lack of urban services in Charlesbridge:

> We had not before this thought it was a grave disadvantage that our street was unlighted. Our street was not drained nor graded; no municipal cart ever came to carry away our ashes; there was not a water-butt within half a mile to save us from fire, nor more than one thousandth part of a policeman to protect us from theft.

But in spite of everything, Howells enjoyed his life in Charlesbridge, and as editor of the *Atlantic Monthly* in 1878, he published an anonymous letter which perhaps paralleled his own sentiments: "In everything except proximity to their business . . . it seems to me the suburban people, in their spacious houses, designed often by the best professional skill, and affording in their interiors light for works of art and room for the varied activities of a refined life, have the best of it." If only the few could afford spacious houses or works of art, almost everyone could enjoy more light and grass in an outlying community.

Through this combination of rapid urban growth, industrial development, transit innovation, and rural ideology, five trends were apparent in all large cities by 1910 and in Philadelphia, New York, and Boston by 1860: (1) at the center of the city, residential density was declining as the area was converted to industrial or commercial use; (2) on the edges of the city, residential density was rising as metropolitan regions tended to spread themselves out; (3) throughout the urbanized areas, the average residential density was declining; in 1850, less than 25 percent of the urban population lived at densities of less than fifty per acre, and by 1890, about 45 percent lived at or below this level of dispersal; (4) throughout the entire metropolitan regions, the density curve representing the variation in density from one ward to the next was leveling—that is, the difference between the most congested and least congested districts was becoming smaller; and (5) the wealth of peripheral residents was increasing relative to that of persons in the core. A sixth tendency, that of decreasing residential density with increasing distance from the center, remained operative.

These important trends toward suburbanization in the nineteenth century are not widely recognized because the earliest suburbs did not long remain suburbs. They lost their independence because municipal governments adopted the philosophy that "bigger is better" and expanded their populations and area by moving their boundaries outward to recapture their departing citizens or to insure that new residents would not be part of a separate community. Without exception, such adjustments were the dominant method of population growth in every American city of consequence before 1920, and in the cases of Phoenix, Houston, Memphis, Dallas, and other large communities which continue to register population gains, it remains the most important cause. If annexation (the addition of unincorporated land to the city) or consolidation (the absorption of one municipal government by an adjacent one) had not taken place, there would now be no great cities in the United States in the political sense of the term. Only New York City would have grown as large as 1 million people, and it would have remained confined to the island of Manhattan. Viewed another way, if annexation had not been successful in the nineteenth century, many large cities would have been surrounded by suburbs even before the Civil War. Such cities as St. Louis, Pittsburgh, Cleveland, and Philadelphia contained in 1970 less than one-half the population of their standard metropolitan areas. Their boundaries have not been altered in almost half a century, and they are now extreme examples of older cities being strangled by a ring of suburbs. A St. Louis school administrator recently complained that suburbanites have "erected a wall of separation which towers above the city limits and constitutes a barrier as effective as did those of ancient Jericho or that of the Potsdamer Platz in Berlin." Yet if these cities had been unable to add territory in the nineteenth century, their central areas would have contained a far smaller percentage of the metropolitan population in 1900 than they in fact contained in 1970.

Appropriately, the most significant annexations in the nineteenth century involved the nation's three largest cities—New York, Chicago, and Philadelphia. In 1854, the City of Brotherly Love expanded its area from 2 to 129 square miles by absorbing such formerly independent suburbs as Spring Garden, Southwark, Kensington, and Moyamensing. Chicago's largest consolidation took place in 1889, when 133 square miles and most of what is now the South Side were added. The new city boundaries included pleasant residential villages such as Hyde Park, Kenwood, and Woodlawn as well as such outlying industrial communities as Grand Crossing and Pullman. New York City was the scene of the most important boundary adjustment in American history when in 1898 Brooklyn, Queens, Staten Island, and part of the Bronx were added to Manhattan. The size of the city increased from 40 to 300 square miles; the population jumped by well over 1 million.

Although smaller cities did not match in size the additions of the major metropolises, every large city shared in the expansion boom. St. Louis increased its area from 4.5 to 14 square miles in 1856 and to 17 square miles in 1870. The biggest change came in 1876, when city voters overwhelmed the opposition of rural St. Louis County, raising the municipal area to 61 square miles and creating an independent city. Boston added about 15 square miles by joining with Roxbury in 1868 and Dorchester in 1870, while New Orleans absorbed Carrolton in 1876, which gave the Crescent City most of the area it occupies today. Baltimore more than doubled its size in 1888; Minneapolis, Cleveland, Cincinnati, and Pittsburgh more than tripled through a series of small nineteenth century additions. Thus, suburbs became neighborhoods, and in the official census reports, cities registered startling population increases until well into the twentieth century. In actuality, what was called the growth of Chicago or Philadelphia or Memphis was actually the building up of residential communities on their edges.

The Emergence of the Modern Suburb

Between 1900 and 1945, the foundations were laid for the creation of a predominantly suburban nation. In older cities in the East and Midwest, annexation fell into disuse. Among twenty large cities which increased their area by 170 percent between 1870 and 1920, the corresponding figure for the half century between 1920 and 1970 was a miniscule 14 percent. But the outward trend continued and expanded, with the wealthy moving from the inner suburbs to the outer suburbs. By the 1920s, sociologists at the University of Chicago had constructed a concentric zone model to describe the way in which residential neighborhoods improved in quality with increasing distance from the urban core. This "North American pattern" became so dominant that a suburban rabbi recently confessed that when he was growing up in Brooklyn, the Five Towns area of Long Island, even more than Israel, represented the "promised land."

Technological developments such as automobiles, telephones, radios, septic tanks, electric lights, and laundry machines increased the appeal of the twentieth century suburb by bringing the amenities and conveniences of the city to widely scattered subdivisions. But the most basic impulse toward suburbia remained as before: the desire for a home. And where was an individual more likely to find a house than in the developing periphery?

Very few of the new neighborhoods and suburbs were "planned" by experts, a defect which advocates of the garden city and the garden suburb hoped to remedy. The garden city idea was conceived by Ebenezer Howard, a London court stenographer who had lived briefly in Chicago. In 1898, he published *Tomorrow*, a small volume which proposed a new kind of community that would combine the best features of town and country. The garden city would be limited to 32,000 people and would be surrounded by a permanent agricultural belt that would produce food for the community and would prevent suburban sprawl. All land would be owned by the community as a whole, and enough industry would be included to insure self-sufficiency. In 1899, the Garden City Association was formed in England, but the more ambitious plans of the organization were not realized. A quarter of a century later, only two such communities had been built.

Howard's plan had even less success in the United States, where no garden city was ever built. The somewhat similar "garden suburb," a planned residential community on the outskirts of a city, did enjoy a temporary popularity, however. The most important garden suburb was built on Long

Island in 1909 by the Russell Sage Foundation. Forest Hills Gardens featured a shopping plaza, a commuter railroad station, curvilinear streets, spacious Tudor-style houses, and a network of small parks. Not far from the Forest Hills project, realtor Alexander Bing built Sunnyside Gardens in Queens fifteen years later. Bing conceived a new town design which eliminated side alleys and used the space saved for small commons in the center. Both of these garden suburbs, however, differed from the garden city concept in that they were not self-sufficient and that they provided homes only for persons of above-average income.

During the 1930s, Ebenezer Howard's ideas threatened to gain an American significance that had previously eluded them when the federal government undertook the greenbelt town program. Designed by Rexford Tugwell, a Columbia University economics professor and member of Roosevelt's brain trust, the plan was to establish, at locations well removed from large cities, new and complete towns that would provide a healthful and safe environment as well as jobs for former residents of urban slums. The greenbelt town program ultimately failed, however; the Roosevelt administration never completed the project, and the three half-finished towns became ordinary suburbs.

Two other government programs had a more lasting influence on the development of metropolitan America. Municipal zoning and the long-term, low-interest mortgage loan were developments of social technology that gave official sanction to the suburban ideal and institutionalized the North American pattern.

Zoning, which is the power to control the use of land and the size of buildings, originated in Germany about 1900. Before that time, many American cities had regulated the construction and height of structures, but New York's comprehensive zoning law of 1916 was the first to limit the general *usage* of land in an important American metropolis. The Gotham ordinance was passed after a group of Fifth Avenue merchants became concerned over "the gathering together of factory operatives at the noon hour on Fifth Avenue." Their objection was that ordinary garment workers were eating lunch from brown paper sacks within sight of the patrons of the nation's most exclusive shops. Their solution was a zoning law that would push the garment district west of Seventh Avenue. In the process, they revolutionized the real estate industry.

In theory, zoning was designed to protect the interests of all citizens by limiting land speculation and congestion. And it was popular. Although it represented an extraordinary growth of municipal power, nearly everyone supported zoning. By 1926, seventy-six cities had adopted ordinances similar to that of New York. By 1936, 1,322 cities (85 percent of the total) had them, and zoning laws were affecting more property than all national laws relating to business.

In actuality, zoning was a device to keep poor people and obnoxious industries out of affluent areas. And in time, it also became a cudgel used by suburban areas to whack the central city. Advocates of land-use restrictions in overwhelming proportion were residents of the fringe. They sought through minimum lot and set-back requirements to insure that only members of acceptable social classes could settle in their privileged sanctuaries. Southern cities even used zoning to enforce racial segregation. And in suburbs everywhere, North and South, zoning was used by the people who already lived within the arbitrary boundaries of a community as a method of keeping everyone else out. Apartments, factories, and "blight," euphemisms for blacks and people of limited means, were rigidly excluded.

While zoning provided a way for suburban areas to become secure enclaves for the well-to-do, it forced the core city to provide economic facilities for the whole area and homes for people the suburbs refused to admit. Simply put, land-use restrictions tended to protect residential interest in the suburbs and commercial interests in the cities, because the residents of the core usually lived on land owned by absentee landlords who were more interested in financial returns than neighborhood preferences. For the man who owned land but did not live on it, the ideal situation was to have his parcel of earth zoned for commercial or industrial use. With more options, the property often gained in value. In Chicago, for example, three times as much land was zoned for commercial use as could ever have been profitably employed for such purposes. This overzoning prevented inner-city residents from receiving the same protection from commercial incursions as was afforded suburbanites. Instead of becoming a useful tool for the rational ordering of land in metropolitan areas, zoning became a way for suburbs to pirate from the city only its desirable functions and residents. Suburban governments became like so many residential hotels, fighting for the upper-income trade while trying to force the deadbeats to go elsewhere.

Federal home loan policies have also been especially beneficial to suburbs. During the 1930s, President Franklin D. Roosevelt and Congress became concerned over the high foreclosure rate as tens of thousands of families proved unable to meet their mortgage payments. Meanwhile, the construction industry was at a virtual standstill. The New Deal responded with federally sponsored mortgage insurance programs and incentives for building. Congressional support for the long-term, monthly payment mortgage with low interest increased even more after World War II, when the government adopted the position that the veteran should own his own home. Through the GI Bill, former servicemen were able to buy homes with as little as one dollar down. By 1972, the federal government had aided more than 10 million families to buy homes, most of them in the suburbs.

Because Congress understood the intensity of the American preference for single-family, detached houses, important provisions in the FHA legislation worked to the advantage of new neighborhoods, most of which were in the suburbs. Home improvement loans were difficult to get and were issued only for short periods. New home loans, by contrast, were available under favorable, long-term conditions. Similarly, loans to contractors for building apartments were inhibited through higher rates. Families were thus encouraged by the government to buy new, single-family, detached homes rather than to repair older ones or to move to apartment buildings.

Guidelines not in the legislation but established by the FHA bureaucracy and the real estate industry also stimulated suburban growth. The agency was run as if it were a private business. To protect its investments, the FHA rated neighborhoods according to the estimated safety of housing loans made there. Four categories were established, and each rating was translated into a color, which was then placed on secret maps in FHA offices. Every block in every city had a rating and a color. High ratings were given to homogeneous and new neighborhoods that were well away from the problems of the city. The lowest rating, red, was assigned to communities which contained such "adverse influences" as smoke, odor, or "inharmonious racial and nationality groups." The presence of older properties and slums dramatically lowered the rating of any area and, because of limited funding, practically insured that a neighborhood would be ineligible for federal funds. As urban renewal critic Jane Jacobs has noted, such credit-blacklisting maps were accurate forecasts because they were self-fulfilling prophecies.

A prospective homeowner could increase his chances of acceptance by the FHA by selecting his house in a white, middle-class neighborhood with "enforced zoning, subdivision regulations, and suitable restrictive covenants." With that sort of logic behind federal financing, only 1 percent of the government insured homes constructed between 1945 and 1965 went to blacks. In accordance with its New Deal mission, the FHA was successful in banishing from the land the specter of frequent mortgage foreclosures, and in providing assistance to families that otherwise could not have arranged for adequate loans. In the process, it provided an enormous subsidy to the suburbs.

The Legacy of Henry Ford

Even more important than zoning and mortgages in determining the shape of the metropolitan landscape have been the road and the car. The gasoline-powered, internal-combustion engine was not invented in the United States; that honor probably goes to Karl Benz and Gottlieb Daimler in Germany in 1885. The first workable American motor vehicle was not built until 1893, when a horseless carriage was fashioned by the Duryea brothers. As late as 1900, when about 8,000 of the curious machines were on American streets, domestic automobile development trailed that of Europe both qualitatively and quantitatively.

Within the space of a single generation, however, Henry Ford turned a novelty of the rich into a necessity of the middle class. Other pioneers such as Ransom E. Olds and Walter Chrysler contributed to the increasing American dominance in automobile production, but it was Ford whose dream of a car for the multitude resulted in the most popular vehicle the world has ever known—the Model T. The tin lizzie was introduced in 1908; when production was halted in 1928 almost sixteen million of them had rolled off the assembly line and every other car on earth was a Ford. Meanwhile, American automobile registrations climbed to 100,000 in 1906, to one million by 1913, and to ten million by 1922. By 1927, when the United States was building about 85 per cent of the world's automobiles, there was one motor vehicle for every five Americans. In the 1940s, a Hollywood movie based on John Steinbeck's novel *The Grapes of Wrath* was exhibited throughout the Soviet Union as an example of the distress of capitalism. After less than two months it was removed from the theaters, however, because the Russian people were less impressed by the poverty they saw on the screen than by the fact that everyone seemed to own a car.

With the automobile came the highway. Prior to 1900, there were almost no paved surfaces between cities in the United States, not from a lack of ability to build them but from a lack of demand. For trips of any distance, the railroad was smoother, faster, and more economical than any other form of overland travel. The motor car, and to a lesser degree the bicycle, changed all this. The Federal Road Act of 1916 offered funds to states that organized highway departments; the Federal Road Act of 1921 designated 200,000 miles of road as "primary" and thus eligible for federal funds on a fifty-fifty matching basis. Meanwhile, the adoption of gasoline taxes, beginning with a one cent per gallon levy in Oregon in 1919, provided the necessary state revenues for a massive road-building program. By 1925, the value of highway construction projects exceeded $1 billion for the first time; thereafter, it fell below that figure only during a few years of the Great Depression and World War II. Bridges such as that over the Delaware River between Philadelphia and Camden (1926) and the George Washington Bridge, which connected New York City with northern New Jersey (1931), also spurred suburban growth and increased the demand for feeder highways.

Most of the early road mileage was only one or two lanes in width, but in urban areas wider thoroughfares were soon proposed. The bucolic and meandering Bronx River Parkway, begun in 1906 and completed in 1923, was the nation's first landscaped highway. Running from Bruckner Boulevard in the Bronx alongside the New York Central tracks to White Plains, it stimulated commuting from such Westchester County suburbs as Scarsdale, Mount Vernon, Bronxville, and New Rochelle. Within ten years, the New York area also witnessed the construction of the Hutchinson River Parkway (1928), the Saw Mill River Parkway (1929), and the Cross County Parkway (1931). The Henry Hudson Parkway, the first metropolitan freeway to have limited access, no grade crossings, and service stations of its own, was begun in New York City in 1934, and in 1940, the nation's first long-distance superhighway, the Pennsylvania Turnpike, was opened.

The highway almost created its own raison d'être; many of the factories, shopping centers, and subdivisions of the suburbs were originally attracted by the transportation routes. Its significance in the growth of automobile suburbs can be illustrated by Detroit. Six major arteries radiate from the Motor City toward Pontiac, Toledo, Lansing, Windsor, Ann Arbor, and Port Huron. The road to Pontiac, Woodward Avenue, is Detroit's main street; it begins at the Detroit River and follows the original Saginaw Trail. The twenty-five mile stretch between the city and Pontiac offers several examples of commuter suburbs that sprang up in response to a good transportation facility—the highway itself.

As Woodward Avenue angles away from Detroit, it passes through communities such as Birmingham and Ferndale, which had a long independent history before they became commuter suburbs, as well as villages such as Royal Oak, which have developed more recently. The Woodward Avenue "family" includes Buckley, a poor neighborhood with homes built of whatever materials were available, as well as Bloomfield Hills, one of the wealthiest communities in the United States. All share a dependence on the highway. In 1923, when a Wider Woodward Project was started to provide an eight-lane concrete road all the way to Pontiac, every town along the way joined in enthusiastic support. When the road was finished in the late 1920s, local boosters proclaimed it the nation's best, and developers began to advertise land in terms of its distance from Woodward Avenue. The new facility enabled executives to travel twenty-five miles to their offices in Detroit in less than forty-five minutes.

The decade of the 1920s was the first in which the road and the car had full impact. In the seven years between 1922 and 1929, new houses were begun at the rate of 833,000 per year, a pace more than double that of any previous seven-year period. New suburbs sprouted on the edges of every major city. Of the seventy-one new incorporations in Illinois and Michigan in the 1920s, two-thirds were Chicago, St. Louis, or Detroit suburbs. Statistics for individual communities were startling. Grosse Pointe, near Detroit, grew by 725 percent in the ten years; Elmwood Park, near Chicago, by 717 percent; and Beverly Hills, near Los Angeles, by 2,485 percent. Long Island's Nassau County almost tripled in population. Appropriately, the central character in F. Scott Fitzgerald's novel of the 1920s, *The Great Gatsby*, came east to "make it" in New York and then promptly purchased a suburban estate on Long Island.

The benefits of this suburban boom were not evenly distributed; the biggest gainers were usually real estate promoters who owned land somewhere near the new highways. Every multilane ribbon of concrete was like the touch of Midas, transforming old pastures into precious property. Of course, not all speculators got rich; some even lost money. Particularly in the latter part of the 1920s, overanxious subdividers platted more land than could be occupied, and many were thus driven into bankruptcy. Those who inaugurated their land promotion schemes earlier generally had better luck, and some of their parklike communities—such as Coral Gables, Florida, and Roland Park in Baltimore—retain their charm today. The most successful such developer was J. C. Nichols, who planned Kansas City's Country Club District around 1912. Offering "spacious ground for permanently protected homes, surrounded with ample space for air and sunshine," this six-thousand-acre residential setting became a national model for open spaces, set-back lines, and self-perpetuating deed restrictions, which were the acceptable way of keeping Jews and Negroes out of the preserve.

As a stimulus to the development of suburbs, the automobile had no greater impact than the mass transit innovations of the nineteenth century. In fact, even in the era of the Model T, some of the most spectacular suburban ventures were expressly tied to the fare boxes of streetcar lines. Niles Center, near Chicago; large parts of Queens in New York; and Shaker Heights, southeast of Cleveland, were all designed partially to increase transit revenues. The Ohio community, a several-thousand-acre tract on the site of an old Shaker religious colony, was the work of the Van Sweringen brothers. They developed an upper-middle-class community renowned for its preservation of parklands, its imaginative street plans, and its rigid architectural and construction standards. In 1920, the Van Sweringen electric rapid transit lines reached Shaker Heights; in the next decade, population grew by 1,000 percent, and real estate valuation increased more than five-fold.

However, the automobile did more than simply add additional layers to the streetcar suburbs which already surrounded every city. Unlike the fixed trolley tracks, which almost always led downtown and thus encouraged transit patrons to maintain their economic and social ties with the core, the private car encouraged crosstown or lateral movement and, if anything, discouraged travel to the increasingly traffic-snarled city center. The streetcar was permanent and inflexible; the automobile would go almost anywhere. In the late 1920s, President Herbert Hoover appointed a commission to examine contemporary trends in American life. Published in 1933 as *Recent Social Trends in the United States,* the report said this about the car:

> In no inconsiderable degree the rapid popular acceptance of the new vehicle centered in the fact that it gave to the owner a control over his movements that the older agencies denied. Close at hand and ready for instant use, it carried its owner from door to destination by routes he himself selected, and on schedules of his own making; baggage inconveniences were minimized and perhaps most important of all, the automobile made possible the movement of an entire family at costs that were relatively small. Convenience augmented utility and accelerated adoption of the vehicle.

The different characteristics of streetcar and automobile can be illustrated by considering the kind of retailing pattern which each encouraged. At the center of every mass transit system was the great department store— John Wanamaker's in Philadelphia; Gimbel's, R. H. Macy's, and A. T. Stewart's in New York; Marshall Field and Carson, Pirie, Scott in Chicago; Hudson's in Detroit; Rich's in Atlanta; Jordan Marsh in Boston. Without exception, these giant downtown stores experienced their greatest growth and relative success between 1870 and 1930, the time of the trolley.

In contrast, the outlying shopping center, whose formula was six square feet of parking for every square foot of selling area, became the symbol of the automobile culture. This new method of retailing was presaged in the 1920s, when Sears, Roebuck and Company embraced the concept of "America on wheels." Executives of this giant Chicago mail-order house decided that their new class A stores would be built in the suburbs. Such locations would offer the advantage of lower rentals, yet because of increasing automobile registrations, they would be within reach of potential customers. The nation's first shopping center, a complex of stores with off-street parking, opened inside Baltimore's city limits in 1907. After Nichols built a magnificent retailing plaza in his Kansas City Country Club District, the former was designated a "neighborhood" center and the latter a "suburban" one. Shortly after World War II, the concept was further expanded by the construction of one-hundred-store "regional" shopping centers remote from downtown. Prototypes such as Northgate, near Seattle; Shopper's World, outside Boston; and Lakewood, outside Los Angeles, were opened by 1950, and within twenty years more than 13,000 such centers had been built in the United States. Meanwhile, downtown areas, especially in older suburbs and smaller cities, became virtual ghost towns of dusty, underused shops.

The Contemporary Suburb

The depression of the 1930s slowed suburban growth as the scarcity of money and jobs encouraged people to stay put. During World War II, armaments production naturally took precedence over the building of homes, although the government did build factories in the suburbs to reduce the danger of enemy air attacks. In Detroit, for example, the Chrysler Tank Arsenal and the Hudson Naval Arsenal were erected beyond the city's boundaries in Warren Township.

The coming of peace in 1945 was followed by a generation of economic prosperity which provided new families with the financial means to act upon their desire for new homes. A vast surge in road construction supplemented the economic boom. Highway expenditures topped $2 billion in 1949, $3 billion in 1953, and $4 billion in 1955. New housing more than kept pace. Between 1946 and 1955, more than twice as many new houses were built as were constructed in the previous *fifteen* years. The peak year of this record-breaking construction decade was 1950, when over 1 million single-family houses were begun, almost half of them financed by the Federal Housing Administration (FHA) or the Veterans' Administration (VA).

The suburban boom continued into the late 1950s and 1960s on a slightly less dramatic scale. An important stimulus was the passage in 1956 of the Interstate Highway Act, which initiated the largest public works project in history. The 42,500-mile, $60 billion road network has been a special favorite of the highway lobby, one of the broadest-based of all pressure groups. It consists of the oil, rubber, automobile, asphalt, and construction industries; the car dealers and renters; the trucking and bus concerns; the banks and advertising agencies that depend on the companies involved; the American Automobile Association; state and local officials who want the federal government to pay for new highways in their areas; and labor unions. President Dwight D. Eisenhower gave four reasons for advocating the interstate highway program: current highways were unsafe, cars too often became snarled in traffic jams, poor roads saddled business with high costs for transportation, and modern highways were needed because "in case of atomic attack on our key cities, the road net must permit quick evacuation of target areas." Not a single word was said about the impact of highways on cities and suburbs, although the concrete thoroughfares and the thirty-five-ton tractor-trailers which used them encouraged the continued outward movement of industries toward the beltways and expressway interchanges. Moreover, the interstate system, paid for with 90 percent federal funds, helped continue the downward spiral of public transportation and virtually guaranteed that future urban growth would perpetuate a centerless sprawl. Soon after the bill was passed by the Senate, Lewis Mumford wrote sadly: "When the American people, through their Congress, voted a little while ago for a $26 billion highway program, the most charitable thing to assume is that they hadn't the faintest notion of what they were doing."

Large-scale builders knew what they were doing; taking advantage of the various subsidies of the federal government, they developed communities of every size, shape, and income level. Orange County, California, the home of Disneyland, became the nation's fastest growing suburban area, but imposing statistics could be cited for the outer rings of every metropolitan area. Cities varied somewhat in the speed of deconcentration, but not so much as is commonly supposed. New cities in the Southwest, for example, experienced a greater out-migration from the core than older cities in the East. The Census Bureau reported the opposite, however, because the newer communities were annexing vast tracts of new subdivisions, whereas the older cities were trapped within outmoded boundaries.

The move to the suburbs was almost self-generating. As larger numbers of affluent citizens moved out, shopping centers and jobs followed. In turn, this attracted more families, more roads, and more industries. The city was caught in a reverse cycle. As businesses and taxpayers left, property values declined or failed to rise proportionately with inflation, houses became older and more deteriorated, and low-income families moved in. The new residents required as many services from the city government as did the old, but they were less able to pay high property taxes. When municipal authorities had to increase expenditures, they levied higher property taxes, thus encouraging more middle-class homeowners to leave, causing the cycle to repeat. In Newark, currently the most financially impoverished major city in the United States, local real estate taxes are more than twice as high as they are in nearby suburbs, which offer better schools and public services.

The families that moved to Anaheim or Levittown or Park Forest or a thousand lesser-known suburbs after World War II were similar to earlier suburban migrants. Their motivation was simple: they wanted a house, and they wanted that house to be in a clean, healthy neighborhood that promised decent schools for their children. Proximity to work was not as important as a house and a yard. To a lesser extent, the suburbanites sought to separate themselves from the problems of race, crime, narcotics, congestion, and confusion. "Escape to Scarborough Manor," suggested the advertisements. "Escape from cities too big, too polluted, too crowded, too strident to call home."

The new homesites did not always provide the better life that the realtors promised, however. Postwar developers, thinking mostly of profits, crammed as many houses as possible onto a given piece of land. Bulldozers removed every vestige of the original vegetation, so that row upon row of look-alike houses could be built quickly. Along the feeder highways, garish commercial strips blinked neon messages from the entrances to fast-food outlets, gas stations, and motels of every variety. Joseph Wood Krutch dubbed the result a "sloburb" and asserted that if an individual were carried into one blindfolded, he would not even be able to tell what section of the nation he was in. And Russell Baker has bemoaned the fact that either America is a shopping center or that the one shopping center in existence is moving around the country at the speed of light.

According to some observers, the life style of the newest suburbs is as artificial as the physical environment. Fathers, weary from ten hours of commuting every week, are supposedly reduced to the status of weekend visitors in their own homes, and women fare no better in their roles as semi-professional chauffeurs. In fact, anthropologist Margaret Mead has argued that women will never assume an equal position in American society as long as they are isolated in bedroom communities.

But for all the criticism, it is necessary to remember that the suburbs have grown and doubtless will continue to grow because they satisfy the needs of those who live there better than any currently available alternative. In the late 1950s, Herbert J. Gans lived in and studied Levittown, New Jersey, a community seventeen miles from Philadelphia built entirely by Levitt and Sons. After more than two years of participant-observation in the new subdivision, the Columbia University sociologist concluded that most residents enjoyed their homes and took pleasure in the social contacts available in the largely residential setting. He did not find the boredom and malaise so often attributed to the suburban family, and he did not find that Levittowners were shaped by their environment. Rather, Gans reported that the attitudes of the residents were generally shaped before the move. All in all, Gans concluded, Levittown was a "good place to live."

In every case, the particular appeal of a given suburb or neighborhood is a personal matter. In recent years, however, it appears that the prospect of escape from the problems of the central city has become increasingly important. For example, race has become a particularly explosive issue. Since the end of the Civil War, blacks have increased their representation in American cities, North and South. In the larger metropolises, the shift was especially noticeable after World War I, when Afro-Americans replaced European immigrants as the primary source of cheap labor and as the most conspicuous occupants of the urban slums. Of course, they were effectively kept out of the newer suburban developments by restrictive covenants, "understandings" among realtors, zoning restrictions, and ultimately, violence. Civil rights laws passed since 1957, and particularly the open-housing law, which was passed within a few months of the Reverend Martin Luther King's assassination in 1968, have removed some of the more overt forms of racial discrimination in housing. But in 1970, only 9 of every 200 suburbanites were black, and *suburbia* will likely continue to be a synonym for *white*.

In recent years, some inner suburbs have become acquainted with problems that were once considered peculiar to the central city. During the 1960s, for example, poverty, unemployment, crime, and narcotics addiction all increased faster in the suburbs than in the core cities. Financial distress has followed, as working-class fringe areas have found themselves unable to pay for quality schools without a substantial industrial or commercial tax base. Hamtramck, Michigan, a smoke-smudged, independent suburb surrounded by Detroit, is the only bankrupt community in the nation.

In the long run, the experience of Hamtramck may not prove unusual, partly because the distinctions between city and suburb are largely transitory; they are opposite sides of the same coin. Suburbanization is a continuing, shifting process. As the core of the city expands, the periphery moves farther out. Many contemporary slums, such as Woodlawn in Chicago or Harlem in New York or Bedford in Brooklyn, were once distant suburbs that offered a bucolic atmosphere quite unlike that of the cities which finally engulfed them. Perhaps today's suburbs will lose their privileged status to newer neighborhoods. In any event, contemporary problems, whether they are related to narcotics, disease, or economic depression, do not respect political and suburban boundaries. Increasingly, all metropolitan residents are coming to live in "Spread City," or as one cynic termed it, "Phantom City," because you cannot tell when you enter or when you leave.

Many people make the easy choice. Their solution to contemporary problems is escape to a place yet farther out on the fringe, where they can pretend that they have nothing whatever to do with the distant city. Meanwhile, blight absorbs more and more of the older communities. Cities can thrive only if people accept the proposition that affluent rings around dying cores will ultimately prove disastrous for both the cities and the suburbs. But the prospects are not bright. A century ago Frederick Law Olmsted outlined his hopes for suburbanization:

> The present outward tendency of town population is not so much an ebb as a higher rise of the same flood (of urbanization), the end of which must be, not a

sacrifice of urban conveniences, but their combination with the special charms and substantial advantages of rural conditions of life.

Then, as now, however, the promise was only for the well-to-do.

Selected Bibliography

There is no general history of suburbs or suburbanization in America. A brief but provocative essay on the subject is Leo F. Schnore, "The Timing of Metropolitan Decentralization: A Contribution to the Debate," *Journal of the American Institute of Planners*, 25 (November 1959), 200–206. The best study of changing residential patterns in the pre–Civil War city is Allen Pred, *The Spatial Dynamics of Urban Industrial Growth: Interpretive and Theoretical Essays* (Cambridge, Mass., 1966). A methodologically interesting account of intraurban geographical mobility is Peter R. Knights, *The Plain People of Boston, 1830–1860: A Study in City Growth* (New York, 1971). Contemporary reports of suburbanization before 1860 include "The Diary of Sidney George Fisher, 1859–1860," *Pennsylvania Magazine of History and Biography*, 87 (April 1963), 189–225; and George Rogers Taylor, "Philadelphia in Slices; By George G. Foster," *Pennsylvania Magazine of History and Biography*, 93 (January 1969).

On the early development of mass transit in the United States see Charles J. Kennedy, "Commuter Services in the Boston Area, 1835–1860," *Business History Review*, 36 (Summer 1962), 153–70; Glen E. Holt, "The Changing Perception of Urban Pathology: An Essay on the Development of Mass Transit in the United States," in Kenneth T. Jackson and Stanley K. Schultz, editors, *Cities in American History* (New York, 1972), 324–43; and George Rogers Taylor, "The Beginnings of Mass Transportation in Urban America," *Smithsonian Journal of History*, 1 (1966), No. 2, 35–50, No. 3, 31–54. For the development of mass transit in the last part of the century, Sam Bass Warner, Jr., *Streetcar Suburbs: The Process of Growth in Boston, 1870–1900* (Cambridge, Mass., 1962), is indispensable. Students interested in comparative history will want to consult H. J. Dyos's meticulous *Victorian Suburb: A Study of the Growth of Camberwell* (Leicester, 1961) and David Ward, "A Comparative Historical Geography of Streetcar Suburbs in Boston, Massachusetts and Leeds, England; 1850–1920," *Annals of the Association of American Geographers*, 54 (1964), 477–89.

On the development of the suburban ideal, the best study is Peter J. Schmitt, *Back to Nature: The Arcadian Myth in Urban America* (New York, 1969). Olmsted's ideas may be examined in Albert Fein, editor, *Landscape into Cityscape: Frederick Law Olmsted's Plans for a Greater New York City* (Ithaca, N.Y., 1968). The reflections of William Dean Howells on deconcentration are contained in his *Suburban Sketches* (Boston, 1871).

For the early part of the twentieth century, the best book on the move away from urban cores is Harlan Paul Douglass, *The Suburban Trend* (New York, 1925). The author differentiated between urban, suburban, and rural zones and noted that suburbs tended to be nonproductive of goods and critical services. Another important book written during the period is Graham R. Taylor, *Satellite Cities: A Study of Industrial Suburbs* (New York, 1915). Amos H. Hawley, *The Changing Shape of Metropolitan America: Deconcentration since 1920* (Glencoe, Ill., 1956) is dry and unconvincing.

On the history of zoning, the standard works are Richard F. Babcock, *The Zoning Game: Municipal Practices and Policies* (Madison, Wis., 1966); Stanislaw J. Makielski, *The Politics of Zoning: The New York Experience* (New York, 1966); and Seymour I. Toll, *Zoned American* (New York, 1969). There is no satisfactory study of the FHA's impact on urban and suburban spatial patterns.

The only recent overview of the growth of cities through municipal annexation is Kenneth T. Jackson, "Metropolitan Government Versus Suburban Autonomy: Politics on the Crabgrass Frontier," in Jackson and Schultz, editors, *Cities in American History*, 442–62. Earlier studies which remain useful are: Richard Bigger and James D. Kitchen, *How the Cities Grew: A Century of Municipal Independence and Expansion in Metropolitan Los Angeles* (Los Angeles, 1952); Roderick D. McKenzie, *The Metropolitan Community* (New York, 1933); and Paul Studenski, editor, *The Government of Metropolitan Areas in the United States* (New York, 1930).

The literature of the post–World War II suburbs has been vast. Two stimulating essays that should be the starting point for anyone interested in the modern suburb are Herbert J. Gans, "Urbanism and Suburbanism as Ways of Life: A Re-Evaluation of Some Definitions," in Arnold Rose, editor, *Human Behavior and Social Processes* (Boston, 1962), 625–48, and Bennett M. Berger, "Suburbia and the American Dream," *The Public Interest*, 2 (Winter 1966), 80–91. The most famous single work is William H. Whyte's classic study, *The Organization Man* (New York, 1956). An equally distinguished and more recent study of a single community is Herbert J. Gans, *The Levittowners: Ways of Life and Politics in a New Suburban Community* (New York, 1967). Other important books on the subject include: Bennett M. Berger, *Working Class Suburb: A Study of Auto Workers in Suburbia* (Berkeley, Calif., 1960); Scott Donaldson, *The Suburban Myth* (New York, 1969); William M. Dobriner, editor, *The Suburban Community* (New York, 1958); Robert C. Wood, *Suburbia: Its People and Their Politics* (Boston, 1958); and Benjamin Chinitz, editor, *City and Suburb: The Economics of Metropolitan Growth* (Englewood Cliffs, N.J., 1965).

Perspectives on the Contemporary City

James F. Richardson

A general discussion of contemporary cities must immediately acknowledge the fact that cities vary significantly from each other—that there is the risk of lumping together apples and oranges in an overview such as this. Cities differ in size, age, rate of growth, and the degree to which they are able to encompass new settlement on their peripheries. Any useful analysis of urban prospects and current and future problems must weigh the importance of these differences. Smaller communities often have highly specialized economies, with a large proportion of their jobs in one or two activities, such as in a factory or in providing services to surrounding farmers. These communities are particularly vulnerable to the winds of economic change. If they lose an industry, they experience great difficulty replacing it, and changing transportation patterns and the decline in the number of farmers reduce their trade functions. Big cities may be sick, but many smaller ones are dying. Economic differences between cities flatten out in larger cities. In contrast to the specialization found in smaller cities, large cities and metropolitan areas have generally similar economic bases and employment patterns. Major industries locate branch facilities in each metropolis or region to maximize marketing opportunities and to cut transportation costs. Large metropolitan areas have resources of capital, labor, and entrepreneurial talent which provide a cushion against catastrophic economic decline, except when the whole economy collapses.

New, rapidly growing cities differ economically and demographically from older, more slowly growing areas. Growth areas attract firms and individuals who have the most mobility and are able to take advantage of the opportunities offered by a new urban center. The initial attraction for people to move to a city may be jobs available in a new industry—automobiles in Detroit in the early twentieth century, for example—or amenities of climate, such as in Los Angeles at the same time. Whatever the motivations of

222

new arrivals, their presence creates economic opportunity for others. A multiplier effect fuels further growth. When the locational advantages of a city have been fully exploited and diseconomies set in, for either firms or individuals, growth will be much slower.

In the contemporary United States, the growing cities and metropolitan areas are in parts of the South and the Southwest; the older metropolises of the northeastern quadrant of the nation, from New York to St. Louis, grow much more slowly. Much current discussion of urban conditions, often labeled the "urban crisis" or the "plight of the cities," draws upon the recent experiences of New York, Newark, Philadelphia, Pittsburgh, Cleveland, Detroit, Chicago, Boston, and St. Louis. In these and similar metropolitan areas, old and growing slowly, if at all, the gap between central cities and suburbs widens. The Kerner Commission warned in the late 1960s that the United States was becoming two nations, separate and unequal—a constantly higher percentage of blacks is becoming mired in core cities while whites expand suburban populations. The census of 1970 confirmed this perception of an accelerating central city–suburban dichotomy. For example, hardly any affluent whites are left in Newark, whose black mayor, Kenneth Gibson, finds himself a receiver in bankruptcy.

American urban history abounds with ambitious projections of great cities—some of them little more than a gleam in a promoter's eye—which never materialized, but New York, Philadelphia, Cleveland, and Chicago never belonged in this category. These were key nodes in the national urban network which developed in the nineteenth century, the winners in the competition for railroads and industry, around which great cities developed.

Contemporary urban scholarship focusing on these cities is the dismal science of this generation. The central cities of the nation's oldest and largest metropolitan areas are caught in a seemingly inexorable vise of economic and human decay manifested in high rates of unemployment, crime, and disease, a declining tax base, mounting deficits, racial polarization, and increasing despair among citizens and public officials. As the essays in this volume indicate, there is nothing particularly new about many of these urban problems. In the nineteenth century, New York, Boston, and Philadelphia suffered from poverty, slums, pollution, inadequate education, crime in the streets, an overloaded transportation and communication network, and municipal governments seemingly overwhelmed by the complexity of their tasks.

However, important differences exist between current urban dilemmas and those of past generations. Edward Banfield argues in *The Unheavenly City* that American cities are better than ever but that expectations outpace performance; psychological perceptions demand a constantly rising—indeed, impossible—level of achievement. The quality of life is significantly higher for the mass of urbanites today than for all but the most favored city dwellers of 1900. However, scholars and public officials in 1900 could look to economic growth and technological innovation for solutions to their problems, but their contemporary counterparts in central cities see the growth and innovation occurring outside the borders of their cities, thus eroding their tax base and weakening their competitive position.

Cities have always grown by attracting newcomers from the country-side, whether from Europe or from rural America; historically, one of the major functions of cities has been to turn rural man into urban man. But the present geographical structure of older metropolitan areas works against the absorption of newcomers into the urban economy. Since the middle of the nineteenth century, disadvantaged immigrants and rural migrants have lived in the inner city; the contemporary association of the inner city with crowding, blight, and social ills has deep historical roots. However, there is the crucial difference: in the nineteenth century, the inner city was the locus of unskilled and semiskilled employment as well as the residence of the poor. Inner-city locations provided maximum access to job opportunities for new arrivals because commercial and industrial activity clustered in the downtown areas, the central business district.

The technology of the nineteenth century encouraged such concentration. Most cities grew up around the intersection of wharves and railroads, and firms wished to be as close as possible to the hub of the intercity and interregional transportation network because of the high costs of intracity transportation and communication. Also, inner-city locations gave firms maximum access to available labor—the corollary to maximum job opportunities for workers—as well as proximity to outside firms and specialists, to suppliers, and to information necessary to conduct business profitably. These external economies led entrepreneurs to pay the high cost of inner-city land and to put up with the inconveniences of congestion. Moreover, in the early stages of an industry's development, firms often find it advantageous to cluster near each other. Pioneers built automobiles in widely scattered locations, but by the first decade of the twentieth century, the industry began to concentrate in Detroit, which proved a convenient site for assembling materials, parts, and labor.

In contrast, contemporary economic and technological considerations favor dispersal rather than concentration. Firms find that building new plants on a regional and international basis is more profitable than expanding or even maintaining production at the original focal point. Thus, automobile assembly is no longer concentrated in Detroit, tire production in Akron, or steel manufacturing in Pittsburgh. New plants are more efficient; they are located near major markets, thus cutting transportation costs, and especially overseas, they have far lower labor costs. Thus, one-industry towns, which could become big cities if the industry were sufficiently large, find themselves involved in a sometimes painful economic realignment.

Within metropolitan areas, industry increasingly locates or relocates on the suburban periphery rather than in the urban core, a process which, although it began before 1900, has accelerated considerably in the years since World War II. During the war, to meet extraordinary production demands, many new plants were built within central cities, for the most part on vacant land abutting the suburbs, because gasoline and tire rationing inhibited development in areas that were inaccessible by public transportation. This limitation was no longer valid after 1945, and industry now seeks locations outside the political boundaries of central cities. The one-story, continuous-flow production line is by far the most efficient; elevators are a notorious bottleneck in older, multistory facilities. One-story plants demand extensive space, space that is either not available or too expensive within the central city. In addition, a labor force which drives to work demands huge areas for parking lots. The federal highway building program, begun in 1956, which increasingly makes trucks the key element in interregional transportation, encourages access to one or more interstate highways as a prime locational consideration. Firms thus also avoid the high transportation and loading costs caused by crowded city streets and limited docking space.

While industry benefits from suburban locations, inner-city workers or would-be workers suffer. Entry-level jobs are usually secured either by applying at the plant gate or by learning from a friend that a plant is hiring, but these mechanisms do not work well when the plant is fifteen miles away. Furthermore, little or no public transportation is available to many suburban locations, and what there is tends to be both time-consuming and expensive, so that workers must drive. Inner-city residents who cannot finance a car are thus shut off from most job opportunities.

Other economic functions such as retail trade and entertainment have also joined the suburban exodus, further curbing employment opportunities for residents of the core and eroding the city's tax base. Downtown department stores do a continuously dwindling percentage of retail sales, as activity shifts to suburban shopping malls. The trend is so far advanced that even older suburban shopping centers face increasing competition from newer clusters farther out from the core. Owners of professional sports teams in New York, Cleveland, Detroit, and Baltimore have proposed or threatened to build new facilities outside city limits. First-run films play in new shopping center "cinemas," while downtown's great movie palaces from an earlier era are torn down, boarded up, or reduced to playing "skin flicks."

Some forms of white-collar employment continue to cluster in central business districts. These areas throb with people and activity during business hours but are increasingly deserted at night, as workers hurry back to their suburban homes. Thus, we have the absurd situation of white-collar workers, primarily white, commuting into downtown from the periphery of the city and the suburbs, while blue-collar workers and domestics, heavily black, reverse commute to suburban homes, factories, and service centers.

Most of the big, old core cities have lost population since 1950, although their metropolitan areas have continued to grow. Urban decline can thus be explained as a process of metropolitan expansion. As Kenneth T. Jackson indicated, suburbs appeared almost as soon as cities, which have always grown by encompassing new territory at the periphery. For more than a century, the original core of cities such as Philadelphia have lost population as improved transportation enabled affluent people to exercise choice about where they would live. With the growth of economic activity, the central business district expanded into surrounding residential areas, and offices, factories, warehouses, and stores displaced townhouses and tenements. As the population grew on the periphery, so did retailing and commercial recreation.

These movements ignored the political boundaries of cities, but for a long time communities met the challenge through annexation. Suburbanites either sought annexation to gain the advantages of city services, or they lacked the power to resist being forcibly joined with the central city. The cities that are now declining in population are those that are no longer able to annex surrounding territory. On the other hand, as Jackson noted, those cities that have exhibited population growth in recent decades have been able to expand their physical boundaries. If these cities, mainly located in the South and West, were restricted to their political limits of 1940, they also would show a drop in population.

The cities in most trouble are those hemmed in by organized communities, which siphon off desirable taxpayers, whether businesses or individuals, from the decaying core. Cleveland, Ohio, is a particularly graphic example. As the Lake Erie Terminus of the Ohio Canal, in the nineteenth century Cleveland attracted railroad builders and iron and later steel manufacturers, who found the city convenient for combining Michigan and Minnesota ore with Pennsylvania and Ohio coal. John D. Rockefeller began his Standard Oil Company there, and an important machine tool industry developed. By 1920, Cleveland was the nation's fifth largest city, but from that date on much of the area's growth occurred outside the boundaries of the city. Cuyahoga County, of which Cleveland is part, contained about 1 percent of the total national population. Because the area represented a good demographic sample of the nation as a whole, firms used it to test new products.

In the years before World War I, Cleveland, under reform mayors Tom Johnson and Newton Baker, epitomized the potentialities of urban America. The city had problems, serious ones, but it also possessed talented and dedicated political leadership. Johnson especially projected an exciting sense of the possibilities of the American city as a community which could contribute to the human development of all its citizens, and he attracted able and energetic followers who shared his vision. Long after his death in 1911, Cleveland's Democrats invoked his name, just as their nineteenth century counterparts called on the spirits of Thomas Jefferson and Andrew Jackson to preserve the purity of the party's principles.

Johnson's followers honored his memory but could not fulfill his dreams. His activities had created enemies as well as admirers, and the men whose interests he had threatened constituted a solid core of opposition. The combination of movement of people and economic activity beyond the physical boundaries of the city and a slowdown in the rate of growth of the area as a whole made men cautious about programs for social reconstruction. Descendants of Connecticut Yankees who first settled the Western Reserve area of Ohio approached any proposal for government spending with a wary eye. As new immigrants and their children came to political maturity in the 1920s and after, Yankees and ethnics found that they shared a common low-tax ideology. After World War I, progressivism generally exhibited a low level of energy, as such issues as prohibition and the Ku Klux Klan took priority. Cleveland was unique in the respect that in 1924 it gave a plurality of its votes to Robert LaFollette, the third-party candidate for president.

In local affairs, Cleveland of the 1920s, like other American cities, equated progress with huge building projects. Public funds constructed a mammoth public auditorium and the lake-front stadium where Otto Graham and Jim Brown later played great football for the Cleveland Browns. The Van Sweringen brothers, railroad and real estate promoters, built the massive Terminal Tower, which, although it was badly designed and located, did help to maintain the focus of the central business district. Some of these projects were completed after the stock market crash of 1929.

The Great Depression struck Cleveland with devastating force. Its heavy industry and machine tool economy proved especially vulnerable to the drying up of investment in new plants and equipment, and at the depth of the downturn, in some parts of the community a majority of workers lacked jobs. The city struggled to collect taxes to provide basic services, and civil servants faced layoffs or pay cuts of up to 25 percent. Municipal government limited itself to the role of caretaker, a role which persisted even after the unintended Keynesianism of World War II ended the depression. Cleveland businessmen seemed exceptionally conservative and limited in vision, and homeowners resisted proposals that threatened to raise their taxes. Frank Lausche, who rose from mayor of Cleveland to governor of Ohio and United States senator, represented perfectly the conservative nature of his city.

In the 1950s and 1960s, the most important cleavages in Cleveland, as in many other cities, shifted from economic and ethnic rivalries to racial polarization. Blacks in the city have long been concentrated on the east side of the Cuyahoga River, although long before the city had a significant black population, east siders and west siders had a strong sense of local loyalty and separateness. The city council contains thirty-three members elected by wards, which further encourages local identity and political fragmentation. The combination of white out-migration and black in-migration has intensified the sense of separation and cleavage between the predominantly white west side and the increasingly black east side. In 1950, Cleveland had 914,808 people, the highest total in the city's history; by 1970, the total population had declined to 750,903. Just as significant as the overall drop was the change in racial composition. In 1950, Cleveland had 765,264 whites and 147,847 blacks; in 1970, there were 458,903 whites and 287,841 blacks. The net loss of over 300,000 whites more than offset the gain of 140,000 blacks. (These statistics do not take into account the probable undercount of the black population by census takers.) In the same period, the Cleveland metropolitan area grew from 1,465,511 to 2,064,194. In 1970, only 3.4 percent of the suburban population was black.

The implications of these changes can be seen most clearly on the neighborhood level. In the 1950s, urban renewal and other clearance projects pushed blacks from the near east side farther out from the center of the city. The Hough area, which stretches from East 55th Street to East 105th Street, was 95 percent white in 1950 and overwhelmingly black in 1960. Landlords in the area took advantage of limited housing opportunities for blacks by systematic rent gouging. The general practice was to charge as much as the traffic would bear, to spend as little as possible for maintenance, and to get out fast. The population of the area had dropped by 1970 as owners abandoned buildings, and those who could moved out. Hough achieved national notoriety in 1966 with its contribution to the "long, hot summers" of the 1960s. Cleveland, like Detroit, Newark, Los Angeles, and many smaller cities, suffered from wide-ranging arson and looting as the rage of young blacks exploded into action. Cleveland's Hough was just one of many urban ghettos in ferment.

Riots intensified fear of crime in the streets and led pessimists to believe that the United States was not only mired in an immoral and unwinnable war abroad but also faced increasing domestic discord and violence. America's failures to achieve racial and economic justice were most visible in metropolitan areas, where prosperous, pleasant white communities surrounded decaying black cores. The political fragmentation of metropolitan areas, with their noose of independent suburbs around the central city, meant that the burdens of poverty and injustice would fall disproportionately on central cities at a time of declining tax bases.

Historically, cities could not expect much from their respective state governments. For a long time, states milked their major cities, taking far more in taxes than they returned in services or state support for local functions. States could justify this treatment on the grounds that in economic relations, cities drained money from the countryside and small towns. Still, legislatures, which were dominated by rural and small-town representatives, lacked knowledge and sympathy for the problems of cities. A good example is the Ohio legislature's treatment of Cleveland. Most cities achieved "home rule," thus becoming free of the shackles of excessively restrictive or interfering state control, only in the twentieth century. Ironically, attainment of home rule coincided with suburban decisions that costs of joining the central city outweighed possible benefits, and suburbs used home rule arguments to resist political expansion by the central city. Ohio's annexation laws make it impossible for Cleveland to expand beyond its present seventy-six square miles.

Since World War I, cities have made periodic attempts to bypass states and establish direct relations with the federal government to deal with some of their problems. The New Deal brought a considerable federal presence to urban communities, thus aiding Democratic political organizations in cities, and the urban renewal program begun in 1949 hoped to revitalize core cities. Various programs adopted during Lyndon Johnson's administration, especially the "war on poverty" and the model cities program, assumed that infusion of federal money and of innovative approaches would reverse the cycle of decay and despair affecting so many cities. But as Raymond A. Mohl noted, to date these expectations have not been met. According to *Regulating the Poor*, by Frances Fox Piven and Richard A. Cloward, expansion of federal programs in cities served more to swell local welfare rolls than anything else. Poverty program lawyers beat down techniques used by local bureaucrats to keep eligible people off welfare rolls; programs supposedly designed to promote economic justice resulted simply in adding more people to the welfare department's case load. Piven and Cloward argue that the experience of the sixties is consistent with a long-range pattern in which the number of welfare recipients bears no relation to the number of people in need but reflects other considerations. When the interest of the powerful is labor-market discipline, rolls are limited in order to force men and women into the labor market and to take whatever work is available at the lowest possible wage. However, if fear of social disorder is greater than the desire for a pool of low-wage labor, rolls expand as a way of defusing social tensions. In effect, potentially dangerous people are bought off with welfare. If fear of social upheaval subsides, rolls shrink to enlarge the number of domestics and other poorly paid service workers. These propositions are asserted rather than proven in their book, but their case is persuasive.

Even if Cloward and Piven are unduly harsh in their assessment of federal programs in the 1960s, it is clear that federal involvement per se is no panacea for cities. Indeed, many federal programs have detracted from rather than contributed to the health of core cities. Federally guaranteed mortgages promoted the growth of all-white suburbs; urban renewal has destroyed substantial amounts of low-rent housing without providing replacements; public housing projects such as Pruitt-Igoe in St. Louis developed into unmitigated social disasters; federal highways have torn huge chunks out of central cities and have divided neighborhoods in the interests of intercity trucking firms and suburban commuters; and recent programs designed to promote private investment in inner-city housing paradoxically have produced windfall profits for speculators while reducing the number of inhabitable units. George Romney, as secretary of the Department of Housing and Urban Development, publicly proclaimed his despair over the failure of the mortgage subsidy program.

In the 1960s, optimists hoped that charismatic mayors such as Jerome Cavanaugh of Detroit, Carl Stokes of Cleveland, and John Lindsay of New York would be able to mobilize local resources, public and private, to respond creatively to the needs of their communities as well as to dramatize effectively the plight of cities generally. But the bright new mayors of the sixties did not succeed in creating the kind of federal involvement that would promote racial and economic justice in cities. The election of 1968 resulted in a hairline victory for those citizens who were most afraid of big cities, of their social turmoil, and of the institutional change that might enhance their viability.

The Nixon administration's greatest concern about cities has been crime in the streets. Federal money for improving the criminal justice system comes through the Law Enforcement Assistance Agency, which gives block grants. Many states have funneled a disproportionate amount of money into rural areas and small towns whose crime problems, while sometimes increasing, are not nearly as severe as those of large cities. When money has gone to cities, some have used it to buy their police forces more sophisticated and destructive weapons. The needs of upgrading police training and performance and improving the courts and correctional system are as yet unmet.

Mayors find Washington unsympathetic, and the burdens of office in their own cities grind down all but the most durable, such as Chicago's

Richard Daley. Now in his fifth term as mayor, Daley also presides over the most effective big-city political organization in the country. As Bruce M. Stave noted, Daley delivers because he combines the roles of chief executive and party leader of a disciplined army of ward chieftains and precinct workers, who hold some 34,000 patronage jobs. Downtown businessmen appreciate City Hall's ability to clear roadblocks and expedite projects; the white working class responds favorably to Daley's plebian style; and poor blacks receive handouts from the machine's functionaries.

At a time when municipal governments seem paralyzed either by absence of power or by too many competing power centers, Chicago at least provides an example of a city government that functions. No one doubts where the locus of power lies. But, as Stave indicates, Daley's centralization does not meet the needs of all segments of the city. New construction rises in the central business district, while appalling slums decay even further a few miles away; some of the poor receive handouts, but little is done about the existence of poverty; government delivers highly visible basic services but smothers initiative and creativity and sometimes the civil rights of those who do not conform.

Mayors who lack Daley's organizational base either find their popularity eroding to the point where reelection is impossible, or they give up voluntarily because of the immense demands the office imposes upon them. John Lindsay must wonder whether New York City is governable. He came into office denouncing the "power brokers" who put the interests of their special constituencies above those of the city as a whole. He has learned that these "brokers" do exercise power and that they cannot be ignored or made to disappear by ritualistic invocations of the public interest. The mayor must also deal with an increasingly militant and demanding bureaucracy that is no longer content to follow the model of a meek, unambitious, and uncomplaining civil servant. New York City has 400,000 municipal employees, who by themselves would be the thirty-first largest city in the United States. Many of these employees are organized into cohesive unions led by tough, determined men who have stopped the subways and let the garbage pile up in pursuit of their goals of more money and better working conditions. Strikes by public employees, almost unthinkable in past generations, became commonplace under Lindsay. By most accounts, the mayor does not relish the tasks of mediating and negotiating; he would much rather articulate lofty goals and aspirations. The nitty-gritty of delivering services to an enormously diverse and complex public through the mechanism of an isolated and fearful bureaucracy, anxious to protect its turf and established procedures, lacks the charm of traveling around the country preaching a gospel of urban salvation. Like other top men in complex organizations, Lindsay has found it easier to make pronouncements and to decree reorganization than to move his underlings in directions they do not want to go. Lindsay cannot rely on the kind of patronage-rich, disciplined political organization that Daley has to keep power and to exercise it in governing his city; New York has too many power centers, including the organized municipal bureaucracy.

Civil service regulations guaranteeing job protection and promotion from within support bureaucrats' ability to resist pressures for change. Like most people, civil servants prefer to move in traditional ways rather than to respond to demands from constituents or superiors for new modes of operation or standards of judgment. Police departments strenuously resist innovation, as do school systems and welfare departments. Mayors thus have serious difficulty in controlling the activities of those who are theoretically subordinate to them; moreover, the vital nature of the services provided by many public servants gives them great power in advancing their interests. City departments are monopolists, which means that they can get away with providing the kind of product or service that is comfortable for them rather than what their constituency wants. If they withhold their labor, residents must go without garbage collection or babysitting for their children in the public schools.

Pay raises, staff additions, and the upward thrust of inflation generally have put cities in a fiscal crunch. Cities provide services, and it is difficult enough to measure, no less increase, the productivity of those engaged in service occupations. Yet the wage and salary structure of the entire economy is strongly influenced by those sectors, such as manufacturing, in which productivity increases are possible. If productivity in industry rises 2 or 3 percent a year, and the wage scale reflects that, a spillover effect will push up wages in the service sector. But productivity does not increase in such occupations as teaching or welfare case work, and the result is rising real costs. Cities thus constantly need more money to maintain the same level of services. In addition, citizens' demands for services rise continuously. They want more—more police and firemen, more recreational facilities, and more special programs in schools.

Cities' fiscal positions suffer from reliance on the property tax, which has few defenders. It does not bear much relation to ability to pay; it is extremely difficult to administer with any fairness; it encourages decay by increasing the burden on property owners who make improvements; and it hits the taxpayer with brutal directness and force. From 1957 to 1967, the percentage of total revenue American cities derived from the property tax declined from 46.3 percent to 37.9 percent. However, the property tax, which is singularly inelastic, remains the largest single source of revenue. Unlike income taxes, revenue from property taxes does not automatically increase as economic activity expands, and the burden remains the same when business activity and income slump. Attempts to raise more money by raising assessments or rates leads businesses and families to seek new locations outside the cities' tax boundaries.

While profit-oriented and tax-paying activities have moved out, religious, cultural, charitable, and educational institutions, which are nonprofit and nontaxpaying, have remained in central-city locations. Again, Cleveland is a case in point. The city possesses a superb art museum, a magnificent public library, and superior medical facilities. Affluent suburbanites probably use these institutions more than central-city residents do, although much of their support in the form of tax-free land and police and fire protection comes from the Cleveland municipal budget. The presence of these facilities does help make urban life urbane, but municipal finances suffer. Central cities must bear the burdens of both poverty-related and culture-related services for the metropolitan area as a whole. Increasingly, where states permit, cities have turned to income taxes to gain some revenue from suburbanites who work in the city and presumably use some of its other facilities. Another possibility is the imposition of user charges on public services, so that people interested in a particular service would pay at least part of its cost. However, opponents respond that such charges would penalize the poor and would give some citizens greater access than others to public facilities.

Property and income taxes and user charges combined still leave cities without sufficient money to meet their needs. The federal government and the states have made some response to cities' fiscal plight by increasing the amount of intergovernmental revenue: in the decade 1957 to 1967, the proportion of total municipal income derived from intergovernmental exchanges rose from 18.9 to 26.5 percent. But the pressing financial needs of older core cities and their less affluent suburbs will not be met without further substantial increases in intergovernmental revenue. In effect, state and federal tax systems must transfer money from affluent to poor across the political boundaries of fragmented metropolises.

The combination of decay at the core and development on the periphery is not so damaging to those cities which have been able to expand their boundaries in the last twenty years or so. Shifts in location of economic activity and residences of the affluent do not threaten their solvency and morale to the same degree as in those cities that are circumscribed by boundaries established a generation or more ago. In the "sunbelt" of the South and Southwest, such cities as Atlanta, Jacksonville, Houston, and Phoenix have expanded dramatically in geographical area and population; their experience has been the direct opposite of Boston, Cleveland, and St. Louis. As proximity to natural resources becomes less important in locational decisions, amenities of climate take precedence. A generation ago about 30 percent of the labor force was resource-bound; the current figure is about 7 percent, reflecting the occupational shift away from heavy industry and toward white-collar and service jobs. More people can thus forsake bleak northern winters for a Mediterranean life style.

Many rapidly growing sun-belt cities do not have to contend with established suburbs that are out to preserve their independence at all costs, nor do they face the unworkable annexation laws prevalent in northern states. Texas has the most liberal annexation laws in the country, a fact reflected in the recent history of Houston. From 1950 to 1970, Houston expanded from 160 square miles to 453 square miles. In the same period, its population rose from 596,163 to 1,232,802. According to Texas law, Houston and other cities do not have to secure approval from residents of areas being annexed. Here, at least, the bulldozer revolution does not lead to formation of new municipalities determined to resist encroachment by central cities.

At the time northern suburbs decided that the costs of joining the central city outweighed possible benefits and began resisting annexation, some central city civic leaders began pressing for metropolitan government. In 1917, the Cleveland Chamber of Commerce pointed out the absurdity of an economic and social unit, the metropolitan area, being politically fragmented and urged that suburbs be annexed to the city. However, by 1925, the chamber no longer supported annexation or integrated metropolitan government, urging instead that coordination be achieved through intergovernmental cooperation. Obviously, between 1917 and 1925, many of the chamber's members forsook the city and decided that suburban residential independence held priority over political integration.

As Bruce M. Stave indicated, much of the history of American urban government can be written in terms of a conflict between centralization and decentralization. At the present time, that conflict takes the form of proposals for metropolitan government versus demands for community control. Some political scientists preach metropolitan government as the only solution to urban ills; only by balancing needs and resources can urban areas survive and prosper. Suburban exclusiveness must oe overcome to prevent communities from attracting industry and zoning out workers at the same time. Advocates of community control contend that urban government is already too remote and inaccessible for most citizens, especially for poor and dark-skinned ones. Central-city blacks realize that metropolitan government might increase resources available for inner-city areas, but they are afraid of being outvoted by suburban white majorities. In the early twentieth century, structural reformers advocated centralization of municipal government to curb the power of political spokesmen, or "bosses," of inner-city, lower-class residents. Blacks, achieving major political office for the first time, fear that metropolitan government would have the same effect on them.

Metropolitan government, which on the surface seems the most logical and rational way to equalize burdens and improve services, thus meets opposition both from suburbanites and central-city voters. Suburbanites do not want to be saddled with the fiscal and social problems of the core city, and blacks do not want to lose opportunities for office and power and the chance to have what suburbanites have long prided themselves on—a government responsive to their needs and interests. Also, any proposal to change an existing structure faces the opposition of those who hold office or have otherwise learned to function comfortably in that structure unless they can see direct, immediate advantages for themselves.

Some recent developments may decrease resistance to structural changes or find alternate methods of achieving some of the same goals. In pursuit of educational equality, courts are increasingly questioning the local property tax as the base of financing schools. Industry-rich districts or affluent communities sometimes spend more than twice as much per student as other communities in the same county. Proposals for equalizing revenues on a state or metropolitan level are gaining ground among legislatures and other public bodies. In the Minneapolis–St. Paul metropolitan area, communities currently share a portion of tax revenues from new industrial or commercial structures. Court decisions may accelerate this trend.

Legal suits now under way are attacking discriminatory zoning. In what can only be described as fiscal civil war, municipalities attempt to attract big taxpayers, especially research laboratories or clean, nonpolluting industry, while at the same time restricting residential building, which might increase school taxes. However, industrial and commercial interests often oppose restrictive zoning. Employers want to increase their labor market, and restricting workers to inner-city and older suburban locations is inconvenient both to workers and employers. Advocates of racial integration realize that governmental activity against obvious racial bias in housing is not enough; only if affluent suburbs are opened to people of lower income can they be racially integrated. A zoning ordinance which mandates a two-acre lot for a single-family residence maintains segregation as effectively as the now illegal restrictive covenant. Some judges seem ready to invalidate such ordinances, especially if the municipality in question makes any attempt to attract industry.

If local governments did not rely so heavily on the property tax, restrictive zoning might not be so popular. As it is, community leaders believe that any departure from fiscal zoning would bring disaster to their communities. Survival rests on securing businesses and residents who pay their own way in taxes. Whites who support integration, in theory at any rate, can deny it in practice through the measures they adopt to support the fiscal viability of their communities. If restrictive zoning and heavy reliance on local property taxes is done away with by court and legislative action, suburbanites will no longer be able to maintain segregation behind a cloak of fiscal responsibility. They will have to ask themselves whether they want to intensify that tendency noted by the Kerner Commission—that we are becoming two nations separate and unequal.

The great advantage of a major urban area is the number of options available—in choice of jobs, residences, recreational and cultural facilities, institutions, and life styles. But this range is open only to those with enough money and the right color of skin. Affluent whites are better off than they have ever been, but blacks and poor whites bear an undue burden of the costs of affluence, whether in pollution or in absolute or relative deprivation. Central-city residents have the worst air to breathe and the fewest environmental amenities. Nor do blacks have any assurance that if they do what is expected of them by the culture—acquiring economic competence, for example—they will be able to share fully in the rewards of affluence.

In the final analysis, the problems of American cities are problems of American civilization. Cleavages of class and race, deeply embedded in American culture, produce metropolises divided against themselves; treating the environment as a store of riches to be looted and exploited, a carryover of pioneer traditions, fouls our air and poisons our water. Lewis Mumford, who has written sensibly and sensitively about cities and civilization for more than forty-five years, bemoans American fascination with power in its various manifestations. He believes that unless we change the course of our civilization, we will soon create "Necropolis," the city of the dead. In Mumford's view, only if society supports life-expanding rather than power-oriented activities can we avoid disaster in our cities and society generally. Observers less "grandly gloomy" than Mumford also believe that major social and institutional changes are needed to make cities viable.

Urban historians such as the authors of this book study the past to make sense of the present and to see what should be avoided in the future. History may not be a "policy science," in the jargon of current urban scholars, but no scholar, policy maker, or citizen can act intelligently without historical depth and perspective. Reading these essays should be the beginning, not the end, of the search for that understanding that is a necessary prelude to constructive social change.

Selected Bibliography

The literature on contemporary cities is enormous, although to date diagnosis and prescription have been more common than cure or improvement. Daniel P. Moynihan, editor, *Toward a National Urban Policy* (New York, 1970), is a useful collection of essays covering a wide range of topics. James Q. Wilson, editor, *The Metropolitan Enigma* (Cambridge, Mass., 1968), contains fewer pieces, and consequently each author has more scope to develop his argument. Raymond Vernon, *The Myth and Reality of Our Urban Problems* (Cambridge, Mass., 1962), is a trenchant critique of the urban thinking dominant in the 1950s. Edward C. Banfield, *The Unheavenly City: The Nature and Future of Our Urban Crisis* (Boston, 1970), provides a neo-Social Darwinist view of contemporary urban ills.

Several useful books on urban economics have appeared in the last few years. Wilbur R. Thompson, *A Preface to Urban Economics* (Baltimore, 1965), a pioneering text, assumes some familiarity with the technical vocabulary of economics, as do some of the pieces in Harvey S. Perloff and Lowdon Wingo, Jr., editors, *Issues in Urban Economics* (Baltimore, 1968). Anthony Downs, *Urban Problems and Prospects* (Chicago, 1970), is an informed discussion by an economist in nontechnical language. Niles Hansen, *Rural Poverty and the Urban Crisis* (Bloomington, Ind., 1970), builds a case for bringing the people to where the jobs are through a policy of assisted migration to medium-sized cities (250,000–750,000) which have shown a capacity for growth. Victor Gruen, *The Heart of Our Cities: The Urban Crisis: Diagnosis and Cure* (New York, 1964), is a planner's prescription for urban revitalization. Roger Starr, *The Living End: The City and Its Critics* (New York, 1966), is a witty antidote to some of the more extreme writing on cities.

Segregation and poverty have also received substantial attention. Karl E. and Alma F. Taeuber, *Negroes in Cities: Residential Segregation and Neighborhood Change* (Chicago, 1965), is a careful statistical study. Charles Silberman, *Crisis in Black and White* (New York, 1964), is a survey by a perceptive journalist written before the urban riots of the 1960s. Paul Jacobs, *Prelude to Riot: A View of Urban America from the Bottom* (New York, 1967), examines the festering grievances leading to rioting in one city, Los Angeles. Jeanne R. Lowe, *Cities in a Race with Time: Progress and Poverty in America's Renewing Cities* (New York, 1967), shows that cosmetic improvements in central business districts do not solve the problems of the poor and deprived in cities. *Report of the National Advisory Commission on Civil Disorders* [Kerner Commission] (New York, 1968), attributes the urban riots of the 1960s to "white racism." In the process, the commission compiled much useful information on cities, their black populations, and the background to the riots. Lee Rainwater, *Behind Ghetto Walls: Black Fami-*

lies in a Federal Slum (Chicago, 1970), probes the structure and functioning of black families under harsh conditions of poverty and environmental decay. He urges significant income redistribution to reduce inequality. Frances Fox Piven and Richard A. Cloward, *Regulating the Poor: The Functions of Public Welfare* (New York, 1971), argues that the welfare system is concerned more with social control than with humanitarianism. Nathan Glazer and Daniel P. Moynihan, *Beyond the Melting Pot* (2d ed., Cambridge, Mass., 1970), was originally published in 1963. The authors have supplied a new introduction which decries the changes in ethnic group relations in New York City in the 1960s. Their analysis illumines the malaise of white ethnics in contemporary urban America.

Useful material on urban housing can be found in Charles Abrams, *The City is the Frontier* (New York, 1965); Lawrence M. Friedman, *Government and Slum Housing: A Century of Frustration* (Chicago, 1968); and George Sternlieb, *The Tenement Landlord* (New Brunswick, N.J., 1966). Sternlieb examined ownership of slum buildings in Newark, New Jersey. On governmental and political problems of cities, Scott Greer, *The Emerging City: Myth and Reality* (New York, 1962), is brief and to the point. Edward C. Banfield and James Q. Wilson, *City Politics* (Cambridge, Mass., 1963), relies heavily on a distinction between public-regarding, middle-class political behavior and private-regarding, lower-class patterns. David Rogers, *The Management of Big Cities: Interest Groups and Social Change Strategies* (Beverly Hills, Calif., 1971), uses New York, Philadelphia, and Cleveland as case studies of the way things get done or do not get done in large cities. Rogers's focus is on the impediments to efficient delivery of services to citizens. Alan K. Campbell, editor, *The States and the Urban Crisis* (Englewood Cliffs, N.J., 1970), examines the actual and potential role of state governments in dealing with urban problems. Alan Trachtenberg, Peter Neill, and Peter C. Bunnell, editors, *The City: American Experience* (New York, 1971), is an imaginative anthology combining photography, fiction, poetry, and scholarly pieces. One could recommend a long list of books by Lewis Mumford who anticipated many current trends and problems in the 1920s and who has been writing with perception, passion, and style ever since. *The Urban Prospect* (New York, 1968), contains brief pieces written over this period which state many of his basic ideas in highly accessible form.

General Bibliographical Note

The purpose of this bibliographical note is to list useful materials for those students who wish to delve further into the study of American urban history. We have not mentioned books or articles already cited in connection with one of the essays.

Review Articles

A number of scholars have reviewed the existing literature and offered suggestions for future work: Dwight W. Hoover, "The Diverging Paths of American Urban History," *American Quarterly*, 20 (Summer 1968), 296–317; Roy Lubove, "The Urbanization Process: An Approach to Historical Research," *Journal of the American Institute of Planners*, 33 (January 1967), 33–39; Eric E. Lampard, "American Historians and the Study of Urbanization," *American Historical Review*, 67 (October 1961), 49–61; Lampard, "Urbanization and Social Change: On Broadening the Scope and Relevance of Urban History," in Oscar Handlin and John Burchard, editors, *The Historian and the City* (Cambridge, Mass., 1963), 225–47; Lampard, "The Dimensions of Urban History: A Footnote to the 'Urban Crisis,'" *Pacific Historical Review*, 39 (August 1970), 261–78; Sam Bass Warner, Jr., "If All the World Were Philadelphia: A Scaffolding for Urban History, 1774–1930," *American Historical Review*, 74 (October 1968), 26–43; R. Richard Wohl, "Urbanism, Urbanity, and the Historian," *University of Kansas City Review*, 22 (October 1955), 53–61; Richard C. Wade, "An Agenda for Urban History," in Herbert J. Bass, editor, *The State of American History* (Chicago, 1970), 43–69; Allen F. Davis, "The American Historian vs. the City," *Social Studies*, 56 (March, April 1965), 91–96, 127–35; Charles N. Glaab, "The Historian and the American City: A Bibliographic Survey," in Philip M. Hauser and Leo F. Schnore, editors, *The Study of Urbanization* (New York, 1965), 53–80; Charles N. Glaab, "The Historian and the American Urban Tradition," *Wisconsin Magazine of History*, 67 (Autumn 1963), 12–25; Dana F. White, "The Underdeveloped Discipline: Interdisciplinary Directions in American Urban History," *American Studies: An International Newsletter*, 9 (Spring 1971), 3–16; Blaine A. Brownell, "American Urban History: Retrospect and Prospect," *Indiana Academy of the Social Sciences, Proceedings*, 3d Series, 5 (1970), 120–28; and Blake McKelvey, "American Urban History Today," *American Historical Review*, 57 (July 1952), 919–29.

Teaching Urban History

In recent years, urban history courses have multiplied rapidly on both secondary and university levels. Useful for actual and prospective teachers are: Dwight W. Hoover, *A Teacher's Guide to American Urban History* (Chicago, 1971); Raymond A. Mohl and Neil Betten, "Gary, Indiana: The Urban Laboratory as a Teaching Tool," *The History Teacher*, 4 (January 1971), 5–17; Bayrd Still and Diana Klebanow, "The Teaching of American Urban History," *Journal of American History*, 55 (March 1969), 843–47; and Bayrd Still, *New York City: A Student's Guide to Localized History* (New York, 1965). Similar guides have been published for a number of other cities.

General Works

Interpretations and surveys of American urban history include W. Stull Holt, "Some Consequences of the Urban Movement in American History," *Pacific Historical Review*, 22 (November 1953), 337–51; Page Smith, *As a City Upon a Hill: The Town in American History* (New York, 1966), which examines the agricultural town and provides a useful counterpoint for urban history; Arthur M. Schlesinger, "The City in American History," *Mississippi Valley Historical Review*, 27 (June 1940), 43–66, which attempted to substitute the city for Turner's frontier as an organizing focus for American history; William Diamond, "On the Dangers of an Urban Interpretation of History," in Eric F. Goldman, editor, *Historiography and Urbanization: Essays in Honor of W. Stull Holt* (Baltimore, 1941), 67–108, is a negative response to Schlesinger; Bayrd Still, "The History of the City in American Life," *The American Review*, 2 (May 1962), 20–34; Richard C. Wade, "The City in History: Some American Perspectives," in Werner Z. Hirsch, editor, *Urban Life and Form* (New York, 1963), 59–79; Raymond A. Mohl and Neil Betten, "The History of Urban America: An Interpretive Framework," *The History Teacher*, 3 (March 1970), 23–34; Charles N. Glaab and A. Theodore Brown, *A History of Urban America* (New York, 1967); Constance McL. Green, *American Cities in the Growth of the Nation* (London, 1957) and *The Rise of Urban America* (New York, 1965); Blake McKelvey, *The Urbanization of America, 1860–1915* (New Brunswick, N.J., 1963) and *The Emergence of Metropolitan America, 1915–1966* (New Brunswick, N.J., 1968); Adna F. Weber, *The Growth of Cities in the Nineteenth Century* (New York, 1899); Charles N. Glaab, "Metropolis and Suburb: The Changing American City," in John Braeman *et al.*, editors, *Change and Continuity in Twentieth-Century America: The 1920's* (Columbus, Ohio, 1968).

Useful regional overviews include Jean Gottmann, *Megalopolis: The Urbanized Northeastern Seaboard of the United States* (New York, 1961); Richard C. Wade, "Urban Life in Western America, 1790–1830," *American Historical Review*, 64 (October 1958), 14–30; Bayrd Still, "Patterns of Mid-Nineteenth Century Urbanization in the Middle West," *Mississippi Valley Historical Review*, 28 (September 1941), 187–206; Daniel J. Boorstin, *The Americans: The National Experience* (New York, 1965), 113–168; and Lewis Atherton, *Main Street on the Middle Border* (Bloomington, Ind., 1954).

Urban Biographies

This is the term used for histories of single cities. Among the best are Constance McL. Green's two-volume history, *Washington: Village and Capital, 1800–1878* (Princeton, N.J., 1962) and *Washington: Capital City, 1879–1950* (Princeton, N.J., 1963); Bessie L. Pierce's three-volume *A History of Chicago, The Beginnings of a City, 1637–1848* (New York, 1937), *From Town to City, 1848–1871* (New York, 1940), and *The Rise of a Modern City, 1871–1893* (New York, 1957); Blake McKelvey's four-volume history, *Rochester: The Water Power City, 1812–1854* (Cambridge, Mass., 1945), *The Flower City, 1855–1890* (Cambridge, Mass., 1949), *The Quest for Quality, 1890–1925* (Cambridge, Mass., 1956), and *An Emerging Metropolis, 1925–1961* (Rochester, N.Y., 1961); Bayrd Still, *Milwaukee: The History of a City* (rev. ed., Madison, Wis., 1965); Sidney Glazer, *Detroit: A Study in Urban Development* (New York, 1965); Leland A. Baldwin, *Pittsburgh: The Story of a City* (Pittsburgh, 1937); Thomas J. Wertenbaker, *Norfolk: Historic Southern Port* (rev. ed., Durham, N.C., 1962); Gerald M. Capers, *The Biography of a River Town: Memphis, Its Heroic Age* (Chapel Hill, N.C., 1939); Marilyn Sibley, *The Port of Houston: A History* (Austin, Tex., 1968); David McComb, *Houston: The Bayou City* (Austin, Tex., 1969); Robert M. Fogelson, *The Fragmented Metropolis: Los Angeles, 1850–1930* (Cambridge, Mass., 1967); John B. Armstrong, *Factory under the Elms: A History of Harrisville, New Hampshire, 1774–1969* (Cambridge, Mass., 1969); Norman H. Clark, *Mill Town: A Social History of Everett, Washington, from Its Earliest Beginnings on the Shores of Puget Sound to the Tragic and Infamous Event Known as the Everett Massacre* (Seattle, 1970); Constance McL. Green, *History of Naugatuck, Connecticut* (Naugatuck, Conn., 1948) and *Holyoke, Massachusetts: A Case History of the Industrial Revolution in America* (New Haven, Conn., 1939); Rollin G. Osterweis, *Three Centuries of New Haven, 1638–1938* (New Haven, Conn., 1953); Charles N. Glaab and Lawrence H. Larsen, *Factories in the Valley: Neenah-Menasha, 1870–1915* (Madison, Wis., 1959); Lawrence L. Graves, editor, *A History of Lubbock* (3 vols., Lubbock, Tex., 1959–61); Herman R. Lantz, *A Community in Search of Itself: A Case History of Cairo, Illinois* (Carbondale, Ill., 1972); and Edgar B. Wesley, *Owatonna: The Social Development of a Minnesota Community* (Minneapolis, 1938).

Colonial Towns and Cities

These communities have been studied extensively in recent years: Van Cleaf Bachman, *Peltries or Plantations: The Economic Policies of the Dutch West India*

Company in New Netherland, 1623–1639 (Baltimore, 1969); Thomas J. Condon, *New York Beginnings: The Commercial Origins of New Netherland* (New York, 1968); James H. Soltow, *The Economic Role of Williamsburg* (Williamsburg, Va., 1965); Carl Bridenbaugh, *Seat of Empire: The Political Role of Eighteenth-Century Williamsburg* (rev. ed., Williamsburg, Va., 1958); Michael Zuckerman, *Peaceable Kingdoms: New England Towns in the Eighteenth Century* (New York, 1970); John Demos, *A Little Commonwealth: Family Life in Plymouth Colony* (New York, 1970); Darrett B. Rutman, *Husbandmen of Plymouth: Farms and Villages in the Old Colony, 1620–1692* (Boston, 1967); Sumner Chilton Powell, *Puritan Village: The Formation of a New England Town* (Middletown, Conn., 1963); Philip J. Greven, Jr., *Four Generations: Population, Land, and Family in Colonial Andover, Massachusetts* (Ithaca, N.Y., 1970); William Haller, Jr., *The Puritan Frontier: Town Planting in New England Colonial Development, 1630–1660* (New York, 1951); Anthony N. B. Garvan, *Architecture and Town Planning in Colonial Connecticut* (New Haven, Conn., 1951); and Arthur L. Jensen, *The Maritime Commerce of Colonial Philadelphia* (Madison, Wis., 1963).

The Revolutionary Era

Valuable works include Benjamin W. Labaree, *Patriots and Partisans: The Merchants of Newburyport, 1764–1815* (Cambridge, Mass., 1962); Arthur M. Schlesinger, *The Colonial Merchants and the American Revolution* (New York, 1918); Virginia D. Harrington, *The New York Merchant on the Eve of the Revolution* (New York, 1935); Leila Sellers, *Charleston Business on the Eve of the American Revolution* (Chapel Hill, N.C., 1934); Jesse Lemisch, "The American Revolution Seen from the Bottom Up," in Barton J. Bernstein, editor, *Towards a New Past: Dissenting Essays in American History* (New York, 1968); Staughton Lynd, "The Mechanics in New York Politics, 1774–1788," *Labor History*, 5 (Fall 1964), 225–46; Pauline Maier, "Popular Uprisings and Civil Authority in Eighteenth-Century America," *William and Mary Quarterly*, 27 (January 1970), 3–35; and Oscar T. Barck, *New York City During the War for Independence* (New York, 1931).

National Period

Titles in this section deal generally with the cities and topics in question (more specialized works are listed under particular headings): Sidney I. Pomerantz, *New York: An American City, 1783–1803* (2d ed., Port Washington, N.Y., 1965); Ralph Weld, *Brooklyn Village, 1816–1834* (New York, 1938); Harold C. Syrett, *The City of Brooklyn, 1865–1898* (New York, 1944); Floyd R. Dain, *Every House a Frontier: Detroit's Economic Progress, 1815–1825* (Detroit, 1956); Charles R. Poinsatte, *Fort Wayne during the Canal Era, 1828–1855: A Study of a Western Community in the Middle Period of American History* (Indianapolis, 1969); Catherine E. Reiser, *Pitts-*

burgh's Commercial Development, 1800–1850 (Harrisburg, Pa., 1951); James Sterling Young, *The Washington Community, 1800–1828* (New York, 1966); Robert G. Albion, *The Rise of New York Port, 1815–1860* (New York, 1939); A. Theodore Brown, *Frontier Community: Kansas City to 1870* (Columbia, Mo., 1963); Robert R. Dykstra, *The Cattle Towns: A Social History of the Kansas Cattle Trading Centers* (New York, 1968); Kenneth W. Wheeler, *To Wear a City's Crown: The Beginnings of Urban Growth in Texas, 1836–1865* (Cambridge, Mass., 1968); Robert L. Martin, *The City Moves West: Economic and Industrial Growth in Central West Texas* (Austin, Tex., 1969); Duane A. Smith, *Rocky Mountain Mining Camps: The Urban Frontier* (Bloomington, Ind., 1967); James B. Allen, *The Company Town in the American West* (Norman, Okla., 1966); Leonard J. Arrington, *Great Basin Kingdom: An Economic History of the Latter-day Saints, 1830–1900* (Cambridge, Mass., 1958); Thomas A. Clinch, *Urban Populism and Free Silver in Montana: A Narrative of Ideology in Political Action* (Missoula, Mont., 1970); Earl Pomeroy, *The Pacific Slope: A History of California, Oregon, Washington, Idaho, Utah, and Nevada* (New York, 1965); Remi A. Nadeau, *The City Makers: The Story of Southern California's First Boom* (Los Angeles, 1965); John G. Clark, *New Orleans, 1718–1812: An Economic History* (Baton Rouge, La., 1970); Robert C. Reinders, *End of an Era: New Orleans, 1850–1860* (New Orleans, 1964); George C. Rogers, Jr., *Charleston in the Age of the Pinckneys* (Norman, Okla., 1968); D. Clayton James, *Antebellum Natchez* (Baton Rouge, La., 1968); Emory M. Thomas, *The Confederate State of Richmond: A Biography of the Capital* (Austin, Tex., 1971); Kenneth Coleman, *Confederate Athens* (Athens, Ga., 1967); Gerald M. Capers, *Occupied City: New Orleans under the Federals, 1862–1865* Lexington, Ky., 1965); Durward Long, "The Making of Modern Tampa: A City of the New South, 1885–1911," *Florida Historical Quarterly*, 49 (April 1971), 333–45; and Rupert B. Vance and Nicholas J. Demerath, editors, *The Urban South* (Chapel Hill, N.C., 1954).

Economic and Geographical Base

Many of the following titles are useful for both theoretical perspectives and empirical data: N. S. B. Gras, *An Introduction to Economic History* (New York, 1922); Eric E. Lampard, "The History of Cities in the Economically Advanced Areas," *Economic Development and Cultural Change*, 3 (January 1955), 81–136; Eugene Smolensky and Donald Ratajczak, "The Conception of Cities," *Explorations in Entrepreneurial History*, 2d. Series, 2 (1965), 90–131; Julius Rubin, "Urban Growth and Regional Development," in David T. Gilchrist, editor, *The Growth of the Seaport Cities, 1790–1825* (Charlottesville, Va., 1967), 3–21; Jeffrey G. Williamson, "Antebellum Urbanization in the American Northeast," *Journal of Economic History*, 25 (December 1965), 592–608; Edward C. Kirkland, *Industry Comes of Age: Business, Labor, and Public Policy, 1860–1897* (New York, 1961); Harold F. Mayer and Clyde F. Kohn, editors, *Readings in Urban Geography* (Chicago, 1959); James H. Johnson, *Urban Geography: An Introductory Analysis* (Elmsford, N.Y., 1967); Hans Blumenfeld, *The Modern Metropolis* (Cambridge, Mass., 1967); Gunnar Alexandersson, *The*

Industrial Structure of American Cities: A Geographic Study of Urban Economy in the United States (Lincoln, Neb., 1956); Allan R. Pred, "Manufacturing in the American Mercantile City, 1800–1840," *Annals of the Association of American Geographers*, 56 (June 1966), 307–38; Bert F. Hoselitz, "The City, the Factory, and Economic Growth," *American Economic Review*, 45 (May 1955), 166–84; George Rogers Taylor, "American Urban Growth Preceding the Railway Age," *Journal of Economic History*, 27 (September 1967), 309–39; Carter Goodrich, *Government Promotion of Canals and Railroads, 1800–1890* (New York, 1960); Edward C. Kirkland, *Men, Cities, and Transportation: A Study in New England History, 1820–1900* (2 vols., Cambridge, Mass., 1948); Glenn C. Quiett, *They Built the West: An Epic of Rails and Cities* (New York, 1934); Julius Rubin, *Canal or Railroad? Imitation and Innovation in the Response to the Erie Canal in Philadelphia, Baltimore, and Boston* (Philadelphia, 1961); Charles N. Glaab, *Kansas City and the Railroads: Community Policy in the Growth of a Regional Metropolis* (Madison, Wis., 1962); Merl E. Reed, *New Orleans and the Railroads: The Struggle for Commercial Empire, 1830–1860* (Baton Rouge, La., 1966); Leonard P. Curry, *Rail Routes South: Louisville's Fight for the Southern Market, 1865–1872* (Lexington, Ky., 1969); James W. Livingood, *The Philadelphia-Baltimore Trade Rivalry, 1780–1860* (Harrisburg, Pa., 1947); Wyatt W. Belcher, *The Economic Rivalry between St. Louis and Chicago, 1850–1880* (New York, 1947); Harry N. Scheiber, "Urban Rivalry and Internal Improvements in the Old Northwest, 1820–1860," *Ohio History*, 71 (October 1962), 227–39; Herbert W. Rice, "Early Rivalry among Wisconsin Cities for Railroads," *Wisconsin Magazine of History*, 35 (Autumn 1951), 10–15; George M. Smerk, "The Streetcar: Shaper of American Cities," *Traffic Quarterly*, 21 (October 1967), 569–84; George W. Hilton and John F. Due, *The Electric Interurban Railways in America* (Stanford, Calif., 1960); William T. Baxter, *The House of Hancock: Business in Boston, 1724–1775* (Cambridge, Mass., 1945).

Useful material on labor can be found in Carl Degler, "The West as a Solution of Urban Unemployment," *New York History*, 36 (1955), 63–85; Melvyn Dubofsky, *When Workers Organize: New York City in the Progressive Era* (Amherst, Mass., 1968); Thomas W. Gavett, *Development of the Labor Movement in Milwaukee* (Madison, Wis., 1965); Grace H. Stimson, *Rise of the Labor Movement in Los Angeles* (Berkeley, Calif., 1955); Louis B. Perry and Richard S. Perry, *A History of the Los Angeles Labor Movement, 1911–1941* (Berkeley, Calif., 1963); and Robert Knight, *Industrial Relations in the San Francisco Bay Area, 1900–1918* (Berkeley, Calif., 1960).

Social History

The subject of social mobility has received considerable attention in recent years, especially from quantitatively oriented scholars: Stephan Thernstrom, "Reflections on the New Urban History," *Daedalus*, 100 (Spring 1971), 359–75; Stephan Thernstrom and Richard Sennett, editors, *Nineteenth-Century Cities: Essays in the New Urban History* (New Haven, Conn., 1969), contains several valuable essays, for example, Stuart Blumin, "Mobility and Change in Ante-Bellum Philadelphia," 165–208, and Herbert G. Gutman, "The Reality of the Rags-to-Riches 'Myth': The Case of the Paterson, New Jersey, Locomotive, Iron, and Machinery Manufacturers, 1830–1880," 98–124; Stephan Thernstrom, "Notes on the Historical Study of Social Mobility," *Comparative Studies in Society and History*, 10 (January 1968), 162–72; Stephan Thernstrom and Peter R. Knights, "Men in Motion: Some Data and Speculations about Urban Population Mobility in Nineteenth-Century America," *Journal of Interdisciplinary History*, 1 (Autumn 1970), 7–35; Richard J. Hopkins, "Occupational and Geographical Mobility in Atlanta, 1870–1896," *Journal of Southern History*, 34 (May 1968), 200–213; Clyde Griffen, "Making It in America: Social Mobility in Mid-Nineteenth Century Poughkeepsie," *New York History*, 51 (October 1970), 479–99; Herman R. Lantz and Ernest K. Alix, "Occupational Mobility in a Nineteenth Century Mississippi Valley River Community," *Social Science Quarterly*, 51 (September 1970), 404–8; Alwyn Barr, "Occupational and Geographic Mobility in San Antonio, 1870–1900," *Social Science Quarterly*, 51 (September 1970), 396–403; William G. Robbins, "Opportunity and Persistence in the Pacific Northwest: A Quantitative Study of Early Roseburg, Oregon," *Pacific Historical Review*, 39 (August 1970), 279–96; Howard P. Chudacoff, *Mobile Americans: Residential and Social Mobility in Omaha, 1880–1920* (New York, 1972). Richard Sennett, *Families against the City: Middle Class Homes of Industrial Chicago, 1872–1890* (Cambridge, Mass., 1970) is interesting but speculative.

Religious institutions receive attention in Carroll Smith Rosenberg, *Religion and the Rise of the American City: The New York City Mission Movement, 1812–1870* (Ithaca, N.Y., 1971); Alvin W. Skardon, *Church Leader in the Cities: William Augustus Muhlenberg* (Philadelphia, 1971); James F. Findlay, Jr., *Dwight L. Moody: American Evangelist, 1837–1899* (Chicago, 1969); and Jacob H. Dorn, *Washington Gladden: Prophet of the Social Gospel* (Columbus, Ohio, 1966). Arthur M. Schlesinger, *The Rise of the City, 1878–1898* (New York, 1933), is a pioneering work of descriptive social history. There are a number of books on Jews in particular cities, including Selig Adler and Thomas E. Connolly, *From Ararat to Suburbia: The History of the Jewish Community of Buffalo* (Philadelphia, 1960); B. G. Rudolph, *From a Minyan to a Community: A History of the Jews of Syracuse* (Syracuse, N.Y., 1970); Isaac M. Fein, *The Making of an American Jewish Community: The History of Baltimore Jewry from 1773 to 1920* (Philadelphia, 1971); Max Vorspan and Lloyd P. Gartner, *History of the Jews of Los Angeles* (San Marino, Calif., 1970); and Bertram W. Korn, *The Early Jews of New Orleans* (Waltham, Mass., 1969). Urban blacks are treated in Robert S. Starobin, *Industrial Slavery in the Old South* (New York, 1970); Gilbert Osofsky, "The Enduring Ghetto," *Journal of American History*, 55 (September 1968), 243–55; Constance M. L. Green, *The Secret City: A History of Race Relations in the Nation's Capital* (Princeton, N.J., 1967); Lawrence B. DeGraaf, "The City of Black Angels: Emergence of the Los Angeles Ghetto, 1890–1930," *Pacific Historical Review*, 39 (August 1970), 323–52; Arvarh E. Strickland, *History of the Chicago Urban League* (Urbana, Ill., 1966); and Guichard Parris and Lester Brooks, *Blacks in the City: A History of the National Urban League* (Boston, 1971).

Government and Politics

The following illuminate the structure and processes of local politics: R. T. Da-land, "Political Science and the Study of Urbanism: A Bibliographical Essay," *American Political Science Review*, 51 (June 1957), 491–509; Kenneth Lockridge and Alan Kreider, "The Evolution of Massachusetts Town Government, 1640 to 1740," *William and Mary Quarterly*, 23 (October 1966), 549–74; Leonard L. Richards, *"Gentlemen of Property and Standing": Anti-Abolition Mobs in Jacksonian America* (New York, 1970); Arthur M. Schlesinger, Jr., *The Age of Jackson* (Boston, 1946); Edward Pessen, *Most Uncommon Jacksonians: The Radical Leaders of the Early Labor Movement* (Albany, N.Y., 1967), which builds on his earlier articles, "Did Labor Support Jackson? The Boston Story," *Political Science Quarterly*, 64 (June 1949), 262–74, and "The Workingmen's Movement of the Jacksonian Era," *Missis-sippi Valley Historical Review*, 43 (December 1956), 428–43; Walter Hugins, *Jack-sonian Democracy and the Working Class: A Study of the New York Workingmen's Movement, 1829–1837* (Stanford, Calif., 1960); William A. Sullivan, "Philadelphia Labor during the Jackson Era," *Pennsylvania History*, 15 (October 1948), 305–20; Michael F. Holt, *Forging a Majority: The Formation of the Republican Party in Pitts-burgh, 1848–1860* (New Haven, Conn., 1969); David Montgomery, *Beyond Equality: Labor and the Radical Republicans, 1862–1872* (New York, 1967); Eric L. McKitrick, "The Study of Corruption," *Political Science Quarterly*, 72 (December 1967), 502–14; Joy J. Jackson, *New Orleans in the Gilded Age: Politics and Urban Progress, 1880–1896* (Baton Rouge, La., 1969); Walton Bean, *Boss Ruef's San Francisco: The Story of the Union Labor Party, Big Business, and the Graft Prosecution* (Berkeley, Calif., 1952); Arthur Mann, *Yankee Reformers in the Urban Age: Social Reform in Boston, 1880–1900* (Cambridge, Mass., 1954); Mark D. Hirsch, "Reflections on Urban History and Urban Reform, 1865–1915," in Donald Sheehan and Harold C. Syrett, editors, *Essays in American Historiography in Honor of Allan Nevins* (New York, 1960), 109–37; James Weinstein, "Organized Business and the City Commis-sion and Manager Movements," *Journal of Southern History*, 28 (May 1962), 166–82; Gerald Kurland, *Seth Low: The Reformer in an Urban and Industrial Age* (New York, 1971); Edwin R. Lewinson, *John Purroy Mitchel: The Boy Mayor of New York* (New York, 1965); Charles Garrett, *The La Guardia Years: Machine and Reform Pol-itics in New York City* (New Brunswick, N.J., 1961); J. Joseph Huthmacher, "Urban Liberalism and the Age of Reform," *Mississippi Valley Historical Review*, 49 (Sep-tember 1962), 231–41; J. Joseph Huthmacher, *Senator Robert F. Wagner and the Rise of Urban Liberalism* (New York, 1968); Jack Tager, *The Intellectual as Urban Reformer: Brand Whitlock and the Progressive Movement* (Cleveland, 1968); James B. Crooks, *Politics and Progress: The Rise of Urban Progressivism in Baltimore, 1895 to 1911* (Baton Rouge, La., 1968); William D. Miller, *Memphis during the Progressive Era, 1900–1917* (Madison, Wis., 1957) and *Mr. Crump of Memphis* (Baton Rouge, La., 1964); John M. Allswang, *A House for All Peoples: Ethnic Politics in Chicago, 1890–1936* (Lexington, Ky., 1971); Alex Gottfried, *Boss Cermak of Chicago: A Study of Political Leadership* (Seattle, 1962); and Kenneth T. Jackson, *The Ku Klux Klan in the City, 1915–1930* (New York, 1967).

Urban Public Services

Much more work needs to be done in this area. Among the useful materials available are Marvin Lazerson, *Origins of the Urban School: Public Education in Massachusetts, 1870–1915* (Cambridge, Mass., 1971); the issue entitled "Urban Education" of the *History of Education Quarterly*, 9 (Fall 1969); Robert S. Pickett, *House of Refuge: Origins of Juvenile Reform in New York State, 1815–1857* (Syracuse, N.Y., 1969); Joseph M. Hawes, *Children in Urban Society: Juvenile Delinquency in Nineteenth-Century America* (New York, 1971); John B. Blake, *Public Health in the Town of Boston, 1630–1822* (Cambridge, Mass., 1959); John Duffy, *Sword of Pestilence: The New Orleans Yellow Fever Epidemic of 1853* (Baton Rouge, La., 1966) and *A History of Public Health in New York City, 1625–1866* (New York, 1968); James H. Cassedy, *Charles V. Chapin and the Public Health Movement* (Cambridge, Mass., 1962); Lawrence H. Larsen, "Nineteenth Century Street Sanitation: A Study in Filth and Frustration," *Wisconsin Magazine of History*, 52 (Spring 1969), 239–47; Richard Skolnik, "George Edwin Waring, Jr.: A Model for Reformers," *New-York Historical Society Quarterly*, 52 (October 1968), 354–78; Frederick M. Bender, "Gas Light, 1816–1860," *Pennsylvania History*, 22 (October 1955), 359–73; Stephen F. Ginsberg, "Above the Law: Volunteer Firemen in New York City, 1836–1837," *New York History*, 50 (April 1969), 165–86, and "The Police and Fire Protection in New York City: 1800–1850," *New York History*, 52 (April 1971), 133–50; Nelson M. Blake, *Water for the Cities: A History of the Urban Water Supply Problem in the United States* (Syracuse, N.Y., 1956); and William W. Sorrels, *Memphis' Greatest Debate: A Question of Water* (Memphis, 1970).

Architecture and Physical Form

Historically oriented works in this area include Christopher Tunnard, *The City of Man* (New York, 1953); Christopher Tunnard and Henry Hope Reed, Jr., *American Skyline: The Growth and Form of Our Cities and Towns* (Boston, 1956); Charles N. Glaab, "Historical Perspective on Urban Development Schemes," in Leo Schnore, editor, *Social Science and the City* (New York, 1968), 197–219; John W. Reps, *Tidewater Towns: City Planning in Colonial Virginia and Maryland* (Charlottesville, Va., 1971), *Town Planning in Frontier America* (Princeton, N.J., 1969), and *Monumental Washington: The Planning and Development of the Capital Center* (Princeton, N.J., 1967); John Burchard and Albert Bush-Brown, *The Architecture of America: A Social and Cultural History* (Boston, 1961); Wayne Andrews, *Architecture, Ambition, and Americans* (New York, 1955); Carl W. Condit, *American Building: Materials and Techniques from the Beginnings of the Colonial Settlements to the Present* (Chicago, 1968); S. B. Sutton, *Civilizing American Cities: A Selection of Fred-*

erick Law Olmsted's Writings on City Landscapes (Cambridge, Mass., 1971); Paul A. Conkin, *Tomorrow a New World: The New Deal Community Program* (Ithaca, N.Y., 1959); Clarence S. Stein, *Toward New Towns for America* (New York, 1957); Kevin Lynch, *The Image of the City* (Cambridge, Mass., 1960); Walter Muir Whitehill, *Boston: A Topographical History* (Cambridge, Mass., 1959); Harold Kirker and James Kirker, *Bulfinch's Boston, 1787–1817* (New York, 1964); John Coolidge, *Mill and Mansion: A Study of Architecture and Society in Lowell, Massachusetts, 1820–1865* (New York, 1942); Edmund H. Chapman, *Cleveland: Village to Metropolis* (Cleveland, 1964); Raymond A. Mohl and Neil Betten, "The Failure of Industrial City Planning: Gary, Indiana, 1906–1910," *Journal of the American Institute of Planners,* 38 (July 1972), 203–15; Carl W. Condit, *The Chicago School of Architecture: A History of Commercial and Public Building in the Chicago Area, 1875–1925* (Chicago, 1964); Stanley Buder, *Pullman: An Experiment in Industrial Order and Community Planning, 1880–1930* (New York, 1967); and Mel Scott, *The San Francisco Bay Area: A Metropolis in Perspective* (Berkeley, Calif., 1959).

Conceptions of the City

This is another area that needs attention. Most of the following are suggestive rather than definitive: Morton and Lucia White, *The Intellectual Versus the City: From Thomas Jefferson to Frank Lloyd Wright* (Cambridge, Mass., 1962); Frank Friedel, "Boosters, Intellectuals, and the American City," in Oscar Handlin and John Burchard, editors, *The Historian and the City* (Cambridge, Mass., 1963), 115–20; Anselm Strauss, *Images of the American City* (New York, 1961); Robert H. Walker, "The Poet and the Rise of the City," *Mississippi Valley Historical Review,* 49 (June 1962), 85–99; Michael H. Cowan, *City of the West: Emerson, America, and Urban Metaphor* (New Haven, Conn., 1967); George A. Dunlap, *The City in the American Novel, 1789–1900* (Philadelphia, 1934); Blanche E. Gelfant, *The American City Novel* (Norman, Okla., 1954); Eugene Arden, "The Evil City in American Fiction," *New York History,* 35 (July 1954), 259–79; and Don S. Kirschner, *City and Country: Rural Responses to Urbanization in the 1920's* (Westport, Conn., 1970).

Statistical Appendix

The Urbanization of the United States

Census Year	Total Population	Urban Population	Percentage Classified as Urban
1790	3,929,214	201,655	5.1
1820	9,638,453	693,255	7.2
1840	17,069,453	1,845,055	10.8
1860	31,443,321	6,216,518	19.8
1890	62,979,766	22,106,265	35.1
1920	106,021,537	54,253,282	51.2
1940	132,164,569	74,705,338	56.5
1950 [a]	151,325,798	96,846,817	64.0
1960 [b]	179,323,175	125,268,750	69.9
1970 [b]	203,211,926	149,324,930	73.5

Source: United States Census, 1970, *Census of Population, U.S. Summary,* 1–42.

[a] From 1950 on the urban population includes those living in unincorporated parts of urbanized areas.

[b] The 1960 and 1970 figures include Hawaii and Alaska.

Selected American Cities: A Statistical Profile

City and Year	Rank in Population	Area in Square Miles	Population	Population of Metropolitan Area	Percentage of City Foreign-Born	Percentage of City Black
Atlanta						
1890	42	9	65,533		2.9	33.3
1930	32	35	270,366	370,920	1.8	36.6
1950	33	37	331,314	726,989	1.3	51.3
1970	27	131	496,973	1,390,164		
Baltimore						
1890	7	30	434,439		15.9	17.7
1930	8	79	804,874	949,247	9.4	23.8
1950	6	79	949,708	1,457,181	5.4	46.4
1970	7	79	905,759	2,070,670		
Birmingham						
1890			26,178		6.3	38.2
1930	34	50	259,678	382,792	2.3	39.9
1950	34	65	326,037	653,059	1.2	42.0
1970	48	80	300,910	739,274		
Boston						
1890	6	39	448,447		29.4	2.6
1930	9	44	781,188	2,307,897	29.9	5.3
1950	10	48	801,444	2,414,368	18.0	16.3
1970	16	46	641,071	2,753,700		
Buffalo						
1890	11	39	255,664		35.0	2.4
1930	13	39	573,076	820,573	20.8	6.5
1950	15	39	580,132	1,089,230	12.1	20.4
1970	28	41	462,768	1,349,211		
Chicago[a]						
1890	2	169	1,099,850		41.0	6.9
1930	2	202	3,376,438	4,364,755	25.5	14.1
1950	2	208	3,620,962	5,586,096	14.5	32.7
1970	2	223	3,366,957	7,612,314		

City / Year						
Cincinnati						
1890	9	25	296,908			
1930	17	71	451,160	759,464	24.1	10.6
1950	18	75	503,998	1,023,245	7.8	15.6
1970	29	78	452,524	1,384,851	4.1	27.6
Cleveland						
1890	10	28	261,353			
1930	6	71	900,429	1,194,989	37.2	8.0
1950	7	75	914,808	1,532,574	25.6	16.3
1970	10	76	750,903	2,064,194	14.5	38.3
Columbus, Ohio						
1890	30	14	88,150			
1930	28	38	290,564	340,400	14.2	11.3
1950	28	39	375,901	563,040	5.3	12.5
1970	21	135	539,677	916,228	2.9	18.5
Dallas						
1890		9	38,067			
1930	33	42	260,475	309,658	10.5	14.9
1950	22	112	434,462	780,827	3.6	13.2
1970	8	266	844,401	1,555,950	1.9	24.9
Denver						
1890	26	17	106,713			
1930	29	58	287,861	330,761	11.4	2.5
1950	24	67	415,786	612,128	5.4	4.4
1970	25	95	514,678	1,227,529		9.1
Detroit						
1890	15	22	205,876			
1930	4	138	1,568,662	2,104,764	40.0	7.7
1950	5	140	1,849,568	3,016,197	25.9	16.4
1970	5	138	1,511,482	4,199,931	14.9	43.7
Houston						
1890		9	27,557			
1930	26	72	292,352	339,216	11.3	21.7
1950	14	160	596,163	935,539	6.1	21.1
1970	6	434	1,232,802	1,985,031	2.9	25.7

Selected American Cities: A Statistical Profile (Cont.)

City and Year	Rank in Population	Area in Square Miles	Population	Population of Metropolitan Area	Percentage of City Foreign-Born	Percentage of City Black
Indianapolis						
1890	27	11	105,436	417,685	13.8	12.1
1930	21	54	364,161	727,122	3.8	15.0
1950	23	55	427,173	1,109,882	2.1	18.0
1970	11	379	744,624			
Jacksonville						
1890	63	10	17,201	148,713	3.5	37.2
1930	49	26	129,549	304,029	2.1	35.5
1950	23	30	204,517	528,865		22.3
1970		766	528,865			
Kansas City						
1890	24	13	132,716	608,186	15.8	9.6
1930	19	59	399,746	848,655	6.6	12.3
1950	20	81	456,622	1,253,916	3.5	22.1
1970	26	239	507,087			
Los Angeles						
1890	5	29	50,395	2,318,526	20.0	3.1
1930	4	440	1,238,048	4,151,687	12.5	10.7
1950	3	451	1,970,358	7,032,075		17.9
1970		464	2,816,061			
Louisville						
1890	20	13	161,129	404,396	2.9	15.4
1930	24	36	307,745	576,900	1.3	15.7
1950	30	40	369,129	826,553		23.8
1970	39	60	361,472			
Memphis						
1890	43	4	64,495	276,126	2.1	38.1
1930	36	46	253,143	529,577	1.1	37.2
1950	26	104	396,000	770,120		38.9
1970	17	217	623,530			

1930	78	43	110,637	132,189	12.4	22.7
1950	42	34	249,276	495,084	10.8	16.3
1970	42	34	334,859	1,267,792		22.7
Milwaukee						
1890	16	17	204,468		39.0	
1930	12	41	578,249	743,414	19.1	1.3
1950	13	50	637,392	1,014,211	10.0	3.6
1970	12	95	717,099	1,403,688		14.7
Minneapolis[b]						
1890	18	48	164,738		36.8	
1930	15	55	464,356	832,258	17.5	0.9
1950	17	54	521,718	1,151,053	9.4	1.6
1970	32	54	434,400	1,813,647		4.4
New Orleans						
1890	12	196	242,039		14.2	
1930	16	196	458,762	494,877	4.6	28.3
1950	16	197	570,445	712,393	2.5	32.0
1970	19	197	593,471	1,045,809		45.0
New York[c]						
1890		44	1,515,301		42.2	
1930	1	299	6,930,446	10,901,424	34.0	4.7
1950	1	299	7,891,957	12,911,994	22.6	9.8
1970	1	299	7,894,862	16,178,700		21.2
Oklahoma City						
1890			4,151			
1930	43	30	185,389	202,163	2.0	7.9
1950	45	51	243,504	392,439	1.1	9.3
1970	37	636	366,481	640,889		13.7

Selected American Cities: A Statistical Profile (Cont.)

City and Year	Rank in Population	Area in Square Miles	Population	Population of Metropolitan Area	Percentage of City Foreign-Born	Percentage of City Black
Philadelphia						
1890	3	130	1,046,964		25.8	
1930	3	130	1,950,961	2,847,148	19.1	11.3
1950	3	127	2,071,605	3,671,605	11.2	18.3
1970	4	129	1,948,609	4,817,914		33.6
Phoenix						
1890			3,152			
1930		10	48,118			4.9
1950		17	106,818	331,700	4.6	6.2
1970	20	248	581,562	967,522	6.7	4.8
Pittsburgh						
1890	13	27	238,617		30.7	
1930	10	51	669,817	1,953,669	16.4	8.2
1950	12	54	676,806	2,213,236	9.6	12.3
1970	24	55	520,117	2,401,245		20.2
St. Louis						
1890	5	61	451,770		25.4	
1930	7	61	821,960	1,293,516	9.9	11.4
1950	8	61	856,796	1,755,334	4.9	18.0
1970	18	61	622,236	2,363,017		40.9
San Antonio						
1890			37,673			
1930		36	231,542	279,271	23.9	
1950		70	408,442	525,852	17.6	7.8
1970	15	184	654,153	864,014		7.6
San Diego						
1890			16,159			
1930	53	74	147,995	181,020		1.8
1950	31	94	334,387	556,808	14.6	5.5
1970	14	99	696,769	1,357,854	7.0	7.6
		317				
San Francisco[d]						
1890	8	42	298,997	1,290,094	27.1	0.6
1930	11	42	634,394	2,135,934	15.5	10.5
1950	11	45	775,357			

Seattle						
1890		13	42,837			
1930	20	69	365,583	420,663	21.4	0.9
1950	19	71	467,591	844,572	11.9	5.8
1970	22	84	530,831	1,421,869		7.1
Washington, D.C.						
1890	14	60	188,932			
1930	14	62	486,869	621,059	8.2	27.1
1950	9	61	802,178	1,507,848	6.3	35.4
1970	9	61	756,510	2,861,123	4.9	71.1

Sources: The census reports for 1890, 1930, 1950, and 1970. The figures for metropolitan areas for 1950 and 1970 are for the boundaries as defined in 1970.

[a] 1950 and 1970 metropolitan area figures include northwest Indiana.
[b] Metropolitan area includes St. Paul.
[c] Metropolitan area includes parts of New Jersey.
[d] Metropolitan area includes Oakland SMSA.

Notes on Contributors

Joseph L. Arnold is associate professor of history at the University of Maryland, Baltimore County, and author of *The New Deal in the Suburbs: A History of the Greenbelt Town Program, 1935–1954* (Columbus, Ohio, 1971).

Neil Betten is associate professor of history at Florida State University and coeditor of *Urban America in Historical Perspective* (New York, 1970).

Jacob H. Dorn is associate professor of history at Wright State University and author of *Washington Gladden: Prophet of the Social Gospel* (Columbus, Ohio, 1967).

Kenneth T. Jackson is associate professor of history at Columbia University. He is author of *The Ku Klux Klan in the City, 1915–1930* (New York, 1967), coeditor of *American Vistas* (2 vols., New York, 1971), and coeditor of *Cities in American History* (New York, 1972).

Zane L. Miller is associate professor of history at the University of Cincinnati and author of *Boss Cox's Cincinnati: Urban Politics in the Progressive Era* (New York, 1968).

Raymond A. Mohl is associate professor of history at Florida Atlantic University, where he specializes in American urban and social welfare history. He is coeditor of *Urban America in Historical Perspective* (New York, 1970) and author of *Poverty in New York, 1783–1825* (New York, 1971). In 1972 and 1973, he held a Younger Humanist Fellowship from the National Endowment for the Humanities.

Humbert S. Nelli is associate professor of history at the University of Kentucky and author of *The Italians of Chicago, 1880–1930: A Study in Ethnic Mobility* (New York, 1970).

James F. Richardson is associate professor of history and urban studies at the University of Akron. He is the author of *The New York Police: Colonial Times to 1901* (New York, 1970) and the editor of *The American City: Historical Studies* (Waltham, Mass., 1972).

Bruce M. Stave is associate professor of history at the University of Connecticut, where he specializes in American urban history. He is author of *The New Deal and the Last Hurrah: Pittsburgh Machine Politics* (Pittsburgh, 1970); editor of *Urban Bosses, Machines, and Progressive Reformers* (Lexington, Mass., 1972); and coeditor of *The Discontented Society: Interpretations of Twentieth-Century American Protest* (Chicago, 1972). From 1968 to 1969, he was Fulbright Professor of American History in India.

Selwyn K. Troen is assistant professor of history at the University of Missouri, Columbia, where he specializes in the history of American education and urban history. During 1972 and 1973 he was a fellow at the Shelby Cullom Davis Center for Historical Studies at Princeton University.

Index